Digital Government and Pu

In every part of the world information and technology are changing society and challenging the structures, roles, and management of traditional government institutions. At the same time, universal needs for human and social development, environmental protection, commercial and financial stability, and scientific and technological advancement demand governmental attention.

In this complex and changing environment, governments are still expected to provide for the public good through legal and political processes, and public programs and services. Digital transformation, electronic government, government 2.0, and electronic governance are just some of the labels used to characterize the ideas and actions that underlie adaptation, transformation, and reform efforts. This book contributes to the ongoing dialog within the digital government research and practice community by addressing leadership and management challenges through the interplay of five interconnected themes: management, policy, technology, data, and context. These themes are evident in a wide range of topics including policy informatics, smart cities, cross-boundary information sharing, service delivery, and open government, among others. Accordingly, it includes chapters that explore these themes conceptually and empirically and that emphasize the importance of context, the need for cross-boundary thinking and action, a public value approach to performance, and the multidimensional capabilities necessary to succeed in a dynamic, multi-stakeholder environment.

The chapters in this book were originally published as a special issue of the journal, *Public Management Review*.

J. Ramon Gil-Garcia is Director of the Center for Technology in Government and Associate Professor of Public Administration and Policy, University at Albany, SUNY. He has published extensively and some of his publications are among the most cited in the field of digital government research worldwide.

Sharon S. Dawes is Professor Emerita of Public Administration and Policy at the University at Albany, SUNY. She was instrumental in creating the field of digital government in her roles as founding Director of the Center for Technology in Government and first President of the Digital Government Society.

Theresa A. Pardo is Associate Vice President for Research and Full Research Professor of Public Administration and Policy, University at Albany, SUNY. She is a member of the National Academy of Public Administration and among the most cited authors in the field of digital government research.

Digital Government and Public Management

Generating Public Sector Innovation at the
Crossroads of Research and Practice

Edited by
**J. Ramon Gil-Garcia, Sharon S. Dawes
and Theresa A. Pardo**

Routledge
Taylor & Francis Group

LONDON AND NEW YORK

First published 2022
by Routledge
2 Park Square, Milton Park, Abingdon, Oxon OX14 4RN

and by Routledge
605 Third Avenue, New York, NY 10158

Routledge is an imprint of the Taylor & Francis Group, an informa business

Introduction, Chapters 2–7 © 2022 Taylor & Francis
Chapter 1 © 2017 Marijn Janssen, Nripendra P. Rana, Emma L. Slade and Yogesh
K. Dwivedi. Originally published as Open Access.

British Library Cataloguing in Publication Data
A catalogue record for this book is available from the British Library

ISBN: 978-1-032-19343-4 (hbk)
ISBN: 978-1-032-19344-1 (pbk)
ISBN: 978-1-003-25874-2 (ebk)

DOI: 10.4324/9781003258742

Typeset in Minion Pro
by Newgen Publishing UK

Publisher's Note
The publisher accepts responsibility for any inconsistencies that may have arisen
during the conversion of this book from journal articles to book chapters, namely the
inclusion of journal terminology.

Disclaimer
Every effort has been made to contact copyright holders for their permission to
reprint material in this book. The publishers would be grateful to hear from any
copyright holder who is not here acknowledged and will undertake to rectify any
errors or omissions in future editions of this book.

Contents

Citation Information

The chapters in this book were originally published in the journal, *Public Management Review*, volume 20, issue 5 (2018). When citing this material, please use the original page numbering for each article, as follows:

For any permission-related enquiries please visit:
www.tandfonline.com/page/help/permissions

Notes on Contributors

Walter Castelnovo, Department of Theoretical and Applied Sciences, University of Insubria, Varese, Italy.

Yu-Che Chen, School of Public Administration, University of Nebraska at Omaha, Omaha, NE, USA.

Sharon S. Dawes, Department of Public Administration and Policy, Rockefeller College of Public Affairs and Policy; Center for Technology in Government, University at Albany, State University of New York, Albany, NY, USA.

François Duhamel, International Business, Universidad de las Américas Puebla, Cholula, México.

Yogesh K. Dwivedi, The Emerging Markets Research Centre (EMaRC), School of Management, Swansea University, Swansea, UK.

J. Ramon Gil-Garcia, Department of Public Administration and Policy, Rockefeller College of Public Affairs and Policy; Center for Technology in Government, University at Albany, State University of New York, Albany, NY, USA; Business School, Universidad de las Americas Puebla, Cholula, Puebla, Mexico.

Isis Gutiérrez-Martínez, Business Administration, Universidad de las Américas Puebla, Cholula, México.

David M. Hondula, Center for Policy Informatics, Arizona State University, Phoenix, AZ, USA; School of Geographical Sciences and Urban Planning, Arizona State University, Tempe, AZ, USA.

Qian Hu, School of Public Administration, University of Central Florida, Orlando, FL, USA.

Marijn Janssen, Faculty of Technology, Policy, & Management, Delft University of Technology, Delft, The Netherlands.

Erik W. Johnston, Center for Policy Informatics, Arizona State University, Phoenix, AZ, USA.

Evan R. Kuras, Center for Policy Informatics, Arizona State University, Phoenix, AZ, USA; Department of Environmental Conservation, University of Massachusetts, Amherst, MA, USA.

Jooho Lee, School of Public Administration, University of Nebraska at Omaha, Omaha, NE, USA.

Justin Longo, Center for Policy Informatics, Arizona State University, Phoenix, AZ, USA; Johnson Shoyama Graduate School of Public Policy, University of Regina, Regina, Canada.

Dolores E. Luna, Industrial Engineering, Universidad de las Américas Puebla, Cholula, México.

Luis F. Luna-Reyes, Rockefeller College of Public Affairs and Policy, University at Albany, SUNY, Albany, NY, USA.

Ines Mergel, Department of Politics and Public Administration, University of Konstanz, Konstanz, Germany.

Theresa A. Pardo, Division for Research; Center for Technology in Government; Department of Public Administration and Policy, Rockefeller College of Public Affairs and Policy, University at Albany, State University of New York, Albany, NY, USA.

Sergio Picazo-Vela, Business Administration, Universidad de las Américas Puebla, Cholula, México.

Nripendra P. Rana, The Emerging Markets Research Centre (EMaRC), School of Management, Swansea University, Swansea, UK.

Emma L. Slade, The Emerging Markets Research Centre (EMaRC), School of Management, Swansea University, Swansea, UK.

Maddalena Sorrentino, Department of Economics, Management and Quantitative Methods and ICONA Research Center, University of Milano, Milano, Italy.

Introduction – Digital government and public management research: finding the crossroads

J. Ramon Gil-Garcia, Sharon S. Dawes and Theresa A. Pardo

ABSTRACT

Information and information technologies have become ubiquitous in the public sector and it is difficult to think of a public problem or government service that does not involve them in some substantial way. Public management (PM) research now incorporates the effects of the availability and quality of data as well as the technologies used in the public sector. From a PM perspective, digital government (DG) could be considered an essential aspect of innovation, co-production, transparency, and the generation of public value. However, studies that attempt to understand the role that DG research plays in PM theory and practice are scarce. As a research field, DG emerged from multiple disciplines, including public administration, information science, management information systems, computer science, communication, and political science. There have been numerous efforts in the last decade to delineate this emergent academic community by assessing the growing body of research represented by hundreds of new peer-reviewed publications every year. This paper reviews these prior studies about the DG community, along with a systematic review of recent articles in top public administration journals from the United States and Europe, to begin to identify and compare key characteristics of these academic communities, including their core researchers, theories, topics, and methods. We argue that their similarities and differences present opportunities for more dialogue between DG and PM scholars that could produce synergies to enhance the production and dissemination of knowledge, yielding greater influence on practice.

1. Introduction

It is hard to imagine any government function or governance process that does not involve extensive use of information and technology. The use of information and communication technologies (ICT) in government, and the explosion of digital information throughout society, offers the possibility of a more efficient, transparent, and effective government. At the same time, these trends challenge traditional notions of administration, management, organization, accountability, and engagement.

Today, at all levels and in all branches of government we find tools, applications, and emergent technologies being applied to the needs of citizens, service users, public servants, and political leaders. Mobile applications, open data, social media, technical and organizational networks, the Internet of things, sensors, data analytics, and more are embedded in the working environment of government. Collectively, we have come to label this set of developments as 'digital government,' a concept that has broadened in scope from an early focus on the use of ICT for government administration to the more recent notion that information and technology influence administration, management, and governance. Digital government (DG) as a phenomenon involves new styles of leadership, new decision-making processes, different ways of organizing and delivering services, and new concepts of citizenship. Our view of DG aligns with UNESCO's definition of e-governance: *'The public sector's use of information and communication technologies* (ICTs) *with the aim of improving information and service delivery, encouraging citizen participation in the decision-making process and making government more accountable, transparent, and effective.'* (UNESCO 2011)

As a domain of study, DG has its roots in computer science, political science, information science, and public administration. Accordingly, it reflects a variety of perspectives, methodologies, and themes that draw on or cross over these traditional scholarly disciplines. For example, Moon, Lee, and Roh (2012) argue that DG is part of the discipline of public administration rather than a coherent area of study in itself. From their perspective, research on DG has evolved as a sub-area of public administration. By contrast, Dawes (2009) argues that DG is inherently multidisciplinary and reflects the convergence of essential questions about governance, individual rights, technical developments, and information collection, use, and dissemination. This dynamic environment demands a more holistic and flexible perspective about the prospects for government and governance in the digital age. Scholl (2006) has argued strongly that DG, while not a discipline in the traditional sense, is a distinct field of study with a multidisciplinary outlook on the challenges of the information society.

Likewise, many scholarly efforts have sought to characterize the development and trajectory of DG research (Erman and Todorovski 2009; Grönlund, Ake y Andersson, Annika 2006; Heeks and Bailur 2007; Meijer and Bekkers 2015; Rodríguez Bolivar, Alcaide Muñóz, and López Hernández 2014; Scholl et al. 2009; 2014; 2016; Wahid et al. 2012; Wirtz and Daiser 2016; Yildiz 2007). Some identified and characterized the core community of DG scholars, including their academic backgrounds, expertise, regional location, research foci, and productivity (Scholl et al. 2009). Others addressed the theories, frameworks, philosophies, concepts, and variables that DG scholars use in their research (e.g. Heeks and Bailur 2007). Still, others have examined the research methods and data employed in DG research (Grönlund, Ake y Andersson, Annika 2006; Wahid et al. 2012). Studies have also examined the influence of DG development on public sector policies and practices (e.g. Dawes, 2013; Gil-Garcia and Pardo 2005: Gil-Garcia, Pardo, and Nam 2015). This last line of work considers the practical impact of government's adoption of a new technology or new types or uses of data as well as the extent to which DG research findings are reflected in practical guidance for public managers.

DG scholars have also identified the field's main themes and topics of investigation, which include government transformation, digital democracy, citizen engagement, access to information, and improved public services, among others (Scholl et al. 2014). They have also identified some of the major unanswered questions still to be investigated (Yildiz 2013), including how to better connect DG studies with mainstream public administration research and how to better measure and evaluate performance and results. These themes have strong theoretical and practical ties to public administration in general and public management (PM) in particular. For example, DG scholars Gil-Garcia and Luna-Reyes (2006) and PM scholars Moon, Lee, and Roh (2012) both used Rosenbloom's (1983, 1998) framework to categorize studies based on their focus of attention: managerial, political, or legal. The managerial approach is related to values such as efficiency, effectiveness, and economy; the political approach is concerned with values of representativeness and accountability; and the legal approach with values of equity, due process, and individual rights.

Clearly, DG research addresses many management values as it explores the implications of technology adoption for service delivery systems, cost-effectiveness, human resources, organizational structures, processes, and performance. The political approach to DG research addresses the effects of information and technology on transparency, accountability, and citizen and community engagement. DG studies focused on legal aspects address such issues as privacy, access to information, and human rights, among others. Combining these various considerations, Dawes and Helbig (2015) offer a conceptual model for understanding DG as a dynamic phenomenon in which policies, management and organization, technology, and data all interact within a given social, political, and economic context.

DG and PM also share strong ties to practice. Hardy and Williams (2011) argue that improving the quality and impact of DG research requires greater consideration of complex governmental contexts and more interdisciplinary and collaborative research that informs not only theory but also policy and practice. To this end, Dawes (2009), like Ospina and Dodge (2005) and others in PM, argues that the relationship between research and practice can be mutually beneficial, if researchers apply their skills, theories, and methods to problems identified by experienced and knowledgeable public managers – especially when they work in active collaboration.

Given these points of connection, we believe more dialogue between PM and DG scholars would benefit both domains. This special issue represents an opportunity to explore how these closely related fields might benefit from greater familiarity and closer collaboration.

This article is organized in five sections, including this brief introduction. Section 2 describes the methodological approach we used for our review of top PM journals and previous studies of published DG research. Section 3 presents our main findings and discusses them in relation to prior findings about the full multidisciplinary DG community. This is done by identifying the core authors, topics, theories, methods, and findings. The description of the overall DG community is based on reviews of published research without disciplinary boundaries and includes authors from multiple disciplines. While it is clear that a few DG scholars are already becoming important links with the PM discipline, there are also many missed opportunities for synergies and mutual learning. Section 4 summarizes the articles included in this special issue as illustrative examples of efforts to integrate theories and concepts from DG and PM. We believe they are good starting points for discussion and for other similar efforts in the future. Finally, section 5 provides some concluding remarks and suggests areas for future research.

2. Methodology

This article relies on reviews of research published in both DG and PM outlets. First, we considered recent research published in eight public administration journals that emphasize PM. The journals shown in Table 1 were selected for their high rankings in the field to assure a sample of high-quality articles. All articles in these eight journals from winter 2010 to spring 2016 were reviewed. Those related to the use of information and technology in the public sector were selected based on the title, abstract, and keywords and then downloaded from the journal web pages. Only research papers were included. There was no particular trend in the number of articles published each year, ranging from a low of two in 2010 to 14 each in 2011 and 2012. Three outlets account for most of the published papers: The *American Review of Public Administration* (25%), *Public Administration Review* (19%), and *Public Management Review* (19%). All publishing houses (Wiley Group, Sage Publications, Routledge, Oxford Press, and Taylor and Francis) are based in either the United States or the United Kingdom. The largest number of articles was published in journals operated by Wiley (37%) or Sage (25%).

Second, we systematically reviewed prior studies of published DG research that attempt to understand and characterize not only the DG academic community but also the scope of DG as a field of study in terms of its theories, methodologies, topics, and practical implications. Some of these studies are based on reviews of papers from specialized conferences, specific journals, or a comprehensive reference library of DG publications[1] compiled by Professor Jochen Scholl (2009, 2014, 2016). Finally, we reviewed titles and abstracts of recent articles published in specialized DG journals such as Government Information Quarterly, Information Polity, and the International Journal of Electronic Government Research. The purpose of this review was to identify the most frequent topics addressed in recent studies. In general, the sources of information about DG research use a larger body of work over a longer time period and are not strictly comparable with our review of recent publications in the PM journals. Both sources present useful information, however, about the make-up of the communities, their areas of interest, their general approach to research, and their links to the world of practice. Thus, they serve as a reasonable starting point for understanding similarities and differences in different publication outlets.

Using these sources of data, we explored five interrelated questions: (1) To what extent do scholars in the two domains overlap? (2) What are the main topics studied and what do they have in common across the two domains? (3) What types of research methods are used and what kinds of data are employed? (4) To what extent

Table 1. Public management journals selected for the study (winter 2010 to spring 2016).

Journal	No. of papers	Per cent
Governance: An International journal of policy, Administration and Institutions	4	7%
International public management journal	5	8%
Journal of policy analysis and management	3	5%
Journal of public administration and theory	6	10%
Public administration	4	7%
Public administration review	11	19%
Public management review	11	19%
The American review of public administration	15	25%
Total	59	100%

do the two bodies of work present practical and policy recommendations in addition to research findings? (5) Where are the opportunities for collaboration and synergy across the two communities?

3. Similarities and differences in digital government and public management research

This section illustrates some of the differences and similarities between DG research published in PM outlets and DG research published in other peer-reviewed outlets. The section follows the order of our questions above and provides brief comparisons of the activities of the DG and PM research communities to begin to explore if and how the two fields are related, aligned, or, ideally, interrelated.

3.1. *Scholarly communities*

Scholl (2015) argues that the study domain of DG has accumulated a relatively large body of knowledge and has formed a well-structured research community, which produces a steady flow of research output. He has been studying the DG research community for a number of years, including its core scholars, their academic backgrounds, the most common outlets in the field, which research methods they use in their studies, and how their publications have changed over time (Scholl et al. 2009, 2014, 2016). In 2009, Scholl identified 55 scholars as the core of the DG research community (Scholl et al. 2009). They were mainly based in Europe and North America, with some representation from Asia in recent years (Scholl et al. 2014). Similarly, Erman and Todorovski (2009) identified a list of the most cited authors in the field by using social network analysis, but their scope was limited to a single international conference. These studies of the DG community differed in their use of data; some authors analysed only journals, others included specific academic conferences, and Scholl (2009, 2014, 2016) analysed all peer-reviewed publications, irrespective of discipline or type of outlet.

In general, the DG research community has grown dramatically in the past 15 years and has a clear core of about 60 senior scholars with at least 20 peer-reviewed publications each in diverse journal and conference outlets. This group also exhibits a diverse disciplinary background that includes computer science, information science, management, public administration, and political science. The DG community is geographically dispersed, although the largest numbers of authors come from Europe, followed by North America and Asia. DG scholarship is commonly authored by multiple researchers, often with two, three, or more authors. Single-author publications are in the minority. A decade ago, Grönlund, Ake y Andersson, Annika (2006) showed that very few of the papers involve authors from more than one institution, although it is more common to have authors from more than one discipline.

By contrast, PM researchers interested in DG topics show a different pattern. Our sample of 59 PM articles involved 125 authors. Among those authors, 92 of them authored only one paper, 11 authored two papers, and only three authors had three or more published papers. From this data, it would seem there is no core community of PM scholars who are publishing about the use of information and technology in government in the top ranking PM journals. However, two authors of papers in our sample are also among the top 20 most influential DG researchers identified in Scholl's (2016) latest study. These two authors have been conducting research and publishing about DG for many years, but their publications not only appear in PM outlets but also in journals and peer-reviewed conferences from other disciplines. Therefore, they have many more publications in outlets outside PM and more publications in prior years not covered in this review. We also looked at the number of authors for each article and their background disciplines. Here, there is some similarity with DG researchers. Of the total of 59 articles, three-quarters were co-authored. However, the most common collaborations only had two authors. Authors tend to be concentrated in the United States, followed by Europe and with some representation from Asia, mainly Korea. However, very few papers are collaborations between authors from different countries. In addition, in two-thirds of the papers, the authors came from the same academic background; they tended to be part of the same school and discipline.

The DG and PM scholarly communities vary across several dimensions: geographic distribution, the existence of a core set of scholars, and authorship patterns. While more DG authors are based in Europe than other parts of the world, more PM authors are based in the United States. Analysis of the DG scholarly community provides strong evidence for a core set of scholars which is not evident in the PM scholarly community that is publishing on DG topics. Authorship patterns are also different. While both communities tend towards multi-author papers with authors coming from the same institution, DG papers tend to have more authors and authors from different disciplines, while PM papers tend towards just two authors, typically from the same discipline.

3.2. Themes, topics, and specific technologies

Several of the DG review papers identified the main topics and themes studied by the DG research community. Erman and Todorovski (2009) used social network analysis to identify the most influential themes. They found (1) state-of-the-art DG research, (2) integration of electronic services (e-services) in public administrations, (3) digital divide, (4) factors of success and failure of DG projects, and (5) roadmaps for future research. Scholl et al. (2014) relied on manuscript titles and keywords to obtain a view of topical directions and scholarly interests in the DG domain. His findings show that the research topics in electronic government between 2009 and 2013 mainly focused on electronic and transformational government, ICTs, public participation, electronic public services, and the digital divide. Our own review of titles and abstracts of articles published in the top DG journals in the last 3 years reveals strong recent interest in social media, open government, open data, e-services, and smart cities.

These themes and topics could include a wide spectrum of DG applications and characteristics, but such comprehensiveness makes it difficult to summarize the essential elements (Gil-Garcia 2012). Gil-Garcia and Luna-Reyes (2006) respond to this difficulty by categorizing the contributions from different authors into four main categories (Gil-Garcia and Luna-Reyes 2006): e-services; electronic management (e-management); electronic democracy (e-democracy); and electronic policy (e-policy). Using these categories, we classified all of the papers in our review of the PM literature (see Table 2). Almost half of the papers (42%) focus on themes related to

Table 2. Classification of PM articles into DG categories.

Main category	Percentage	Elements
E-democracy	42%	Participation, transparency, accountability
E-management	27%	Management, planning, personnel
E-services	25%	Services
E-policy	5%	Policies, governance
Total	100%	

e-democracy. The most frequent elements were participation, transparency, and accountability. This category included topics such as citizen engagement, fiscal transparency, social media, open government and open data, and budget transparency. The e-management category was the second most frequent (27%), with elements like planning and personnel issues. In this category, we found research on such topics as organizational change with the use of ICT, e-adoption, innovation, emergency response, discretion, and trust. The third most common category was e-services (25%). These papers refer to specific topics such as service delivery, accessibility, government websites, and wireless broadband. Finally, only three papers (5%) fell under the category of e-policy with research themes related to technology adoption and regulation.

A number of DG-related concepts appear frequently in our review of the PM literature such as IT adoption, e-participation, trust, transparency, citizen participation, use of ICT, and social media. Most of the PM papers referred to the content and use of websites or government portals and the information included in these portals. Ten papers addressed Web 2.0 technologies, primarily related to social media use such as Twitter. Ten others focused on a specific technology or device such as mobile, internet, call centres, open architecture, or specific software tools or devices. A few papers referred to intranets, GIS technology, and wireless broadband.

A topical comparison across the PM and DG scholarly communities begins to illustrate common interests across the two domains. For example, many topics found in the DG reviews – participation, open government and open data, and the digital divide – map quite easily to the area of e-democracy, the category with the highest number of PM publications. Further, DG scholarship in areas such as DG success factors and smart cities maps well to the e-management category, the second highest among the PM papers. Finally, both communities appear to be investing in research on the broad area of e-services, and in the design and impact of particular technologies and tools such as social media.

3.3. Research methods and data sources

The third aspect of DG research we reviewed is the methods and data used in the published papers. Early in the development of DG research, normative statements and literature reviews dominated, but there has been a reduction in purely conceptual or descriptive research (Moon, Lee, and Roh 2012; West 2003; Yildiz 2007). Accordingly, studies have continuously increased in methodological diversity and theoretical rigor (Moon, Lee, and Roh 2012). Case studies are widely used as a research methodology to examine particular aspects of ICT and information use in government and to better understand complexity and offer practical and public policy implications (Moon, Lee, and Roh 2012). In the context of developing

Table 3. Comparison of methodological approaches.

DG research (Scholl et al. 2009)	Methodology	PM research (Current study)
45.50%	Quantitative	69%
9%	Qualitative	12%
45.50%	Mixed	8%
0%	Literature review	10%

countries, Wahid et al. (2012) identified the case study as the most employed methodology and also found other methods such as surveys, experiments, and action research.

In contrast, PM research on DG topics has used primarily quantitative methods (see Table 3). First, we looked for an explicit section that describes the paper's methods, data, and research questions. We found 15 articles did not describe their methodology in a clear manner, which represents around 25% of the sample. For the articles that did describe their methods, we followed Scholl's et al. (2009) definition of quantitative and qualitative methods and, as mentioned above, found that the majority of the studies (69%) used quantitative methods. The quantitative tools most employed are descriptive statistics, different types of regression models, structural equation models, citation analysis, and factor analysis. Twelve per cent of the studies used qualitative methods such as case studies and content analysis. In addition, six papers were literature reviews which we classified separately since they do not use empirical data. Very few papers used a mixed-method strategy.

We also considered the type of data collection methods. Heeks and Bailur (2007) distinguished between the studies that relied on primary or secondary data and identified whether those studies used multiple methods versus quantitative or qualitative methods exclusively. They write, 'Of classifiable papers, just under two-thirds used primary data (though this included papers where practitioners reflected on their own experiences), and just over one-third used only secondary data' (Heeks and Bailur 2007, 256). More recently, Wirtz and Daiser (2016) identified specific quantitative and qualitative tools such as structural equation modelling, ANOVA, regression, and confirmatory factor analysis, among others. Likewise, Scholl et al. (2009) analysed which general methods the core researchers preferred. Although he found scholars draw from a wide range of methods (from qualitative studies based on grounded theory at one end of the continuum to purely quantitative methods like algorithmic studies and simulations at the other end), he simply distinguished between 'qualitative' and 'quantitative' studies to gain an overall perspective on the field.

Of the 59 PM articles in our review, 11 used primary data (19%), 25 used secondary data (42%), and 17 used both (29%). In six (10%), it was unclear whether the data were primary or secondary. Primary sources included online surveys and questionnaires, in-depth interviews, web and social media content analysis, and document analysis. Most secondary data came from national surveys, online records and databases, reports, and online media and websites. Although no comparable information is available about previous DG research overall, for our sample of PM papers we also studied the geographic focus and level of government addressed by each paper. Almost half focused on local governments (49%), with national-level studies accounting for one-third (31%) and regional or state-level studies making up only 12%. In terms of geographical regions, 39% of the papers focused on the United States, 20% on Europe (including Spain, Germany, Italy, and the Netherlands), and 14% on countries in Asia (namely, Korea and China). One paper focused on Oceania (New Zealand), one on Latin America (Brazil), and none on Africa. We found seven articles (12% of the total) focused on a group of countries from different continents, which we labelled international studies. A final 7% were conceptual papers without a regional or national focus.

As noted above, DG is a rapidly growing and evolving area of research. A notable feature of the evolution of DG research is a reduction in the proportion of conceptual and descriptive work with a shift towards papers with more methodological and theoretical rigor (Moon, Lee, and Roh 2012). The early years of DG research included heavy reliance on case studies as a tool to begin unearthing the complexity of the phenomenon and to build theory. This balance is shifting away from case studies towards a pattern that is more like that generally seen in PM, where close to 50% of the papers analysed use quantitative methods either exclusively or in combination with qualitative work. In addition, the use of primary data is more common in DG research than in our sample of PM articles.

3.4. *Practical and policy recommendations*

As in other fields strongly related to practice, DG scholars seek to provide practical recommendations derived from sound research (Fountain 2003). Dawes (2013) argues for a connection between practice and knowledge where researchers use academic theories, standards, and methods to serve the real needs of government as expressed by government professionals in partnership projects. The profound know-how of government organizations and public policymakers should enhance and frame research questions, possibilities, and the presentation of results (Dawes, 2013). Gil-Garcia and Pardo (2005) also argue that practical tools and guides should be grounded in the latest research and practice to best serve both groups. Understanding and reducing risk in DG initiatives is a high priority for both researchers and practitioners. Therefore, we would expect most DG papers to provide practical implications and recommendations. Early research on DG focused on the potential for ICTs to help governments become more efficient and reduce their costs (Ho 2002; Moon, Lee, and Roh 2012; Rodríguez Bolivar, Alcaide Muñóz, and López Hernández 2014). However, efficiency is only one potential impact that deserves investigation. More recent work addresses factors underlying effectiveness such as leadership and trust as well as social and political impacts like transparency and participation. Previous reviews of DG research analysed papers in terms of whether they provide practical recommendations. For instance, in 2007 Heeks and Bailur found that less than half the articles they reviewed had any specific practical recommendations. Among those articles that did provide practical recommendations, three-quarters gave a single sentence or, at best, a single paragraph of recommendations. In recent years, there has been greater attention to practical implications, but it continues to need more emphasis in scholarship. Similarly, in our review of the PM literature, we found 53% of the articles included some practical recommendations in their final comments or in their findings and results sections. The nature and extent of these recommendations should be studied with more detail in the near future.

4. Digital government and public management research in action: some illustrative examples

The articles included in this special issue illustrate the value of combining DG and PM research. We argue that these fields jointly offer a powerful perspective and integrating concepts from the two can help us to better understand complex social problems and provide empirically grounded implications and practical recommendations. One article, for instance, argues that trustworthiness is a significant concept in DG, but has its origin in public administration. Another presents a framework about collaborative governance, but explicitly integrates the role of technology and its interplay with management, collaboration, performance, and the context in which these dynamics are embedded. A third shows how government collaboration with private organizations for DG projects negatively moderates the effect of resources and positively moderates the effect of processes on public value creation. Another paper illustrates how the outcomes of public sector reforms are shaped not only by legislative forces and ubiquitous technological enablement but also, and more prominently, by environmental dynamics. The next article studies the barriers to the adoption of DG, describing how online open innovation platforms seek to increase government innovation by posting public sector problem statements, then collecting and evaluating ideas submitted by citizens. Another article focuses on environmental hazards and how precision governance reflects an administrative capacity in which policy decisions are enhanced by the use of information about individual and collective preferences. The final article focuses on the connection between research and practice by analysing how current public affairs graduate programs prepare students for governing in the digital age and offers suggestions for how to better incorporate information management, use, and technology into public affairs curricula in the United States.

In their article entitled 'Trustworthiness of digital government services: deriving a comprehensive theory through interpretive structural modelling', Janssen et al. describe the origins of the concept of trustworthiness in public administration and how it has become a very important concept in DG research. They highlight the influence of trust on the relationship between citizens and governments. The article develops a theory to explain the factors affecting citizens' perceptions of e-government trustworthiness, based on a comprehensive review of the public administration and information systems literature. They highlight 20 pertinent variables, identifying and categorizing their interrelationships by employing interpretive structural modelling. The findings reveal that current conceptualizations of DG trustworthiness take a too-narrow view. The findings can help government policymakers better understand the interrelated factors associated with trustworthiness in the context of DG services and implement them in effective strategic planning.

Likewise, Chen and Lee integrate insights from collaborative governance, network management, and cross-boundary information sharing to develop a framework that outlines the interplay among context, management, collaborative dynamics, technology, and performance. Their article, 'Collaborative data networks for public service: governance, management, and performance', aims to advance the theory and practice of managing collaborative data networks for information and decision support services in over 400 U.S. metropolitan areas. This study applies the framework to conduct an exploratory in-depth case study of a metropolitan transportation data network to examine this interplay. The findings suggest ways to improve the performance of collaborative data networks.

Also related to inter-organizational networks and collaboration, Picazo-Vela et al. argue that collaborative approaches to PM are generally known to represent sources of public value. However, certain theoretical and empirical gaps in understanding this process of value creation persist. Their article, 'Value of inter-organizational collaboration in digital government projects', adopts a resource-based lens to analyse how public and private collaborations moderate relations among resources, processes, and the creation of public value. Their results show that collaboration with private organizations negatively moderates the effect of resources on public value creation and positively moderates the effect of processes on public value creation. Collaboration within the public sector positively moderates the effect of resources, but not the effect of processes.

Castelnovo and Sorrentino's article, 'The digital government imperative: a context-aware perspective', applies a 'context-aware' research approach to explore Italy's DG trajectory, using the ICT-enabled program that introduced the One-Stop Business Shop to exemplify its analytical potential. The interpretive lens captures the political, institutional, and external forces at play to illustrate how the outcomes of public sector reforms are shaped not by legislative strong-arming and ubiquitous technological enablement, but by the environmental dynamics. To demonstrate the central role of contextual factors in achieving the desired change, the study conducts a qualitative exploratory analysis that opens doors left mostly closed by the deterministic view of the mainstream literature on digital reform.

Studying the barriers to adoption of DG, Mergel describes how online open innovation platforms like Challenge.gov are used to post public-sector problem statements, then collect and evaluate ideas submitted by citizens with the goal of increasing government innovation. Her article, 'Open innovation in the public sector: drivers and barriers for the adoption of Challenge.gov', uses quantitative data extracted from contests posted to Challenge.gov and qualitative interviews with 36 public managers in 14 federal departments. The article contributes to the discovery and analysis of intra-, inter-, and extra-organizational factors that drive or hinder the implementation of open innovation in the public sector. The analysis shows that system-inherent barriers hinder public sector organizations from adopting this procedural and technological innovation. When the mandate of the innovation policy aligns with the mission of the organization, however, it opens opportunities for change in innovation acquisition and standard operating procedures.

The next article focuses on environmental hazards and how precision governance represents an administrative capacity in which policy decisions are enhanced with information about individual and collective preferences and contexts. Hondula et al. introduce the prospects for precision governance of natural hazards through the use of both big and individual data technologies, describing what is enabled and what concerns arise with their use. The article, 'Toward precision governance: infusing data into public management of environmental hazards', grounds the authors' perspective with a topical focus on mitigating the health risks of high temperatures in the chronically hot setting of Phoenix, Arizona in the United States. Their study, which examines individually experienced temperature data, provides compelling evidence that the transition towards data-driven precision governance will enhance hazard preparedness and response efforts.

Hu closes this special issue with the article 'Preparing public managers for the digital era: incorporating information management, use, and technology into public affairs graduate curricula'. This study examines how current public affairs graduate programs prepare students for governing in the digital age and offers suggestions for how to better incorporate information management, use, and technology into public affairs curricula in the United States. Through surveys of graduate program directors and content analysis of course syllabi, this study shows that current curricula have failed to keep pace with rapid changes in industry and society. Courses on information management, use, and technology need to balance their focus on technology with their focus on government. It remains a challenge to integrate information management, use, and technology topics into mainstream management and policy foci.

5. Concluding remarks: towards better synergy between digital government and public management

The analysis presented in this paper tells a story about the characteristics of two scholarly communities. Not surprisingly, we found that the DG and PM scholarly communities vary across several dimensions and also share important similarities. Perhaps most important, there is clear potential for complementary and collaborative work that can contribute to both fields of study. The papers in this special issue, demonstrate how the overlap in interests and the divergence in methods and approaches can produce research that is theoretically robust, methodologically sound, and useful in practice. We hope, other researchers will take this integrative perspective in future studies and argue that this should help advance our current knowledge about the use of information technologies in the public sector.

Towards this end, Dawes (2009) outlined a conceptual framework for considering future research about governance in the digital age. Taking a sociotechnical approach, she proposes that DG is a dynamic open system characterized by six dimensions or themes. These include the purpose and role of government, recognition of broad societal trends, attention to the nature of changing technologies, human elements of choice and self-determination, information creation and management, and ongoing interaction, change, and complexity. Research that takes such a holistic view of digital-age governance requires collaboration among DG and PM researchers. The main purpose of this special issue is to highlight the opportunities for joint efforts and encourage scholars to pursue them. These communities have much in common and also have useful differences that can allow them to challenge one another and produce new knowledge that benefits society.

Note

1. The E-Government Reference Library is available at http://faculty.washington.edu/jscholl/egrl/

Disclosure statement

No potential conflict of interest was reported by the authors.

References

Dawes, S. S. 2013. *Advancing Digital Government: "The Research-Practice-Knowledge Connection"*, Gestión Y Política Pública, CIDE, México, Volumen Temático Sobre Gobierno Electrónico, 49–67. Mexico: CIDE.

Dawes, S. S., and N. C. Helbig. 2015. "The Value and Limits of Government Information Resources for Policy Informatics." In *Governance in the Information Era: Theory and Practice of Policy Informatics*, edited by E. Johnston. New York: Routledge.

Dawes, S. S. 2009. "Governance in the Digital Age: A Research and Action Framework for an Uncertain Future." *Government Information Quarterly* 26 (2): 257–264. doi:10.1016/j.giq.2008.12.003.

Erman, N., and L. Todorovski. 2009. "Mapping the E-Government Research with Social Network Analysis." In *International Conference on Electronic Government*, edited by M. A. Wimmer, H. J. Scholl, M. Janssen, and R. Traunmüller, 13–25. Berlin: Springer.

Fountain, J. E. 2003. *Information, Institutions and Governance: Advancing a Basic Social Science Research Program for Digital Government, Research Working Paper 03-004*. Cambridge, MA: Kennedy School of Government, Harvard University.

Gil-Garcia, J. R. 2012. *Enacting Electronic Government Success: An Integrative Study of Government-Wide Websites, Organizational Capabilities, and Institutions (Vol. 31)*. New York: Springer.

Gil-Garcia, J. R., and L. F. Luna-Reyes. 2006. "Integrating Conceptual Approaches to E-Government." In *Encyclopedia of E-Commerce, E-Government and Mobile Commerce*, edited by M. Khosrow-Pour. Hershey, PA: Idea Group Inc.

Gil-Garcia, J. R., and T. A. Pardo. 2005. "E-Government Success Factors: Mapping Practical Tools to Theoretical Foundations." *Government Information Quarterly* 22 (2): 187–216. doi:10.1016/j.giq.2005.02.001.

Gil-Garcia, J. R., T. A. Pardo, and T. Nam. 2015. "What Makes a City Smart? Identifying Core Components and Proposing an Integrative and Comprehensive Conceptualization." *Information Polity* 20 (1): 61–87. doi:10.3233/IP-150354.

Grönlund, Ake y Andersson, Annika. 2006. "E-Gov Research Quality Improvements since 2003: More Rigor, but Research (Perhaps) Redefined." In *Egov 2006, Lncs 4084*, edited by M. A. Wimmer, H. J. Scholl, A. Grönlund, and K. V. Andersen, 1–12. Berlin Heidelberg: Springer-Verlag.

Hardy, C. A., and S. P. Williams. 2011. "Assembling E-Government Research Designs: A Transdisciplinary View and Interactive Approach." *Public Administration Review* 71 (3): 405–413. doi:10.1111/j.1540-6210.2011.02361.x.

Heeks, R., and S. Bailur. 2007. "Analyzing E-Government Research: Perspectives, Philosophies, Theories, Methods, and Practice." *Government Information Quarterly* 24: 243–265. doi:10.1016/j.giq.2006.06.005.

Ho, A. T. 2002. "Reinventing Local Governments and the E-Government Initiative." *Public Administration Review* 62 (4): 434–441.

Meijer, A., and V. Bekkers. 2015. "A Metatheory of E-Government: Creating Some Order in a Fragmented Research Field." *Government Information Quarterly* 32 (3): 237–245. doi:10.1016/j.giq.2015.04.006.

Moon, M. J., J. Lee, and C.-Y. Roh. 2012. "The Evolution of Internal IT Applications and E-Government Studies in Public Administration: Research Themes and Methods." *Administration & Society* 2014. Published online on October 1, 2012. doi:10.1177/0095399712459723.

Ospina, S., and J. Dodge. 2005. "Narrative Inquiry and the Search for Connectedness: Practitioners and Academics Developing Public Administration Scholarship." *Public Administration Review* 65 (4, July/August). doi:10.1111/j.1540-6210.2005.00468.x.

Rodríguez Bolivar, M. P., L. Alcaide Muñóz, and A. M. López Hernández. 2014. "Scientometric Study of the Progress and Development of E-Government Research during the Period 2000–2012." *Information Technology for Development*. doi:10.1080/02681102.2014.927340.

Rosenbloom, D. H. 1983. "Public Administrative Theory and the Separation of Power." *Public Administration Review* 43: 219–226. doi:10.2307/976330.

Rosenbloom, D. H. 1998. *Public Administration: Understanding Management, Politics, and Law in the Public Sector*. New York: McGraw-Hill.

Scholl, H. J. 2006. "Is E-Government Research a Flash in the Pan or Here for the Long Shot?" In *Electronic Government: Fifth International Conference, EGOV 2006, Vol. LNCS 4084*, edited by M. A. Wimmer, H. J. Scholl, A. Grönlund, and K. V. Andersen, 13–24. Krakow, Poland: Springer.

Scholl, H. J. 2009. "Profiling the EG Research Community and Its Core." In *Egov 2009, Lncs 5693*, edited by M. A. Wimmer, H. J. Scholl, A. Grönlund, and K. V. Andersen, 1–12. Berlin: Springer-Verlag.

Scholl, H. J. 2014. "The EGOV Research Community: An Update on Where We Stand." In *Egov 2014, Lncs 8653*, edited by M. Janssen, H. J. Scholl, M. A. Wimmer, and F. E. Bannister, 1–16. New York: Springer.

Scholl, H. J. 2015. "Electronic Government: A Study Domain Past its Infancy." In *E-Government: Information, Technology, and Transformation*, edited by H. J. Schnoll. New York: Routledge.

Scholl, H. J. 2016. "Making Sense of Indices and Impact Numbers: Establishing Leading EGOV Scholars'"Signatures"." In *International Conference on Electronic Government and the Information Systems Perspective*, 3–18. New York: Springer International Publishing.

UNESCO. 2011. ICTs as Tools for Improving Local Governance; Accessed January 2017. http://portal.unesco.org/ci/en/ev.php-URL_ID=3038&URL_DO=DO_TOPIC&URL_SECTION=201.html

Wahid, F. 2012. "The Current State of Research on Egovernment in Developing Countries: A Literature Review." In *Egov 2012, Lncs 7443*, edited by H. J. Scholl, M. Janssen, C. E. Moe, and L. S. Flak, 1–12. London: Springer.

West, D. 2003. Urban E-Government, 2003. http://www.insidepolitics.org/egovt03city.html

Wirtz, B. W., and P. Daiser. 2016. "A Meta-Analysis of Empirical E-Government Research and Its Future Research Implications." *International Review of Administrative Sciences* 74 (3): 421–433.

Yildiz, M. 2007. "E-Government Research: Reviewing the Literature, Limitations, and Ways Forward." *Government Information Quarterly* 24: 646–665. doi:10.1016/j.giq.2007.01.002.

Yildiz, M. 2013. "Big Questions of E-Government Research." *Information Polity* 17: 343–355.

Trustworthiness of digital government services: deriving a comprehensive theory through interpretive structural modelling

Marijn Janssen ⓘ, Nripendra P. Rana, Emma L. Slade
and Yogesh K. Dwivedi

ABSTRACT
Having its origin in public administration, trustworthiness is a significant concept in digital government research, influencing the relationships between citizens and governments. However, the interrelationships between the facets of trustworthiness are given inadequate attention. Therefore, the aim of this research was to develop a theory detailing the factors affecting citizens' perceptions of e-government trustworthiness. A comprehensive review of public administration and information systems literature highlighted 20 pertinent variables. The interrelationships of these variables were identified and categorized according to their driving and dependence power by employing interpretive structural modelling. The proposed model was then drawn based on the level partitioning of variables and interrelationships of the variables determined using the final reachability matrix. The findings reveal that current conceptualizations of digital government trustworthiness take a too narrow view. The findings can help government policy makers with understanding the interrelated factors associated with trustworthiness in the context of digital government services and implement them in effective strategic planning.

Introduction

Governments are struggling with their relationships with the public. Studies have shown that the trust of citizens in government has declined dramatically over recent decades (e.g. Hibbing and Theiss-Morse 2001; Rosenstone and Hansen 1993). Digital government – or e-government – technologies are regarded as key to improving relationships between government and the public (Morgeson III et al., 2011; Ravishankar 2013; Shareef et al. 2016a). Some regard e-government as a powerful tool for improving the internal efficiency of the government, the quality of service delivery, and public participation and engagement (Dwivedi et al., 2016a; Dawes 2008; Gil-García and Pardo 2005; Parent, Vandebeek, and Gemino 2005; Rana and Dwivedi 2015; Rana et al. 2015a, 2016). Others find e-government to be a means of helping to establish trustworthy institutions and building or restoring citizen's trust in government (Bellamy and Taylor 1998; Tolbert and Mossberger 2006; West 2005; Sandeep and Ravishankar 2014).

Trust is important in the e-services context to help users overcome perceptions of uncertainty and risk (McKnight, Choudhury, and Kacmar 2002), which may inhibit citizens' use of e-government technologies. Although scholars in the public admin-istration field have discussed the significance of trust (e.g. Behn 1995; Nachmias 1985; Ruscio 1996), not much empirical research on this subject is yet found (Cho and Poister 2013). Originating in the public administration literature, trustworthiness has become central to e-government research (Carter and Belanger 2005; Welch, Hinnant, and Moon 2005). The concept of *trustworthiness* refers to the properties through which a trusted entity (whether another person or an institution) serves the interests of the trustor (citizen or business) (Levi and Stoker 2000). Belanger, Hiller, and Smith (2002) defined trustworthiness as the perception of conviction in the trusted entity's reliability and integrity. This perception usually involves concerns related to security and privacy.

Despite its importance for the e-government context (Das, DiRienzo, and Burbridge 2010), causality of trust in governance remains an under-investigated area (Vigoda-Gadot and Yuval 2003). Carter and Belanger (2005) recommend further research into the specific components of e-government trustworthiness. Although Yang and Anguelov (2013) provide comprehensive preliminary discussions of factors contributing to the trustworthiness of public services, public sector literature has not yet holistically considered the factors affecting citizens' perceptions of e-government trustworthiness.

The interpretive structural modelling (ISM) method helps to impose order and direction on the complexity of the relationships among the variables of a system (Sage 1977). Therefore, the aim of this research is to conduct ISM to develop a theory detailing the factors affecting citizens' perceptions of e-government trust-worthiness. By doing so, this work will attempt to answer the following research question: which factors affect citizens' perceptions of e-government trustworthi-ness and how are they related to each other? The research endeavours to make a cross-disciplinary contribution through application of knowledge from public sector, e-government, and information systems literature. We limit the scope of e-government to government-to-citizen e-government transactional and interac-tional services in accordance with other researchers (e.g. Lee and Rao 2009; Shareef et al. 2011).

The remainder of the paper is as follows. First, a literature review of public administration and information systems research uncovers a variety of factors linked to e-government trustworthiness. In the next section, the ISM method employed to determine the power of the antecedents is described. In the further sections, the results and their implications are discussed. Finally, the paper is concluded, outlining limitations and suggestions for future research.

Literature review

Trust and trustworthiness are fundamentally distinct but closely related concepts (Yang and Anguelov 2013). Cho and Lee (2011) discuss the differences between trust and trustworthiness at length, determining that trustworthiness centres around the characteristics of a trustee whereas trust concerns a trustor's psychological state.

Therefore, trust is an individual's perception of the trustworthiness owned or displayed by another (Grimmelikhuijsen and Meijer 2014; Yang and Anguelov 2013).

In contrast to the context of e-commerce, there are unlikely to be competing e-government services, making trust even more vital to prevent citizens reverting to traditional offline interactions with government (Teo, Srivastava, and Jiang 2008). Cho and Lee (2011) argue that focussing on the trustworthiness rather than on trust is more practically useful in order to guide public managers' trust-building activities. In a similar vein, Yang and Anguelov (2013) argue that trustworthiness can be directly controlled or influenced by public sector managers and decision makers.

There have been two overarching focal points in terms of trustors in public administration research: public sector servants and citizens. Considering the former, existing research has explored the role of perceived trustworthiness as a managerial resource within US federal agencies (Cho and Lee 2011), the role of trust in public servants' organizational identification (Campbell and Im 2015), and the effects of different types of trust on employee satisfaction and organizational commitment (Cho and Park 2011). Focussing on citizens as the trustors, public sector research has explored the effect of e-government adoption and/or satisfaction on citizens' trust in government (e.g. Hong 2013; Morgeson, VanAmburg, and Mithas 2011; Welch, Hinnant, and Moon 2005), the effect of transparency on citizens' perceptions of trustworthiness (Grimmelikhuijsen and Meijer 2014), and the role of organizational politics and ethics as predictors of citizens' trust in governance (Vigoda-Gadot 2007).

Even though gaining citizens' trust is a high priority for public organizations (Park and Blenkinsopp 2011), Robinson et al. (2013) argue that limited work has been conducted to examine the factors contributing to citizens' perceptions of trustworthiness of specific agencies, programmes, or services and find that models of trust need to be specific to the context. Most theory and empirical research on the impact of e-government on citizens' trust in government remains at the macro-level and misses out on the deeper understanding of the interaction between the factors directly or indirectly influencing the trustworthiness of e-government (Smith 2010, 2011). This lack of empirical data is partially due to the relatively contemporary nature of e-government implementation that has meant limited time and opportunities to study the wider social, economic, and political implications of e-government projects (Weare 2002).

Trustworthiness of e-government and associated variables

Trustworthiness of e-government is based on characteristics of e-government that may generate citizens' trust. Mayer, Davis, and Schoorman (1995) identified three core dimensions of trustworthiness: *ability, benevolence*, and *integrity*. These three principles are associated with competence, good intentions, and honesty and consistency, respectively (see McKnight, Choudhury, and Kacmar 2002; Yang and Anguelov 2013). A number of public sector studies have employed these dimensions of trustworthiness in government and e-government (e.g. Cho and Lee 2011; Grimmelikhuijsen and Meijer 2014; Shareef, Archer, and Dwivedi 2015; Yang and Anguelov 2013). Despite criticisms of adopting unidimensional scales of trust, other studies have captured trustworthiness as a unidimensional scale (e.g. Park and Blenkinsopp 2011), sometimes even using just one of the three aforementioned dimensions as a measure of trustworthiness (e.g. Robinson et al. 2013).

Lee and Rao (2009) focus on 'trust in e-government agent', measuring benevolence, integrity, and competence beliefs as reflective indicators of a second-order
construct, whereas Tan, Benbasat, and Cenfetelli (2008) model competence, integrity, and benevolence as predictors of customer trust. Dashti, Benbasat, and
Burton-Jones (2009) argue that citizens' trust in e-government reflects their evaluation of the officials responsible for developing, maintaining, and monitoring the
system rather than the system itself. This suggests that the dimensions of trustworthiness, that is, ability, benevolence, and integrity, are relevant for e-government. However, Dashti, Benbasat, and Burton-Jones (2009) include
trustworthiness as a measurement item of the latent variable 'trust in e-government.' Teo, Srivastava, and Jiang (2008) modelled trust in government and trust in
Internet as predictors of trust in e-government website. Carter and Belanger (2005)
proposed a model of e-government trustworthiness comprised trust of the Internet
and trust of government, but cross-loading led to the combination of the observed
variables to form one trustworthiness construct. These various measurements and
conceptualizations demonstrate the inconsistency in the use of 'trust' and 'trustworthiness' as constructs in e-government research.

Given that citizens hold the government accountable when services provided by
third parties go wrong, Yang and Anguelov (2013) argue that *trust in government* is
inextricably linked to trustworthiness of public services, which implies that trust in
government is linked to trustworthiness of e-government. Dashti, Benbasat, and
Burton-Jones (2009) differentiate trust in government and trust in e-government by
the visibility of the public servants and their direct contact with the public. They
found support for their hypothesis that trust in government would positively affect
trust in e-government, suggesting that citizens' rely partly on their offline experience
with public servants to evaluate their less visible counterparts who operate e-government; if government behaves sincerely offline, then it appears that citizens are more
likely to believe that e-government will behave similarly. These findings are in line
with Vigoda-Gadot & Yuval's (2003, p.504) arguments that 'as customers of public
services, citizens tend to generalize their attitudes.'

In addition to trust in government, Belanger and Carter (2008) propose that initial
trust in e-government is composed of *trust of the Internet* as the enabling technology
of e-government services and find that both of these constructs significantly affect
intention to use e-government services. However, when modelled as predictors of
trust in e-government website, trust in technology was only found to be a significant
predictor for active users (Teo, Srivastava, and Jiang 2008), evidencing a contextual
effect of trust of the Internet.

E-government provides a vehicle for increased dissemination of information and
hence improved *transparency*. Transparency has been found to increase citizens' trust
in local government (e.g. Tolbert and Mossberger 2006) as well as being a predictor
of trust and satisfaction (Park and Blenkinsopp 2011). However, Grimmelikhuijsen
and Meijer (2014) found that prior knowledge and disposition to trust government
moderated the relationship between transparency and perceived trustworthiness,
suggesting that the link between transparency and trustworthiness is more compli-
cated. Although much of the empirical evidence suggests transparency is an antecedent of trustworthiness, Margetts (2011) makes an interesting point about the
limits of transparency and potential detrimental effects of highlighting incompetence
as a result of transparency. This suggests that presenting wrong or inaccurate

information as a result of transparency may negatively affect trustworthiness of e-government.

Citizens want to know that public servants are listening and will respond to their needs (Ravishankar 2013; Yang and Anguelov 2013) and interaction between two parties helps to develop trust (see Welch, Hinnant, and Moon 2005). *Responsiveness* relates to perceptions about the willingness of a service provider to help the customer and can positively affect customer trust (Gefen 2002). E-government websites create opportunities for convenient and quick interactions between citizens and public servants (Tolbert and Mossberger 2006). Responsiveness of public servants behind the e-government system may make a citizen feel cared about by the government, which may increase perceptions of trustworthiness. Tolbert and Mossberger (2006) found that responsiveness was directly linked to increased trust of local government. Tan, Benbasat, and Cenfetelli (2008) found responsiveness to be a core attribute of service quality, concluding that such a feature is central to e-government service design. The finding of Welch et al. (2005) – that individuals with more concern about the responsiveness of government are less satisfied – suggests an important relationship between responsiveness and satisfaction with e-government.

Welch, Hinnant, and Moon (2005) argue that factors such as *accountability* may be just as important as concerns over the technical systems enabling e-government services. 'To be accountable is to provide information about one's performance, to take corrective action as necessary, and to be responsible for one's performance' (Wang and Wan Wart 2007, p.270), suggesting that transparency and responsiveness are inextricably linked to accountability. Although accountability is influenced by information quality, information asymmetry blurs insight. Baldwin, Gauld, and Goldfinch (2012) explored public servant attitudes towards ICT and e-government in New Zealand. Using a mixture of closed- and open-ended questions, it was revealed that while some of the 240 respondents saw increased accountability as a result of e-government, others envisaged the opposite. From the citizen perspective, accountability as a result of e-government may precede trustworthiness of e-government (see Sandeep and Ravishankar 2014).

Privacy and *security* relate to the safety of information (Shareef et al. 2016b; Teo, Srivastava, and Jiang 2008). Transactional services require citizens to disclose personal information before a transaction can be completed (Beldad et al. 2012); thus, 'privacy and security are reoccurring issues in e-commerce and e-government research' (Carter and Belanger 2005, p.9). Perceived privacy and security of information is critical to instil users' confidence. Asgarkhani's (2005) report on a pilot study of a digital government project in New Zealand documented concerns about data security and confidentiality with regard to online government services. For both experienced and inexperienced users, confidence in online privacy statements has been found to be very important in predicting trust in e-government (Beldad et al. 2012). Shareef et al. (2011) also found that beliefs in security contribute to developing trust in e-government.

Spatial separation when conducting transactions via e-government also involves an element of risk from sources of attack such as third-party hacking. *Perceived risk* is related to the uncertain outcome of a behaviour (Lee and Rao 2009). Evidence of the relationship between perceived risk and trust in e-government remains largely convoluted. Belanger and Carter (2008) found trust of the government, but not trust of the Internet, to have a significant negative effect on perceived risk of e-government services, and that perceived risk had a negative effect on intention to use e-government. Horst, Kuttschreuter, and Gutteling (2007) found perceived risk of e-services to negatively affect trust in e-government. Unusually, Shareef et al. (2011) found perceived uncertainty to have a positive effect on trust, which they argued was a result of the respondents' enjoyment of the virtual characteristics of e-government in the presence of security and technical ability.

In the context of e-government services, *system quality* is a subjective assessment of the e-government website. Lee and Rao (2009) found that website quality has a significant effect on citizens' confidence in the competence of an e-government service provider. Among respondents with e-government experience, it has been found that the quality of previous online government transactions plays an important role in shaping trust in government (Beldad et al. 2012). Another measure of perceived quality, *service quality* is a subjective assessment of a service received against expectations of that service (Parasuraman, Zeithaml, and Berry 1988; Shareef et al. 2014). Carter and Belanger (2005) argue that those who have a positive experience of e-government services will be more likely to use the service again. Parent, Vandebeek, and Gemino (2005) found e-government service quality to have a significant effect on trust in government. Tan, Benbasat, and Cenfetelli (2008) also found service quality to highly influence the three core constructs of trustworthiness. In the opposite direction, Teo, Srivastava, and Jiang (2008) found trust in e-government website to significantly predict both system quality and service quality. The meta-analysis of Rana et al. (2015b) found support of the significant effects of system and service quality on satisfaction, which has also been confirmed in public administration literature (e.g. Van Ryzin et al. 2004).

Citizen *satisfaction* with e-government results from a number of factors (Welch, Hinnant, and Moon 2005). Van Ryzin et al. (2004) found that overall satisfaction drives trust in local government officials and research by Vigoda-Gadot (2007) found satisfaction to be the strongest predictor of trust in governance. It has also been found that those individuals who are more satisfied with e-government and government Web sites also trust the government more, and those individuals who trust government more are also more likely to be satisfied with e-government (Welch, Hinnant, and Moon 2005). The effect of trust in e-government website on satisfaction was found to be partially mediated by system quality and service quality in the study of Teo et al. (2008), with service quality having a slightly stronger influence than system quality.

Robinson et al. (2013) found various individual factors such as *political attitude* to have substantive impacts on trust in administrative agencies and argue that although these are seldom measured in public administration research, their significant influence makes their inclusion in further research important. Shareef et al. (2011) found *perceived ability to use* to have substantial effects on both trust in e-government and adoption intentions. Grimmelikhuijsen and Meijer (2014) found that *prior knowledge* and *disposition to trust* government moderated the relationship between transparency and perceived trustworthiness. Disposition to trust is based on characteristics of the trustor (Belanger and Carter 2008) – the extent to which an individual displays an inclination to trust others and depend on them (McKnight, Choudhury, and Kacmar 2002). Therefore, disposition to trust is personality based (Mayer, Davis, and Schoorman 1995) rather than context specific and so cannot be manipulated by government agencies (Belanger and Carter 2008). Disposition to trust is especially pivotal when the situation is ambiguous and/or there is little information about the trustee's ability, benevolence, and integrity. Belanger and Carter (2008) found disposition to trust to significantly influence trust of the Internet and trust of the government. Lee and Rao (2009) also found disposition to trust to increase trust in e-government, whereas Beldad et al. (2012) did not find support for this.

'While e-government has the potential to improve government transparency, responsiveness, and accountability, e-services will only be adopted if citizens deem them trustworthy' (Belanger and Carter 2008, p.166). *Use* of e-government has been found to be related to a number of factors already highlighted. Morgeson III et al. (2011) found that e-government adoption may lead to improved citizen confidence in the future performance of that e-government agency and Welch, Hinnant, and Moon (2005) found that e-government website use is positively related to e-government satisfaction. Teo, Srivastava, and Jiang (2008) found trust in e-government website to have a direct effect on intention to continue using e-government and Tolbert and Mossberger (2006) found a significant relationship between trust and use of a local government website. On the other hand, Parent, Vandebeek, and Gemino (2005) found that e-government usage is not sufficient to induce trust in government but intensifies existing levels of trust if these are already positive.

Method

The previous section highlighted how trustworthiness of e-government services is impacted by a number of variables. However, the direct and indirect relationships between the variables describe the situation far more precisely than when they are considered in isolation. ISM is an interactive learning process: a group's adjudication decides whether and how a number of variables are related, an overall structure is extracted from the complex set of variables based on the relationships interpreted by the group, and then the specific relationships and overall structure are portrayed in a directed graph (digraph) model through a hierarchical configuration. ISM has been used by other researchers in the area to explore e-governance service delivery based on its critical success factors (Lal and Haleem 2009). ISM is a sound method for this research in order to develop insight into the collective understanding of the relationships between trustworthiness of e-government and the various variables identified in the literature review. The steps involved in the ISM technique are shown in Figure 1.

Structural self-interaction matrix (steps 2, 3, 4, and 5)

For analysing the criteria, a contextual relationship of 'helps achieve' or 'influences' is chosen. In this exercise, seven experts – three public sector professionals and four academics – whom have a mixed experience of information systems, e-government, and public administration were chosen to provide their expert views on the inter-relationships of the twenty constructs selected through the review of literature (see Appendix for construct definitions and table used for the expert survey). To express the relationships between different factors of e-government trustworthiness, four symbols were used to denote the direction of a relationship between the parameters i and j (here $i < j$):

[1] **V** – construct i helps achieve or influences j; [2] **A** – construct j helps achieve or influences i; [3] **X** – constructs i and j help achieve or influence each other; [4] **O** – constructs i and j are unrelated.

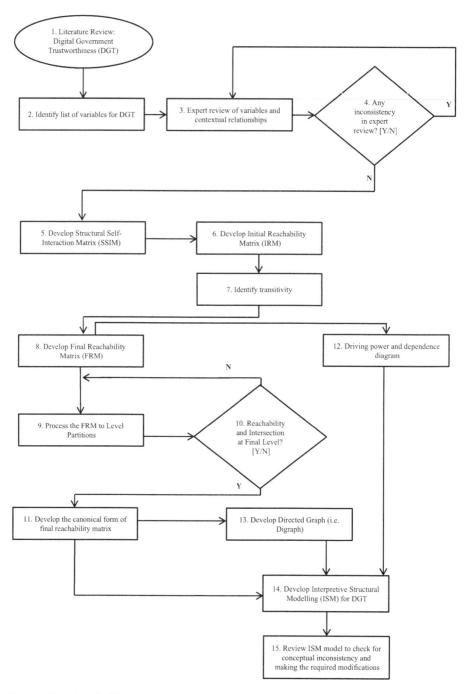

Figure 1. Flow chart for ISM method.

By collating the contextual relationships decided by each expert, the structural self-interaction matrix (SSIM) is developed (Table 1). The following statements explain the use of symbols V, A, X, O in SSIM: [1] Privacy concerns (Variable 5)

Table 1. Structural self-interactional matrix (SSIM).

VR[i/j]	20	19	18	17	16	15	14	13	12	11	10	9	8	7	6	5	4	3	2	1
1	X	A	A	X	V	O	O	X	A	A	A	A	A	A	A	A	X	X	X	
2	X	A	O	O	V	X	A	X	X	A	X	A	A	O	X	X	X	X		
3	X	O	X	O	V	O	O	V	A	O	O	O	A	O	A	V	V			
4	V	A	A	O	V	A	A	X	A	A	O	A	A	O	X	X				
5	V	O	A	A	V	A	A	V	A	A	A	A	A	O	X					
6	X	A	A	A	V	A	A	X	A	A	A	A	A	O						
7	V	O	V	V	O	O	O	O	O	O	O	O	O							
8	V	O	X	O	V	O	X	V	O	O	X	X								
9	V	V	V	O	V	O	X	O	V	V	O									
10	V	X	V	V	V	O	O	V	O	X										
11	V	O	O	V	V	O	V	V	V											
12	V	A	X	V	V	V	X	V												
13	V	A	O	O	X	X	A													
14	V	V	V	O	V	V														
15	V	O	O	O	V															
16	X	A	A	A																
17	V	O	A																	
18	V	O																		
19	V																			
20																				

1: Trust in government; 2: trust in technology; 3: disposition to trust; 4: perceived risk; 5: privacy concerns; 6: perceived security; 7: political attitudes; 8: transparency; 9: perceived prior knowledge; 10: accountability; 11: responsiveness; 12: service quality; 13: satisfaction; 14: system quality; 15: perceived ability to use; 16: use; 17: benevolence; 18: integrity; 19: competence; 20: trustworthiness of e-government; VR[i/j]: variable i/variable j.

help achieve or influence trustworthiness of e-government (Variable 20) (V); [2] system quality (Variable 14) helps achieve or influences trust in technology (Variable 2) (A); [3] satisfaction (Variable 13) and use (Variable 16) help achieve or influence each other (X); [4] transparency (Variable 8) and competence (Variable 19) are unrelated (O).

Reachability matrix (steps 6, 7, and 8)

Next, the SSIM was converted into a binary matrix, called the initial reachability matrix, by substituting V, A, X, and O with 1 and 0 as per the case. The substitution of 1s and 0s is as per the following rules: [1] if the (i, j) entry in the SSIM is V, the (i, j) entry in the reachability matrix becomes 1 and the (j, i) entry becomes 0; [2] if the (i, j) entry in the SSIM is A, the (i, j) entry in the reachability matrix becomes 0 and the (j, i) entry becomes 1; [3] if the (i, j) entry in the SSIM is X, both the (i, j) entry and (j, i) entry in the reachability matrix become 1; [4] if the (i, j) entry in the SSIM is O, both the (i, j) entry and (j, i) entry in the reachability matrix become 0. Following these rules, the initial reachability matrix for the trustworthiness factors of e-government is shown in Table 2.

After including transitivity, the final reachability matrix is shown in Table 3. Table 3 also shows the driving and dependence power of each variable. The driving power for each variable is the total number of variables, including itself, which it may help to achieve. On the other hand, dependence power is the total number of variables, including itself, which may help in achieving it. These driving powers and dependence powers will be used later in the classification of variables into the four groups including autonomous, dependent, linkage, and drivers.

Table 2. Initial reachability matrix.

VR	1	2	3	4	5	6	7	8	9	10	11	12	13	14	15	16	17	18	19	20
1	1	1	1	1	0	0	0	0	0	0	0	0	1	0	0	1	1	0	0	1
2	1	1	1	1	1	1	0	0	0	1	0	1	1	0	1	1	0	0	0	1
3	1	1	1	1	1	0	0	0	0	0	0	0	1	0	0	1	0	1	0	1
4	1	1	0	1	1	1	0	0	0	0	0	0	1	0	0	1	0	0	0	1
5	1	1	0	1	1	1	0	0	0	0	0	0	1	0	0	1	0	0	0	1
6	1	1	1	1	1	1	0	0	0	0	0	0	1	0	0	1	0	0	0	1
7	1	0	0	0	0	0	1	0	0	0	0	0	0	0	0	0	1	1	0	1
8	1	1	1	1	1	1	1	0	1	1	1	0	0	1	0	1	0	1	0	1
9	1	1	0	1	1	1	0	1	1	0	0	1	1	0	1	1	0	1	1	1
10	1	1	0	0	1	1	0	1	0	1	1	0	1	0	0	1	1	1	1	1
11	1	1	0	1	1	1	0	0	0	1	1	1	1	1	0	1	1	0	0	1
12	1	1	1	1	1	1	0	0	0	0	0	1	1	1	1	1	1	1	0	1
13	1	1	0	1	0	1	0	0	0	0	0	0	1	0	1	1	0	0	0	1
14	0	1	0	1	1	1	0	1	0	0	0	1	1	1	1	1	0	1	1	1
15	0	1	0	1	1	1	0	0	1	0	0	0	1	0	1	1	0	0	0	1
16	0	0	0	0	0	0	0	0	0	0	0	0	1	0	0	1	0	0	0	1
17	1	0	0	0	1	1	0	0	0	0	0	0	0	0	0	1	1	0	0	1
18	1	0	1	1	1	1	0	1	0	0	0	1	0	0	0	1	1	1	0	1
19	1	1	0	1	0	1	0	0	0	1	0	1	1	0	0	1	0	0	1	1
20	1	1	1	0	0	1	0	0	0	0	0	0	0	0	0	1	0	0	0	1

1: Trust in government; 2: trust in technology; 3: disposition to trust; 4: perceived risk; 5: privacy concerns; 6: perceived security; 7: political attitudes; 8: transparency; 9: perceived prior knowledge; 10: accountability; 11: responsiveness; 12: service quality; 13: satisfaction; 14: system quality; 15: perceived ability to use; 16: use; 17: benevolence; 18: integrity; 19: competence; 20: trustworthiness of e-government; VR: variable.

Table 3. Final reachability matrix.

VR	1	2	3	4	5	6	7	8	9	10	11	12	13	14	15	16	17	18	19	20	DRP
1	1	1	1	1	1*	1*	0	0	0	1*	0	1*	1	0	1*	1	1	1*	0	1	14
2	1	1	1	1	1	1	0	1*	1*	1	1*	1	1	1*	1	1	1*	1*	1	1	19
3	1	1	1	1	1	1*	0	1*	0	1*	0	1*	1	0	1*	1	1*	1	0	1	15
4	1	1	1*	1	1	1	0	0	0	1*	0	1*	1	0	1*	1	1*	0	0	1	13
5	1	1	1*	1	1	1	0	0	0	1*	0	1*	1	0	1*	1	1*	0	0	1	13
6	1	1	1	1	1	1	0	0	0	1*	0	1*	1	0	1*	1	1*	1*	0	1	14
7	1	1*	1*	1*	1*	1*	1	1*	0	0	0	1*	1*	0	0	1*	1	1	0	1	14
8	1	1	1	1	1	1	0	1	1	1	1*	1*	1	1	1*	1	1*	1	0	1	18
9	1	1	1*	1	1	1	0	1	1	1	0	1	1	1*	1	1	1*	1	1	1	18
10	1	1	1*	1*	1	1	0	1	1*	1	1	1*	1	1*	1*	1	1	1	1	1	19
11	1	1	1*	1	1	1	0	1*	0	1	1	1	1	1	1*	1	1	1*	1*	1	18
12	1	1	1	1	1	1	0	1*	1*	1*	0	1	1	1	1	1	1	1	1*	1	18
13	1	1	1*	1	1*	1	0	0	1*	1*	0	1*	1	0	1	1	1*	0	0	1	14
14	1*	1	1*	1	1	1	0	1	1*	1*	0	1	1	1	1	1	1*	1	1	1	18
15	1*	1	1*	1	1	1	0	1*	1	1*	0	1*	1	0	1	1	0	1*	1*	1	16
16	1*	1*	1*	1*	0	1*	0	0	0	0	0	0	1	0	1*	1	0	0	0	1	9
17	1	1*	1*	1*	1	1	0	0	0	0	0	0	1*	0	0	1	1	0	0	1	10
18	1	1*	1	1	1	1	0	1	1*	1*	0	1	1*	1*	1*	1	1	1	0	1	17
19	1	1	1*	1	1*	1	0	1*	0	1	1*	1	1	1*	1*	1	1*	1*	1	1	18
20	1	1	1	1*	1*	1	0	0	0	1*	0	1*	1*	0	1*	1	1*	1*	0	1	14
DNP	20	20	20	20	19	20	1	12	9	17	5	18	20	9	18	20	18	15	8	20	309

1*: Shows transitivity; 1: trust in government; 2: trust in technology; 3: disposition to trust; 4: perceived risk; 5: privacy concerns; 6: perceived security; 7: political attitudes; 8: transparency; 9: perceived prior knowledge; 10: accountability; 11: responsiveness; 12: service quality; 13: satisfaction; 14: system quality; 15: perceived ability to use; 16: use; 17: benevolence; 18: integrity; 19: competence; 20: trustworthiness of e-government; DNP: dependence power; DRP: driving power; VR: variable.

Level partitions (steps 9 and 10)

The matrix is partitioned by assessing the reachability and antecedent sets for each variable (Warfield 1974). The final reachability matrix leads to the reachability and antecedent set for each factor relating to trustworthiness of e-government. The reachability set $R(s_i)$ of the variable s_i is the set of variables defined in the columns that contained 1 in row s_i. Similarly, the antecedent set $A(s_i)$ of the variable s_i is the set of variables defined in the rows, which contain 1 in the column s_i. Then, the interaction of these sets is derived for all the variables. The variables for which the intersection of reachability and intersection sets results into reachability sets (i.e. $R(s_i) \cap A(s_i) = R(s_i)$) are the top-level variables of the ISM hierarchy. The top-level variables of the hierarchy would not help to achieve any other variable above their own level in the hierarchy.

Once the top-level variables are identified, they are separated out from the rest of the variables. Then, the same process is repeated to find out the next level of variables, and so on. These identified levels help in building the diagraph and the final ISM model (Agarwal, Shankar, and Tiwari 2007; Dwivedi et al., 2016b; Hughes et al. 2016; Singh, Garg, and Deshmukh 2007). In the present context, the variables along with their reachability set, antecedent set, and the top level are shown in Table 4. The process is completed in five iterations (Tables 4–8) documented below. In Table 4, nine variables namely 1 (trust in government), 2 (trust in technology), 3 (disposition to trust), 4 (perceived risk), 6 (perceived security), 13 (satisfaction), 15 (perceived ability to use), 16 (use), and 20 (trustworthiness of e-government) are found at level I, as the elements for these variables at reachability and intersection set are the same. So, they will be positioned at the top of the hierarchy (i.e. level I) of the ISM model. As a result, the rows corresponding to variables 1, 2, 3, 4, 6, 13, 15, 16, and 20 are removed from further inclusion (see Table 5). The same process of deleting the rows corresponding to the previous level and marking the next level position to the new table is repeated until the final variable in the table is reached.

In Table 5, the variables 5 (privacy concerns) and 17 (benevolence) are put at level II, as the elements (i.e. elements 5, 10, 12, and 17 for variable 5 and elements 5 and 17 for variable 17) for these variables at reachability and intersection set are the same. Thus, they will be positioned at level II in the ISM model.

In Table 6, variables 8 (transparency), 10 (accountability), 12 (service quality), 14 (system quality), and 18 (integrity) are put at level III as, the elements (i.e. 8, 10, 12, 14, and 18) at reachability set and intersection set for these variables are the same. Thus, they will be positioned at level III in the ISM model.

In Table 7, variables 7 (political attitude), 11 (responsiveness), and 19 (competence) are put at level IV as the elements at reachability set and intersection set for these variables are the same. Thus, they will be positioned at level IV in the ISM model.

In Table 8, variable 9 (perceived prior knowledge) is put at level V, as the element (i.e. 9) at reachability set and intersection set for this variable is the same. Thus, it will be positioned at level V in the ISM model.

Developing canonical matrix (step 11)

A canonical matrix is developed by clustering variables in the same level, across the rows and columns of the final reachability matrix as shown in Table 9. This matrix is

Table 4. Partition on reachability matrix: interaction 1.

Element P(i)	Reachability set: R(P_i)	Antecedent set: A(P_i)	Intersection set: R(P_i) ∩ A(P_i)	Level
1	1,2,3,4,5,6,10,12,13,15,16,17,18,20	1,2,3,4,5,6,7,8,9,10,11,12,13,14,15,16,17,18,19,20	1,2,3,4,5,6,10,12,13,15,16,17,18,20	I
2	1,2,3,4,5,6,8,9,10,11,12,13,15,16,17,18,19,20	1,2,3,4,5,6,7,8,9,10,11,12,13,14,15,16,17,18,19,20	1,2,3,4,5,6,8,9,10,11,12,13,14,15,16,17,18,19,20	I
3	1,2,3,4,5,6,8,10,12,13,15,16,17,18,20	1,2,3,4,5,6,7,8,9,10,11,12,13,14,15,16,17,18,19,20	1,2,3,4,5,6,8,10,12,13,15,16,17,18,20	I
4	1,2,3,4,5,6,10,12,13,15,16,17,20	1,2,3,4,5,6,7,8,9,10,11,12,13,14,15,17,18,19,20	1,2,3,4,5,6,10,12,13,15,16,17,20	
5	1,2,3,4,5,6,10,12,13,15,16,17,20	1,2,3,4,5,6,7,8,9,10,11,12,13,14,15,17,18,19,20	1,2,3,4,5,6,10,12,13,15,17,20	
6	1,2,3,4,5,6,10,12,13,15,16,17,18,20	1,2,3,4,5,6,7,8,9,10,11,12,13,14,15,16,17,18,19,20	1,2,3,4,5,6,10,12,13,15,16,17,18,20	I
7	1,2,3,4,5,6,7,8,12,13,16,17,18,20	7	7	
8	1,2,3,4,5,6,8,9,10,11,12,13,14,15,16,17,18,19,20	2,3,7,8,9,10,11,12,14,15,18,19	2,3,8,9,10,11,12,14,15,18,19	
9	1,2,3,4,5,6,8,9,10,12,13,14,15,16,17,18,19,20	2,8,9,10,12,13,14,15,18	2,8,9,10,12,13,14,15,18	
10	1,2,3,4,5,6,8,9,10,11,12,13,14,15,16,17,18,19,20	1,2,3,4,5,6,8,9,10,11,12,13,14,15,18,19,20	1,2,3,4,5,6,8,9,10,11,12,13,14,15,18,19,20	
11	1,2,3,4,5,6,8,10,11,12,13,14,15,16,17,18,19,20	2,8,10,11,19	2,8,10,11,19	
12	1,2,3,4,5,6,9,10,12,13,14,15,16,17,18,19,20	1,2,3,4,5,6,7,8,9,10,11,12,13,14,15,18,19,20	1,2,3,4,5,6,8,9,10,12,13,14,15,18,19,20	
13	1,2,3,4,5,6,9,10,12,13,15,16,17,20	1,2,3,4,5,6,7,8,9,10,11,12,13,14,15,16,17,18,19,20	1,2,3,4,5,6,9,10,12,13,15,16,17,20	
14	1,2,3,4,5,6,8,9,10,12,13,14,15,16,17,18,19,20	2,8,9,10,11,12,14,18,19	2,8,9,10,12,14,18,19	
15	1,2,3,4,5,6,8,9,10,12,13,15,16,18,19,20	1,2,3,4,5,6,8,9,10,11,12,13,14,15,16,17,18,19,20	1,2,3,4,5,6,8,9,10,12,13,15,16,18,19,20	I
16	1,2,3,4,6,13,15,16,20	1,2,3,4,5,6,7,8,9,10,11,12,13,14,15,16,17,18,19,20	1,2,3,4,6,13,15,16,20	I
17	1,2,3,4,5,6,13,16,17,20	1,2,3,4,5,6,7,8,9,10,11,12,13,14,17,18,19,20	1,2,3,4,5,6,13,17,20	I
18	1,2,3,4,5,6,8,9,10,12,13,14,15,16,17,18,20	1,2,3,6,7,8,9,10,11,12,14,15,19	1,2,3,6,8,9,10,12,14,15,18,20	
19	1,2,3,4,5,6,8,10,11,12,13,14,15,16,17,18,19,20	2,8,9,10,11,12,14,15,19	2,8,10,11,12,14,15,19	
20	1,2,3,4,5,6,10,12,13,15,16,17,18,20	1,2,3,4,5,6,7,8,9,10,11,12,13,14,15,16,17,18,19,20	1,2,3,4,5,6,10,12,13,15,16,17,18,20	I

L: Level; VR: variable.

Table 5. Partition on reachability matrix: interaction 2.

Element $P(i)$	Reachability set: $R(P_i)$	Antecedent set: $A(P_i)$	Intersection set: $R(P_i) \cap A(P_i)$	Level
5	5,10,12,17	5,7,8,9,10,11,12,14,17,18,19	5,10,12,17	II
7	5,7,8,12,17,18	7	7	
8	5,8,9,10,11,12,14,17,18,19	7,8,9,10,11,12,14,18,19	8,9,10,11,12,14,18,19	
9	5,8,9,10,12,14,17,18,19	8,9,10,12,14,18	8,9,10,12,14,18	
10	5,8,9,10,11,12,14,17,18,19	5,8,9,10,11,12,14,18,19	5,8,9,10,11,12,14,18,19	
11	5,8,10,11,12,14,17,18,19	8,10,11,19	8,10,11,19	
12	5,8,9,10,12,14,17,18,19	5,7,8,9,10,11,12,14,18,19	5,8,9,10,12,14,18,19	
14	5,8,9,10,12,14,17,18,19	8,9,10,11,12,14,18,19	8,9,10,12,14,18,19	
17	5,17	5,7,8,9,10,11,12,14,17,18,19	5,17	II
18	5,8,9,10,12,14,17,18	7,8,9,10,11,12,14,18,19	8,9,10,12,14,18	
19	5,8,10,11,12,14,17,18,19	8,9,10,11,12,14,19	8,10,11,12,14,19	

Table 6. Partition on reachability matrix: interaction 3.

Element $P(i)$	Reachability set: $R(P_i)$	Antecedent set: $A(P_i)$	Intersection set: $R(P_i) \cap A(P_i)$	Level
7	7,8,12,18	7	7	
8	8,9,10,11,12,14,18,19	7,8,9,10,11,12,14,18,19	8,9,10,11,12,14,18,19	III
9	8,9,10,12,14,18,19	8,9,10,12,14,18	8,9,10,12,14,18	
10	8,9,10,11,12,14,18,19	8,9,10,11,12,14,18,19	8,9,10,11,12,14,18,19	III
11	8,10,11,12,14,18,19	8,10,11,19	8,10,11,19	
12	8,9,10,12,14,18,19	7,8,9,10,11,12,14,18,19	8,9,10,12,14,18,19	III
14	8,9,10,12,14,18,19	8,9,10,11,12,14,18,19	8,9,10,12,14,18,19	III
18	8,9,10,12,14,18	7,8,9,10,11,12,14,18,19	8,9,10,12,14,18	III
19	8,10,11,12,14,18,19	8,9,10,11,12,14,19	8,10,11,12,14,19	

Table 7. Partition on reachability matrix: interaction 4.

Element $P(i)$	Reachability set: $R(P_i)$	Antecedent set: $A(P_i)$	Intersection set: $R(P_i) \cap A(P_i)$	Level
7	7	7	7	IV
9	9,19	9	9	
11	11,19	11,19	11,19	IV
19	11,19	9,11,19	11,19	IV

Table 8. Partition on reachability matrix: interaction 5.

Element $P(i)$	Reachability set: $R(P_i)$	Antecedent set: $A(P_i)$	Intersection set: $R(P_i) \cap A(P_i)$	Level
9	9	9	9	V

another more convenient form of the final reachability matrix (i.e. Table 3) as far as drawing the ISM model is concerned. This matrix helps in the generation of the digraph and later on structural model.

Classification of e-government trustworthiness factors (step 12)

The trustworthiness factors are classified into four categories based on driving power and dependence power. They include autonomous, dependent, linkage, and drivers (Mandal and Deshmukh 1994). The driving power and dependence power of each of these trustworthiness factors are shown in Table 3. Thereafter, the driver power–dependence power diagram is shown in Figure 2.

Table 9. Canonical form of final reachability matrix.

VR	1	2	3	4	6	13	15	16	20	5	17	8	10	12	14	18	7	11	19	9	LVL
1	1	1	1	1	1	1	1	1	1	1	1	0	1	1	0	1	0	0	0	0	I
2	1	1	1	1	1	1	1	1	1	1	1	1	1	1	1	1	0	1	1	1	I
3	1	1	1	1	1	1	1	1	1	1	1	1	1	1	0	1	0	0	0	0	I
4	1	1	1	1	1	1	1	1	1	1	1	0	1	1	0	0	0	0	0	0	I
6	1	1	1	1	1	1	1	1	1	1	1	0	1	1	0	1	0	0	0	0	I
13	1	1	1	1	1	1	1	1	1	1	1	0	1	1	0	0	0	0	0	1	I
15	1	1	1	1	1	1	1	1	1	1	0	1	1	1	0	1	0	0	1	1	I
16	1	1	1	1	1	1	1	1	1	0	0	0	0	0	0	0	0	0	0	0	I
20	1	1	1	1	1	1	1	1	1	1	1	0	1	1	0	1	0	0	0	0	I
5	1	1	1	1	1	1	1	1	1	1	1	0	1	1	0	0	0	0	0	0	II
17	1	1	1	1	1	1	0	1	1	1	1	0	0	0	0	0	0	0	0	0	II
8	1	1	1	1	1	1	1	1	1	1	1	1	1	1	1	1	0	1	1	1	III
10	1	1	1	1	1	1	1	1	1	1	1	1	1	1	1	1	0	1	1	1	III
12	1	1	1	1	1	1	1	1	1	1	1	1	1	1	1	1	0	0	1	1	III
14	1	1	1	1	1	1	1	1	1	1	1	1	1	1	1	1	0	0	1	1	III
18	1	1	1	1	1	1	1	1	1	1	1	1	1	1	1	1	0	0	0	1	III
7	1	1	1	1	1	1	0	1	1	1	1	1	0	1	0	1	1	0	0	0	IV
11	1	1	1	1	1	1	1	1	1	1	1	1	1	1	1	1	0	1	1	0	IV
19	1	1	1	1	1	1	1	1	1	1	1	1	1	1	1	1	0	1	1	0	IV
9	1	1	1	1	1	1	1	1	1	1	1	1	1	1	1	1	0	0	1	1	V
LVL	I	I	I	I	I	I	I	I	I	II	II	III	III	III	III	III	IV	IV	IV	V	

1: Trust in government; 2: trust in technology; 3: disposition to trust; 4: perceived risk; 5: privacy concerns; 6: perceived security; 7: political attitudes; 8: transparency; 9: perceived prior knowledge; 10: accountability; 11: responsiveness; 12: service quality; 13: satisfaction; 14: system quality; 15: perceived ability to use; 16: use; 17: benevolence; 18: integrity; 19: competence; 20: trustworthiness of e-government; DNP: dependence power; DRP: driving power; VR: variable.

This figure has four quadrants that represent the autonomous, dependent, linkage, and drivers sections. For example, a factor (i.e. 16) that has a driving power of 9 and dependence power of 20 is positioned at a place with dependence power of 20 in the X-axis and driving power of 9 on the Y-axis. Based on its position, it can be defined as a strong dependent variable. Similarly, a factor (i.e. 11) having a driving power of 18 and a dependence power of 5 can be positioned at dependence power of 5 at the X-axis and driving power of 18 on the Y-axis. Based on its position, it can be defined as a driving variable.

The objective behind the classification is to analyse the driver power and dependency of the trustworthiness factors. The first cluster includes autonomous trustworthiness factors that have weak driver power and weak dependence. These factors are relatively disconnected from the system. In the context of the current research, no factors belong to this cluster. The second cluster consists of the dependent variables that have weak driver power but strong dependence. Use (variable 16) and benevolence (variable 17) belong to this cluster.

The third cluster has the linkage variables that have strong driver power and strong dependence. Any action on these variables will have an effect on the others and also a feedback effect on themselves (Talib, Rahman, and Qureshi 2011a). Most of the variables including 1 (trust in government), 2 (trust in technology), 3 (disposition to trust), 4 (perceived risk), 5 (privacy concerns), 6 (perceived security), 8 (transparency), 10 (accountability), 12 (service quality), 13 (satisfaction), 15 (perceived ability to use), 18 (integrity), and 20 (trustworthiness of e-government) belong to this cluster. Though the lower level variables induce or influence these variables, these also have significant driving power to influence some other variables, which are

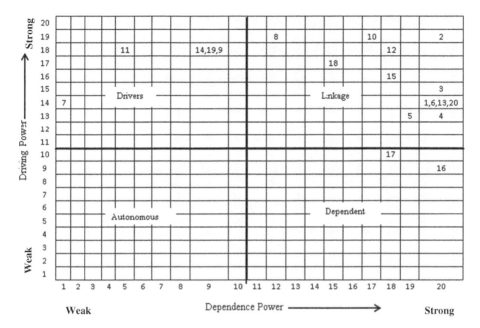

Figure 2. Driving power and dependence diagram.

at the top of the model. In fact, most of the variables on the top level of the ISM model (see Figure 3) are linkage variables interrelated to each other, which clearly indicate that they have strong driving powers to influence other linkage variables at the same top level. The fourth cluster includes drivers or independent variables with strong driving power and weak dependence. The variables including 7 (political attitude), 9 (perceived prior knowledge), 11 (responsiveness), 14 (system quality), and 19 (competence) belong to this cluster.

Formation of ISM (steps 13, 14, and 15)

From the canonical form of the reachability matrix (see Table 9), the structural model is generated by means of vertices and nodes and lincs of edges. If there is a relationship between the e-government trustworthiness factors *i* and *j*, this is shown by an arrow that points from *i* to *j*. This graph is called directed graph or digraph. After removing the indirect links as presented in the ISM method, the digraph is finally converted into an ISM-based model as shown in Figure 3.

From Figure 3, it is observed that perceived prior knowledge (variable 9) plays a significant driving role in improving e-government trustworthiness and so it comes at the base of the ISM hierarchy (i.e. level V). The variables such as trust in government (variable 1), trust in technology (variable 2), disposition to trust (variable 3), perceived risk (variable 4), perceived security (variable 6), satisfaction (variable 13), perceived ability to use (variable 15), use (variable 16), and trustworthiness of e-government (variable 20) depend on the other variables for improving them for the

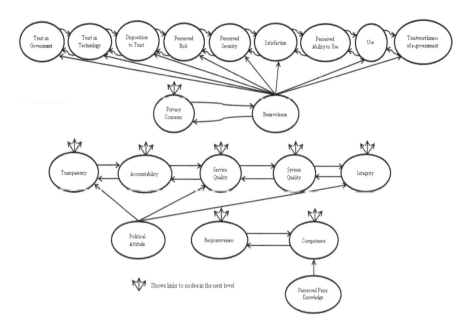

Figure 3. ISM-based model for examining e-government trustworthiness.

effective implementation of the e-government services. These variables have appeared at the top of the hierarchy (i.e. level I).

Perceived prior knowledge (variable 9), political attitude (variable 7), responsiveness (variable 11), and competence (variable 19) provide the basis for successful e-government services. The level of convenience or the degree of immediate feedback provided by the government (i.e. responsiveness), as well as the degree to which e-government possesses the skills needed to enable it to perform tasks in serving the public (i.e. competence), leads to improved transparency, accountability, service quality, system quality, and integrity of the e-government system providing services to citizens. Prior studies on e-government have shown responsiveness as the core attribute to improve service quality (e.g. Tan, Benbasat, and Cenfetelli 2008; Tolbert and Mossberger 2006).

Transparency (variable 8), accountability (variable 10), service quality (variable 12), system quality (variable 14), and integrity (variable 18) will influence privacy concerns and benevolence (i.e. degree to which citizens believe that e-government cares about them and wants to help them). The strong relationship of service quality with benevolence at the next upper level is also supported by prior research (e.g. Tan, Benbasat, and Cenfetelli 2008).

Privacy concerns (variable 5) and benevolence (variable 17) impact trust in government (variable 1), trust in technology (variable 2), disposition to trust (variable 3), perceived risk (variable 4), perceived security (variable 6), satisfaction (variable 13), perceived ability to use (variable 15), use (variable 16), and trustworthiness of e-government (variable 20) at the next, and final, level of the ISM model. Privacy concerns may play an even more important role when individuals' personal information is used for exploring and availing certain transactional e-government services. This is the reason why such services are more directly linked to individual's trust, risk, and satisfaction aspects. This also implies that privacy concerns are prerequisites to predisposition to trust, trust, risk, security, satisfaction, perceived ability to use, use, and lastly to trustworthiness of e-government.

The strong interrelationships between trust and satisfaction in the ISM model are also supported by Welch, Hinnant, and Moon (2005) who argued that higher levels of individuals' trust in government leads to their satisfaction with e-government services and web sites, and that the more satisfied individuals are with e-government or government web sites leads to greater trust in the government. The relationships between trust and risk, risk and security, security and satisfaction, and use and trustworthiness have also been highlighted by the previous literature on e-government (e.g. Belanger and Carter 2008; Chan et al. 2010; Karavasilis, Zafiropoulos, and Vrana 2010; Schaupp and Carter 2010).

Findings and discussion

Trustworthiness of e-government plays a vital role as far as citizens' use of e-government services is concerned. To be able to effectively design and implement the framework for e-government trustworthiness, we need to know the factors that significantly influence it, whether directly or indirectly. Using ISM, the interrelationships between the wide-variety of variables associated with e-government trustworthiness identified in the literature review were revealed to provide a comprehensive conceptualization that was lacking in the existing research. The major findings of this study are as follows:

(1) Autonomous variables generally appear as weak drivers and weak dependents and are relatively disconnected from the system. These variables do not have much influence on the other variables of the system (Singh, Garg, and Deshmukh 2007). The driving power-dependence power diagram indicates that there are no autonomous variables.

(2) Use (variable 16) and benevolence (variable 17) are weak drivers but strong dependent variables. They are situated further up the ISM hierarchy (see Figure 3). These variables represent the desired objectives for any successful e-government implementation and adoption and are classified largely as dependent variables. Hence, practitioners, policy makers, and managers should take special care to handle these (Talib, Rahman, and Qureshi 2011b).

(3) The largest number of variables falls in the quadrant of linkage variables in context of the current driving power-dependence power diagram. These variables include trust in government (variable 1), trust in technology (variable 2), disposition to trust (variable 3), perceived risk (variable 4), perceived security (variable 6), transparency (variable 8), accountability (variable 10), service quality (variable 12), satisfaction (variable 13), perceived ability to use (variable 15), integrity (variable 18), and trustworthiness of e-government (variable 20). This quadrant is primarily known for strong driving power and strong dependence power. Therefore, it can be inferred that among all twenty variables chosen in this research, 13 variables identified for e-government trustworthiness are unstable (see Singh, Garg, and Deshmukh 2007; Talib, Rahman, and Qureshi 2011b).

(4) The variables in the driving power-dependence power diagram including political attitude (variable 7), perceived prior knowledge (variable 9), responsiveness (variable 11), and competence (variable 19) are almost at the bottom of the ISM model with strong driving power. These variables will help the e-government implementation agencies to achieve their desired objectives and are classified as independent variables or drivers (Agarwal, Shankar, and Tiwari 2007). Therefore, these variables need consistent attention from management focussed on improving e-government trustworthiness.

(5) The ISM-based model (see Figure 3) indicates that the variables trust in government, trust in technology, disposition to trust, perceived risk, perceived security, satisfaction, perceived ability to use, use and trustworthiness of e-government are at the top of the model and hence indicate the most significant set of dependent variables of the developed framework. Similarly, perceived prior knowledge falls as the bottom-most variable of the ISM model with one of the highest driving powers. This indicates that perceived prior knowledge would drive other variables to achieve the desired objectives.

The findings of this study provide both theoretical and practical contributions. Considering theoretical contributions, the study has integrated the literature related to trustworthiness from both public management and e-government domains. Very few previous studies have examined factors contributing to trustworthiness of public services and those that have (e.g. Yang and Anguelov 2013) did not consider a wide range of associated variables nor did they focus on citizen's trustworthiness of e-government services. Therefore, this is the first study to provide a comprehensive framework of e-government in the citizen context. Additionally, this is the first study to utilize the ISM method in this area, thus also offering a methodological contribution.

eflecting on practical contributions, the proposed ISM-based model for identification and ranking of factors influencing e-government trustworthiness provides decision makers and practitioners a more realistic representation of the problem in the course of implementing e-government. The utility of the proposed ISM method lies in imposing order and direction on the complexity of relationships among these factors, which would help decision makers and practitioners of e-government to better utilize their available resources for maximizing the trustworthiness of their e-government services. The framework allows government policy makers to effectively incorporate these factors at the implementation (i.e. supply-side perspective of e-government services) and adoption (i.e. demand-side perspective of e-government services) phases, which can help avoid failure of emerging digital government projects (Dwivedi et al. 2015).

The findings of this study can serve as an eye opener for those government organizations that implement e-government services and lack prior perceived knowledge about e-government to its stakeholders, responsiveness demonstrated by its providers, its competence and service and system quality as some of those prominent factors, which are found to be the basic factors of e-government trustworthiness. ISM also helps in classifying variables into autonomous, dependent, linkage, and driver categories. Management may use their resources towards the identified factors among these categories to accomplish the optimization of resources. Moreover, the systematic framework proposed in this research has a widespread application and can be used to improve government's effectiveness, performance, and managing abilities towards generating citizens' trust in e-government services.

Conclusion

Most research that considers the impact of e-government on citizens' trust in government remain at the macro-level and miss out on the deeper understanding of the interaction between the factors that directly or indirectly influence trustworthiness of e-government. The key objective of the present study was to identify and develop a hierarchy of factors influencing trustworthiness of e-government services in the citizen context. Based on a comprehensive literature review, nineteen factors were found to be associated with trustworthiness of e-government, identified as benevolence, integrity, trust in government, trust in technology, transparency, responsiveness, competence, accountability, privacy concerns, perceived security, perceived risk, system quality, service quality, satisfaction, political attitude, perceived ability to use, perceived prior knowledge, disposition to trust, and use. The review highlighted that the relationships between these factors was ill-understood and there was no single work addressing all these factors. Furthermore, there was a lack of model testing and framework development in the area of public administration research. Utilizing ISM, the interrelationships between the twenty constructs were analysed. The findings indicated that trustworthiness of e-government and its use were considered as the ultimate dependent variables, clearly implying that higher levels of trustworthiness can lead to improved use and vice-versa. The driving power and dependence diagram also indicate that the factors such as political attitude (variable 7), perceived prior knowledge (variable 9), responsiveness (variable 11), system quality (variable 14), and competence (variable 19) are factors with relatively weak dependence but strong driving power whereas factors such as use (variable 16) and benevolence (variable 17) are factors with relatively weak driving but strong dependence power. All other factors were found to demonstrate strong driving as well as dependence power. These findings can be helpful for managers, practitioners, and policy makers in framing their further strategies for effectively and successfully implementing e-government services for citizens.

The most prominent contribution of this research lies in the development of contextual relationships among various identified factors influencing e-government trustworthiness through a single multi-level framework. However, like any other research, this study is not without limitations. First, the present model has not been statistically tested and validated. It is likely that relationships are context dependent. Second, this paper is limited only to implication of ISM methodology in modelling the practices of trustworthiness in e-government. Future research should extend this work with empirical validation of the proposed framework across different e-government services in various other contexts.

Disclosure statement

No potential conflict of interest was reported by the authors.

ORCID

Marijn Janssen ⓘ *http://orcid.org/0000-0001-6211-8790*

References

Agarwal, A., R. Shankar, and M. K. Tiwari. 2007. "Modeling Agility of Supply Chain." *Industrial Marketing Management* 36 (4): 443–457. doi:10.1016/j.indmarman.2005.12.004.

Asgarkhani, M. 2005. "Digital Government and Its Effectiveness in Public Management Reform: A Local Government Perspective." *Public Management Review* 7 (3): 465–487. doi:10.1080/14719030500181227.

Baldwin, J. N., R. Gauld, and S. Goldfinch. 2012. "What Public Servants Really Think of E-Government." *Public Management Review* 14 (1): 105–127. doi:10.1080/14719037.2011.589616.

Behn, R. 1995. "The Big Questions of Public Management." *Public Administration Review* 55 (4): 313–324. doi:10.2307/977122.

Belanger, F., and L. Carter. 2008. "Trust and Risk in E-Government Adoption." *Journal of Strategic Information Systems* 17 (2): 165–176. doi:10.1016/j.jsis.2007.12.002.

Belanger, F., J. Hiller, and W. Smith. 2002. "Trustworthiness in Electronic Commerce: The Role of Privacy, Security, and Site Attributes." *Journal of Strategic Information Systems* 11 (3–4): 245–270. doi:10.1016/S0963-8687(02)00018-5.

Beldad, A., T. van der Geest, M. De Jong, and M. Steehouder. 2012. "A Cue or Two and I'll Trust You: Determinants of Trust in Government Organizations in Terms of Their Processing and Usage of Citizens' Personal Information Disclosed Online." *Government Information Quarterly* 29 (1): 41–49. doi:10.1016/j.giq.2011.05.003.

Bellamy, C., and J. A. Taylor. 1998. *Governing in the Information Age.* Buckingham: Open University Press.

Campbell, J. W., and T. Im. 2015. "Identification and Trust in Public Organizations: A Communicative Approach." *Public Management Review* 17 (8): 1065–1084. doi:10.1080/14719037.2014.881531.

Carter, L., and F. Belanger. 2005. "The Utilization of E-Government Services: Citizen Trust, Innovation and Acceptance Factors." *Information Systems Journal* 15 (1): 5–25. doi:10.1111/j.1365-2575.2005.00183.x.

Chan, F. K., J. Y. Thong, V. Venkatesh, S. A. Brown, P. J. Hu, and K. Y. Tam. 2010. "Modeling Citizen Satisfaction with Mandatory Adoption of an E-Government Technology." *Journal of the Association for Information Systems* 11 (10): 519–549.

Cho, Y. J., and J. W. Lee. 2011. "Perceived Trustworthiness of Supervisors, Employee Satisfaction and Cooperation." *Public Management Review* 13 (7): 941–965. doi:10.1080/14719037.2011.589610.

Cho, Y. J., and H. Park. 2011. "Exploring the Relationships among Trust, Employee Satisfaction, and Organizational Commitment." *Public Management Review* 13 (4): 551–573. doi:10.1080/14719037.2010.525033.

Cho, Y. J., and T. H. Poister. 2013. "Human Resource Management Practices and Trust in Public Organizations." *Public Management Review* 15 (6): 816–838. doi:10.1080/14719037.2012.698854.

Das, J., C. DiRienzo, and J. Burbridge. 2010. "Global E-Government and the Role of Trust: A Cross Country Analysis." *International Journal of Electronic Government Research* 5 (1): 1–18. doi:10.4018/jegr.2009010101.

Dashti, A., I. Benbasat, and A. Burton-Jones. 2009. "Developing Trust Reciprocity in Electronic-Government: The Role of Felt Trust." European and Mediterranean Conference on Information Systems, 13-14th July, Izmir.

Dawes, S. S. 2008. "The Evolution and Continuing Challenges of E-Governance." *Public Administration Review* 68: s86–s102. doi:10.1111/puar.2008.68.issue-s1.

Dwivedi, Y. K., M. Janssen, E. Slade, N. P. Rana, V. Weerakkody, J. Millard, A. J. H. Hidders, and D. Snijder. 2016b. "Driving Innovation through Big Open Linked Data (BOLD): Exploring Antecedents Using Interpretive Structural Modelling." *Information Systems Frontiers.* doi:10.1007/s10796-016-9675-5.

Dwivedi, Y. K., M. A. Shareef, A. C. Simintiras, B. Lal, and V. Weerakkody. 2016a. "A Generalised Adoption Model for Services: A Cross-Country Comparison of Mobile Health (M-Health)." *Government Information Quarterly* 33 (1): 174–187. doi:10.1016/j.giq.2015.06.003.

Dwivedi, Y. K., D. Wastell, S. Laumer, H. Z. Henriksen, M. D. Myers, D. Bunker, A. Elbanna, M. N. Ravishankar, and S. C. Srivastava. 2015. "Research on Information Systems Failures and Successes: Status Update and Future Directions." *Information Systems Frontiers* 17 (1): 143–157. doi:10.1007/s10796-014-9500-y.

Gefen, D. 2002. "Customer Loyalty in E-Commerce." *Journal of the Association of Information Systems* 3 (1): 27–51.

Gil-García, J. R., and T. A. Pardo. 2005. "E-Government Success Factors: Mapping Practical Tools to Theoretical Foundations." *Government Information Quarterly* 22 (2): 187–216. doi:10.1016/j.giq.2005.02.001.

Grimmelikhuijsen, S. G., and A. J. Meijer. 2014. "Effects of Transparency on the Perceived Trustworthiness of a Government Organization: Evidence from an Online Experiment." *Journal of Public Administration Research and Theory* 24 (1): 137–157. doi:10.1093/jopart/mus048.

Hibbing, J. R., and E. Theiss-Morse. 2001. "Introduction: Studying the American People's Attitudes toward Government, When Do Americans Tend to Be Dissatisfied with Government." In *What Is It about Government that Americans Dislike?* Eds. J. R. Hibbing and E. Theiss-Morse, 1–7. Cambridge: Cambridge University Press.

Hong, H. 2013. "Government Websites and Social Media's Influence on Government-Public Relationships." *Public Relations Review* 39 (4): 346–356. doi:10.1016/j.pubrev.2013.07.007.

Horst, M., M. Kuttschreuter, and J. M. Gutteling. 2007. "Perceived Usefulness, Personal Experiences, Risk Perception and Trust as Determinants of Adoption of E-Government Services in the Netherlands." *Computers in Human Behavior* 23 (4): 1838–1852. doi:10.1016/j.chb.2005.11.003.

Hughes, D. L., Y. K. Dwivedi, N. P. Rana, and A. C. Simintiras. 2016. "Information Systems Project Failure – Analysis of Causal Links Using Interpretive Structural Modelling." *Production Planning & Control* 27: 1313–1333. doi:10.1080/09537287.2016.1217571.

Karavasilis, I., Zafiropoulos, K., and Vrana V. 2010. "Extending TAM to Understand E-Governance Adoption by Teachers in Greece." In *WSKS 2010, Part II, CCIS 112*, edited by

M. D. Lytras, P. Ordonez de Pablos, A. Ziderman, A. Roulstone, H. Maurer, and J.B. Imber, 57–68. Berlin: Springer.

Lal, R., and A. Haleem. 2009. "A Structural Modelling for E-Governance Service Delivery in Rural India." *International Journal of Electronic Governance* 2 (1): 3–21. doi:10.1504/IJEG.2009.024962.

Lee, J., and H. R. Rao. 2009. "Task Complexity and Different Decision Criteria for Online Service Acceptance: A Comparison of Two E-Government Compliance Service Domains." *Decision Support Systems* 47 (4): 424–435. doi:10.1016/j.dss.2009.04.009.

Levi, M., and L. Stoker. 2000. "Political Trust and Trustworthiness." *Annual Review of Political Science* 3 (1): 475–507. doi:10.1146/annurev.polisci.3.1.475.

Mandal, A., and S. G. Deshmukh. 1994. "Vendor Selection Using Interpretive Structural Modelling (ISM)." *International Journal of Operations and Production Management* 14 (6): 52–59. doi:10.1108/01443579410062086.

Margetts, H. 2011. "The Internet and Transparency." *The Political Quarterly* 82 (4). 518–521. doi:10.1111/poqu.2011.82.issue-4.

Mayer, R. C., J. H. Davis, and F. D. Schoorman. 1995. "An Integrative Model of Organizational Trust." *Academy of Management Review* 20 (3): 709–734.

McKnight, D. H., V. Choudhury, and C. Kacmar. 2002. "Developing and Validating Trust Measures for E-Commerce: An Integrative Approach." *Information Systems Research* 13 (3): 334–359. doi:10.1287/isre.13.3.334.81.

Morgeson, I. I. I., F. V. D. VanAmburg, and S. Mithas. 2011. "Misplaced Trust? Exploring the Structure of the E-Government-Citizen Trust Relationship." *Journal of Public Administration Research and Theory* 21 (2): 257–283. doi:10.1093/jopart/muq006.

Nachmias, D. 1985. "Determinants of Trust with the Federal Bureaucracy." In *Public Personnel Policy: The Politics of Public Service*, ed. D. H. Rosenbloom, 133–143. Port Washington, NY: Associated Faculty.

Parasuraman, A., V. Zeithaml, and L. Berry. 1988. "SERVQUAL: A Multiple-Item Scale for Measuring Consumer Perceptions of Service Quality." *Journal of Retailing* 64 (1): 12–40.

Parent, M., C. A. Vandebeek, and A. C. Gemino. 2005. "Building Citizen Trust through E-Government." *Government Information Quarterly* 22 (4): 720–736. doi:10.1016/j.giq.2005.10.001.

Park, H., and J. Blenkinsopp. 2011. "The Role of Transparency and Trust in the Relationship between Corruption and Citizen Satisfaction." *International Review of Administrative Sciences* 77 (2): 254–274. doi:10.1177/0020852311399230.

Rana, N. P., and Y. K. Dwivedi. 2015. "Citizen's Adoption of an E-Government System: Validating Extended Social Cognitive Theory (SCT)." *Government Information Quarterly* 32 (2): 172–181. doi:10.1016/j.giq.2015.02.002.

Rana, N. P., Y. K. Dwivedi, B. Lal, M. D. Williams, and M. Clement. 2015a. "Citizens' Adoption of an Electronic Government System: Towards a Unified View." *Information Systems Frontiers* 1–20. http://link.springer.com/article/10.1007/s10796-015-9613-y.

Rana, N. P., Y. K. Dwivedi, and M. D. Williams. 2015b. "A Meta-Analysis of Existing Research on Citizen Adoption of E-Government." *Information Systems Frontiers* 17 (3): 547–563. doi:10.1007/s10796-013-9431-z.

Rana, N. P., Y. K. Dwivedi, M. D. Williams, and V. Weerakkody. 2016. "Adoption of Online Public Grievance Redressal System in India: Toward Developing a Unified View." *Computers in Human Behavior* 59: 265–282. doi:10.1016/j.chb.2016.02.019.

Ravishankar, M. N. 2013. "Public ICT Innovations: A Strategic Ambiguity Perspective." *Journal of Information Technology* 28 (4): 316–332. doi:10.1057/jit.2013.18.

Robinson, S. E., X. Liu, J. W. Stoutenborough, and A. Vedlitz. 2013. "Explaining Popular Trust in the Department of Homeland Security." *Journal of Public Administration Research and Theory* 23 (3): 713–733. doi:10.1093/jopart/mus025.

Rosenstone, S. J., and M. Hansen. 1993. *Mobilization, Participation, and Democracy in America*. New York, NY: Macmillan.

Ruscio, K. P. 1996. "Trust, Democracy, and Public Management: A Theoretical Argument." *Journal of Public Administration Research and Theory* 6 (3): 461–477. doi:10.1093/oxfordjournals.jpart.a024321.

Sage, A. P. 1977. *Interpretive Structural Modelling: Methodology for Large Scale Systems*, 91–164. New York, NY: McGraw-Hill.

Sandeep, M. S., and M. N. Ravishankar. 2014. "The Continuity of Underperforming ICT Projects in the Public Sector." *Information and Management* 51 (6): 700–711. doi:10.1016/j.im.2014.06.002.

Schaupp, L. C., and L. Carter. 2010. "The Impact of Trust, Risk and Optimism Bias on E-file Adoption." *Information Systems Frontiers* 12 (3): 299–309. doi:10.1007/s10796-008-9138-8.

Shareef, M. A., N. Archer, and Y. K. Dwivedi. 2015. "An Empirical Investigation of Electronic Government Service Quality: From the Demand Side Stakeholder Perspective." *Total Quality Management & Business Excellence* 26 (3–4): 339–354. doi:10.1080/14783363.2013.832477.

Shareef, M. A., Y. K. Dwivedi, V. Kumar, and U. Kumar. 2016a. "Reformation of Public Service to Meet Citizens' Needs as Customers: Evaluating SMS as an Alternative Service Delivery Channel." *Computers in Human Behavior* 61: 255–270. doi:10.1016/j.chb.2016.03.002.

Shareef, M. A., Y. K. Dwivedi, S. Laumer, and N. Archer. 2016b. "Citizens' Adoption Behavior of Mobile-Government (Mgov): A Cross-Cultural Study." *Information Systems Management* 33 (3): 268–283. doi:10.1080/10580530.2016.1188573.

Shareef, M. A., Y. K. Dwivedi, T. Stamati, and M. D. Williams. 2014. "SQ Mgov: A Comprehensive Service-Quality Paradigm for Mobile Government." *Information Systems Management* 31 (2): 126–142. doi:10.1080/10580530.2014.890432.

Shareef, M. A., V. Kumar, U. Kumar, and Y. K. Dwivedi. 2011. "E-Government Adoption Model (GAM): Differing Service Maturity Levels." *Government Information Quarterly* 28 (1): 17–35. doi:10.1016/j.giq.2010.05.006.

Singh, R. K., S. K. Garg, and S. G. Deshmukh. 2007. "Interpretive Structural Modelling of Factors for Improving Competitiveness of Smes." *International Journal of Productivity and Quality Management* 2 (4): 423–440. doi:10.1504/IJPQM.2007.013336.

Smith, M. L. 2010. "Building Institutional Trust through E-Government Trustworthiness Cues." *Information Technology & People* 23 (3): 222–246. doi:10.1108/09593841011069149.

Smith, M. L. 2011. "Limitations to Building Institutional Trustworthiness through E-Government: A Comparative Study of Two E-Services in Chile." *Journal of Information Technology* 26 (1): 78–93. doi:10.1057/jit.2010.17.

Talib, F., Z. Rahman, and M. N. Qureshi. 2011a. "An Interpretive Structural Modelling Approach for Modelling the Practices of Total Quality Management in Service Sector." *International Journal of Modelling in Operations Management* 1 (3): 223–250. doi:10.1504/IJMOM.2011.039528.

Talib, F., Z. Rahman, and M. N. Qureshi. 2011b. "Analysis of Interaction among the Barriers to Total Quality Management Implementation Using Interpretive Structural Modeling Approach." *Benchmarking: An International Journal* 18 (4): 563–587. doi:10.1108/14635771111147641.

Tan, C. W., I. Benbasat, and R. T. Cenfetelli. 2008. "Building Citizen Trust Towards E-Government Services: Do High Quality Websites Matter?" *41st Hawaii International Conference on Systems Sciences*, 7-10th January, Waikoloa.

Teo, T. S. H., S. C. Srivastava, and L. Jiang. 2008. "Trust and Electronic Government Success: An Empirical Study." *Journal of Management Information Systems* 25 (3): 99–132. doi:10.2753/MIS0742-1222250303.

Tolbert, C., and K. Mossberger. 2006. "The Effects of E-Government on Trust and Confidence in Government." *Public Administration Review* 66 (3): 354–369. doi:10.1111/puar.2006.66.issue-3.

van Ryzin, G. G., D. Muzzio, S. Immerwahr., L. Gulick, and E. Martinez. 2004. "Drivers and Consequences of Citizen Satisfaction: An Application of the American Customer Satisfaction Index Model to New York City." *Public Administration Review* 64 (3): 331–341. doi:10.1111/puar.2004.64.issue-3.

Vigoda-Gadot, E. 2007. "Citizens' Perceptions of Politics and Ethics in Public Administration: A Five-Year National Study of Their Relationship to Satisfaction with Services, Trust in Governance, and Voice Orientations." *Journal of Public Administration Research and Theory* 17 (2): 285–305. doi:10.1093/jopart/muj018.

Vigoda-Gadot, E., and F. Yuval. 2003. "Managerial Quality, Administrative Performance and Trust in Governance Revisited." *The International Journal of Public Sector Management* 16 (7): 502–522. doi:10.1108/09513550310500382.

Wang, X. H., and M. Wan Wart. 2007. "When Public Participation in Administration Leads to Trust: An Empirical Assessment of Managers' Perceptions." *Public Administration Review* 67 (2): 265–278. doi:10.1111/j.1540-6210.2007.00712.x.

Warfield, J.W. 1974. "Developing Interconnected Matrices in Structural Modelling." *IEEETranscript on Systems, Men and Cybernetics* 4 (1): 81-87.

Weare, C. 2002. "The Internet and Democracy: The Causal Links between Technology and Politics." *International Journal of Public Administration* 25 (5): 659–691. doi:10.1081/PAD-120003294.

Welch, E. W., C. C. Hinnant, and M. J. Moon. 2005. "Linking Citizen Satisfaction with E-Government and Trust in Government." *Journal of Public Administration Research and Theory* 15 (3): 371–391. doi:10.1093/jopart/mui021.

West, D. M. 2005. *Government: And Digital Technology Public-Sector Performance.* Princeton, NJ: Princeton Press.

Yang, K., and L. G. Anguelov. 2013. "Trustworthiness of Public Service." In *Public Administration Reform: Market Demand from Public Organizations,* edited by Y. K. Dwivedi, M. A. Shareef, S. K. Pandey, and V. Kumar, 59–75. New York, NY: Routledge.

Appendix [A]: Constructs' definitions and relationship matrix used for ISM survey

NB: Please remember to consider these constructs from the perspective of citizens.

[1] **Trust of government** – Belief that government will behave as expected in a socially responsible manner; [2] **Trust of Internet** – Belief that the Internet will behave as expected in a socially responsible manner; [3] **Disposition to trust** – The extent to which an individual displays an inclination to trust others; [4] **Perceived risk** – Feelings of uncertainty or anxiety about the behaviour and seriousness of the possible outcomes; [5] **Privacy concerns** – The inhibitors of disclosing personal information; [6] **Perceived security** – Perceived protection from any type of financial or non-financial risk; [7] **Political attitudes** – Acitizen's political orientation; [8] **Transparency** – Availability of information about the internal workings or performance of government; [9] **Perceived prior knowledge** – Newness of information disclosed to a citizen; [10] **Accountability** – The answerability of government to the public on e-government services performance; [11] **Responsiveness** – The level of convenience or degree of immediate feedback provided, usually to resolve a problem; [12] **Service quality** – Attitudes towards the level of service provided by e-government; [13] **Satisfaction** – Level of contentment regarding e-government services; [14] **System quality** – Attitudes towards the level of quality of the e-government systems; [15] **Perceived ability to use** – Personal judgements of the possession of skills required to use a technology; [16] **Use** – Citizens' use of e-government; [17] **Benevolence** – Degree to which citizens believe that e-government cares about them and want to help them; [18] **Integrity** – Degree to which citizens believe that e-government adheres to standards and principles that the public find acceptable; [19] **Competence** – Degree to which e-government possess the skills needed to enable it to perform its tasks in serving the public; [20] **Trustworthiness of e-government** – Characteristics of e-government that may generate citizens' trust.

Table A1. Relationship matrix used for survey.

VR[i/j]	20	19	18	17	16	15	14	13	12	11	10	9	8	7	6	5	4	3	2	1
1																				
2																				
3																				
4																				
5																				
6																				
7																				
8																				
9																				
10																				
11																				
12																				
13																				
14																				
15																				
16																				
17																				
18																				
19																				
20																				

[**Legend:** 1 = Trust in Government, 2 = Trust in Technology, 3 = Disposition to Trust, 4 = Perceived Risk, 5 = Privacy Concerns, 6 = Perceived Security, 7 = Political Attitudes, 8 = Transparency, 9 = Perceived Prior Knowledge, 10 = Accountability, 11 = Responsiveness, 12 = Service Quality, 13 = Satisfaction, 14 = System Quality, 15 = Perceived Ability to Use, 16 = Use, 17 = Benevolence, 18 = Integrity, 19 = Competence, 20 = Trustworthiness of E-Government, VR = Variable, i = row, j = column]

Collaborative data networks for public service: governance, management, and performance

Yu-Che Chen and Jooho Lee

ABSTRACT
This study aims to advance the theory and practice of managing collaborative data networks for information and decision-support services that exist in over 400 US metropolitan areas. Integrating insights from collaborative governance, network management, and cross-boundary information sharing, this study develops a framework to outline the interplay between context, management, collaborative dynamics, technology, and performance. This study further utilizes the framework to conduct an exploratory in-depth case study of a metropolitan transportation data network to examine such interplay. The findings suggest ways to improve the performance of collaborative data networks and their implications are discussed.

Introduction

In the digital government area, there is a growing need for collaborative governance across organizational boundaries to leverage technology to provide an integrated and customized view of public service (Dawes, Cresswell, and Pardo 2009). Such cross-boundary collaboration is particularly critical in a federalist administrative system for integrating data that have been collected in individual jurisdictions but need to be integrated to create a service-oriented view.

The primary research question is 'How can we govern and manage cross-boundary collaborative networks with the use of information and communication technology (ICT) to improve the performance of information and decision-support service?' This question focuses on collaborative data governance networks, which are critical to the success of generating quality information for cross-boundary public services such as transportation. Moreover, this question aims to understand the role of ICT in improving performance of such networks. To advance our understanding of collaborative data networks, this study attempts (1) to develop a conceptual framework that integrates insights from three streams of research: electronic government (e-government), collaborative governance, and network management and (2) to explore network governance and management as well as the role of ICT in achieving a high level of network performance. The link between governance, management, and performance has been identified as one main area of research for network management literature (O'Toole 2015).

To address the research question, this study conducted an in-depth case study of metropolitan planning organizations (MPOs) and their collaborative governance networks in metropolitan areas for transportation information and decision-support services. It is a federal mandate to establish a MPO for any metropolitan area with a population of 50,000 or above. Such MPOs manage a network of local governments for better planning. In examining these MPOs, this study's focus is on transportation data for local governments and regional entities to make planning decisions. The collection of transportation data is typically done by autonomous local jurisdictions. As a result, information sharing across jurisdictions becomes a necessity to create an integrated view of metropolitan transportation. Such transportation data also present opportunities for effective use of ICT, which aligns with the goal of this study.

The following section provides a brief description of the relevant bodies of literature on collaborative data governance networks. Then, a conceptual framework drawing from these relevant bodies of literature is outlined. Next is a discussion of research design, methods, and data. The next section provides case description, analysis, and findings. This article then discusses the practical and theoretical implications of the findings. It concludes with a summary of the main points and opportunities for future research.

Literature review

E-government literature on cross-boundary information sharing

The existing e-government literature on cross-boundary information sharing provides insight for this research. For politics and policy, Dawes, Cresswell, and Pardo (2009) articulate the need for legal authority in effective information sharing. Having an information policy is critical because policy issues tend to be the biggest barrier to successful information sharing (Dawes, Cresswell, and Pardo 2009; Yang and Maxwell 2011). Politics is central to information technology (IT) projects that span over functional areas and organizational boundaries (Hellberg and Grönlund 2013; Dawes 1996). The different interests between IT departments and other business departments, as articulated by Kraemer et al. (1989), is a source of politics.

One of the fundamental issues for effective information sharing is to develop shared values across organizations. In fact, implementation of data interoperability can be significantly hampered by conflicts in values such as the emphasis on privacy at the expense of other basic objectives of interoperability (Hellberg and Grönlund 2013). Another key organizational factor for effectiveness is past collaborative experience among organizations that speaks to the mutual trust needed for cross-boundary information sharing (Yang and Maxwell 2011). Moreover, the difference in operational procedures can also pose a barrier to successful information sharing due to the complexity and amount of negotiation involved to address these differences (Yang, Zheng, and Pardo 2012). To achieve effective information sharing, incentives constitute a key tool (Yang and Maxwell 2011).

Technology and data are also important factors in effective cross-boundary information and service collaboration (Dawes, Cresswell, and Pardo 2009; Bekkers 2007). Especially, different IT capabilities can present a challenge for information sharing and service integration. Technical assistance and training is likely needed for those organizations and individuals lacking the prerequisite knowledge and skills to be effective participants in cross-boundary settings. For cross-boundary data sharing, issues such as variety of data definitions and formats present significant challenges for creating a meaningful and personalized view of disparate data coming from various organizations (Comfort 2007).

Collaborative governance for information service

The studies of collaborative governance have identified both the context and condition of success (Emerson, Nabatchi, and Balogh 2012; Ansell and Gash 2008). Important contextual factors include the existing policy and legal framework, levels of conflicts (trust), interdependence, incentives, and leadership (Emerson, Nabatchi, and Balogh 2012; Ansell and Gash 2008). A policy and legal framework for the governance regime provides the shared institutional foundation for collaboration (Bingham 2008). Such a framework facilitates the creation of shared understanding that is needed for inter-organizational collaboration (Wood and Gray 1991). A high level of conflict preceding the formation of a collaborative governance presents a major challenge to that collaborative governance (Emerson, Nabatchi, and Balogh 2012). The degree of interdependence is an important motivation for collaboration across organizational boundaries (Rethemeyer 2009; Rethemeyer and Hatmaker 2008). Incentives for organizational and individual participants constitute another important contextual consideration. Lastly, leadership and management are crucial for the success of collaborative governance networks (Provan and Kenis 2008).

In terms of process and dynamics of collaborative governance, Emerson, Nabatchi, and Balogh (2012) provide three main areas of activities: principled engagement, shared motivation, and capacity-building for joint action. The guiding principles for principled engagement include fair and representative participation, and discourse informed by diverse participant perspectives. Shared motivation involves the process of fostering mutual trust, shared understanding, and securing and carrying out commitment by individual participating organizations (Emerson, Nabatchi, and Balogh 2012, 13–14). Shared motivations can foster commitment that can be translated into concrete plans and actions. Capacity-building for joint action is a critical area of activities for collaborative dynamics. To build capacity, Emerson, Nabatchi, and Balogh (2012) argue for the need for institutions (procedures and arrangements), leadership, and resources to guide and effectuate joint actions at both organizational and individual levels.

Network management

Network management literature has highlighted structural characteristics to help identify relevant leadership and management activities (O'Toole 2015; Provan and Lemaire 2012). Structural characteristics include who has what operational authority, the grouping of various organizations and individuals for network governance (i.e. boards, committees), communication channels and mechanisms, and the prior history of collaboration (Agranoff 2007).

Network management matters in performance (Meier and O'toole 2001; McGuire and Silvia 2010). Specific network management activities can involve activating key network members, mobilizing their support and commitment, framing the key issues and objectives for the network, and synthesizing the diverse interests to create a network whole (McGuire 2006, 2002). These network activities share the generic goals and objectives of network management such as building mutual trust (social capital), creating shared goals and understanding, and wide distribution of needed resources.

Network performance can be measured by result-oriented outcomes and process-oriented outcomes (Provan and Milward 2001; Chen 2008). Examples of result-oriented outcomes include the number of children in stable families through a children's service network or the number of job placements by a network of job-training organizations. Process-oriented outcomes are those dealing with increase in mutual trust, shared understanding, and social capital. These performance measures need to be in alignment with the goals and objectives of a network. Another important perspective of network performance is the level at which performance is measured. Provan and Milward (2001) argue the importance of differentiating network effectiveness at the levels of individuals, programme, and community as well as caution against the potential trade-offs between performance scores at these levels.

An integrated conceptual framework for information and decision-support networks

The development of the proposed integrated conceptual framework draws from the aforementioned bodies of literature and is adapted to networks providing information and decision-support services. The core elements are the context and initial conditions (i.e. existing level of trust), collaborative processes, network leadership and management activities, ICT use, and performance. Figure 1 depicts the framework with these key components and potential relationships.

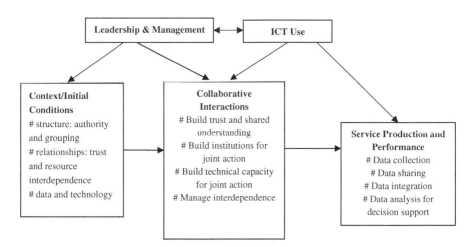

Figure 1. An integrated conceptual framework of managing a collaborative network for information and decision-support services.

Context and initial conditions

The structural characteristics include both authority and grouping (Agranoff 2007). Authority refers to the legal and/or administrative authority of various network-participating organizations to make decisions. Such authority usually has a legal or administrative source. The distribution of authority is a main source of potential power imbalance and conflict. Grouping is about the institutional and organizational design with regard to the governance of the network. Grouping specifies the main governing body of the network, the representation of various network-participating organizations, and the existence and organization of potential subnetworks. A sub-network could be the group of public employees and organizations for a functional area (i.e. finance, planning) as opposed to a subgroup of elected officials.

Initial conditions are critical for appropriate institutional design, collaborative processes, and management strategies (O'Toole 2015; Emerson, Nabatchi, and Balogh 2012; Ansell and Gash 2008). The initial level of mutual trust resulting from a prior history of collaboration and/or conflict is a critical consideration for the network leadership and management effort. Another important condition to examine is interdependence as captured mainly in the resource flow (Park and Rethemeyer 2014). Such interdependence shapes the degree of motivation for participating in a particular network and the level of commitment at the implementation stage. A higher level of interdependence is likely to foster shared motivation once articulated and perceived by the key network member organizations.

The information and decision-support networks necessitate the consideration of data and technology (Dawes, Cresswell, and Pardo 2009; Yang and Maxwell 2011), although these have not been identified as one of the core components in collaborative governance. Data are the building blocks of information interoperability and analytics for decision support. A network-wide common data collection method and definition can significantly reduce the effort involved in information interoperability. The characteristics of ICT being deployed also make a difference. From the network and collaborative governance perspective, heterogeneity of the technologies used and technical capabilities of implementing them can be an impediment to quality information and decision-support service.

Collaborative processes

Collaborative processes are the interactions and activities that address the specific context and initial conditions of a network collaboration. For trust-building, networks can raise the level of mutual trust by exercising the norm of reciprocity and delivering on their commitments. The information and decision-support networks are likely to follow a similar process to build trust. However, differences could arise in the focus on information-related activities, in which participating organizations reciprocate with each other by sharing information and maintaining the capacity to deliver data to the entire network as a whole in a timely and reliable manner. At the same time, fostering a shared understanding of the goals and nature of the service challenge in a network context is important (Ansell and Gash 2008). Meetings and communications should aid in such a shared understanding.

Building institutions/rules for joint action is another main area of collaborative interactions. For collaborative networks, governance institutions correspond to authority and grouping. For instance, a governance board has the authority to decide on information standards and data ownership issues. These authority rules, as well as the rules on data standards, are critical for the effectiveness of information and decision-support networks. From an operational perspective, there need to be rules on who needs to share what information and when for conducting joint actions across the entire network.

Building technical capacity for joint action requires addressing heterogeneity in data standards as well as technological capability among various participating organizations and individuals. One way to build such technical capacity is to create a central information system to facilitate information sharing across organizational boundaries. Coupled with appropriate user training for use of the system, the network can build the capacity of individual participating organizations by applying the same technical standards for data collection and quality assurance before sharing with the entire network.

Since networks are designed to implement interdependent tasks, the collaborative process should focus on managing interdependence. Providing tangible financial incentives for individual organizations to share information is a way to manage information–resource interdependence. Only when a network has all the various pieces of information from various contributing organizations, can it provide an enterprise or holistic perspective of the operation and service.

Leadership and management activities and use of ICT

Leadership and management activities entail leading and managing the collaborative processes. Recognizing major gaps in the conditions for success is an important first step in helping a network to achieve its goals. This recognition requires situational awareness to develop an appropriate strategy. If the network's primary issue is a lack of mutual trust among participating organizations, leadership and management should focus on trust-building by fostering shared understanding and employing regular, meaningful communication via face-to-face and other means. If trust is in place and the primary barrier is the lack of a common data standard, effort should be directed to building institutions for joint action in the area of developing common data standards. Addressing the issue of information policy and data standards is particularly prominent in the success of cross-boundary information sharing to create a service-oriented view of information and service (Dawes, Cresswell, and Pardo 2009).

Moreover, a network manager needs to understand the interplay between these processes of trust-building, institutional design, capacity-building, and interdependence management. The network manager may need to simultaneously engage in various management activities such as activating, mobilizing, and synthesizing. One of the most productive tools while engaging in all these activities is the utilization of tangible and intangible incentives. A positive payoff is needed for network participants to overcome the tendency to advance only the narrow interests of the home organization rather than those of the network.

Network leaders and managers can utilize ICT for managing collaborative processes as well as for direct service provision. For collaborative process management, ICT applications such as video conferencing and centralized project management software can facilitate regular communication as well as the demonstration of reciprocity and commitments. Moreover, a centralized information management system can be part of a network's technical assistance to participating organizations and individuals with limited technical capability to build technical capability for joint action. The use of applications can aid in information service production. For instance, a modelling module in a geographic information system (GIS) can aid in the impact analysis of a regional planning master plan.

Performance of network service production and delivery

For this study, the discussion of performance focuses primarily on the networks providing information and decision-support services. A task-oriented perspective examines the main components and processes needed for the production and delivery of information and decision-support services. The initial task is the data collection by participating organizations. Quality of data collection, use of a network-wide standard, and timeliness of data collection are potential performance measures. The second task is data sharing across the network. Quality can mean whether such sharing has reached its target network audience with the appropriate format in a timely way. The third task is a network administrative organization's compliance with and integration of data from participating organizations and sources into a standardized view of data. Quality is measured by the level of standardization and whether data are relevant to making decisions. The last task involves the analysis of data and the communication of results to support the decision-making process. Both the timeliness of such analysis and the effectiveness of communication as perceived by users can be relevant performance measures.

Research design, methods, and data

This study employs an exploratory case study method to answer the research questions. This method helps address a current research gap in understanding the process aspects of information and decision-support network management and the interplay between context, collaborative processes, management, and performance. Although case study does not offer confirmative statistical correlation in a large N study, it provides opportunities to improve conceptual validity, generate new hypotheses, and explore causal mechanisms and complex interactions (George and Bennett 2005; Yin 2003).

The case selected is a governance network run by a MPO that spans two Midwestern states. The focus of the study is on the network activity associated with transportation planning, which requires the MPO to compile, integrate, and analyse transportation data to provide information services to participating governments and to support their transportation-related decisions. The MPO, however, does not have authority over participating governments in terms of data collection. As a result, metropolitan transportation data collection and compilation are commonly done in a collaborative manner in a network of governments and organizations.

The primary data collection included document reviews and interviews. In March and April 2015, our research team had meetings with key staff members in the MPO to introduce this research project and ask for their support. The MPO allowed us to access internal documents (e.g. Memorandum of Agreement for Transportation Planning and Programming) and introduced potential interviewees. This study reviewed key internal and publicly available documents on the structure and activities of the MPO and transportation planning. This study also conducted interviews with seven key stakeholders, including three participating governments (two from a county government and one from a city government) that provide data to the MPO, and four staff members in the MPO (a programme director, two planners, and a GIS coordinator). Interview questions were designed to capture key variables in our research framework (see selected interview questions in Appendix A). These interview transcripts provide information on the workflow, specific data collected, technology, staffing, incentives, collaborative activities and interactions, and areas for improvement.

Data analysis followed the guidelines and processes of case data analysis as suggested by Yin (2003) as well as Miles, Michael Huberman, and Saldana (2014). Based on the documents and interviews, we established the history and context of the case. The case analysis follows the main components identified in the proposed framework (see Figure 1) while allowing for the emergence of nuances and patterns. We have also examined the processes of production and delivery of information and decision-support service by establishing the workflow for data gathering and analysis as well as communication of the results. Additionally, we have identified key factors for success by identifying the themes of the interview data.

Case description and analysis

Organizational context

The specific case of collaborative data governance is the Metropolitan Area Planning Agency (MAPA). MAPA was established in the 1970s as the chief planning agency for the Omaha-Council Bluffs metropolitan area spanning metropolitan territory in Nebraska and Iowa with a combined population of approximately 865,000 according to the US 2010 Census. The main governance body of MAPA is a 63-member council of officials, representing each of the 63 governmental units that comprise MAPA. Most decisions are made by the Policy Board of Directors (PBD), which is comprised members from local governments in both the State of Nebraska and the State of Iowa.[1] The main areas of responsibilities for MAPA include transportation data and planning as well as community and economic development. The biggest area of responsibilities is transportation data for regional planning.

MAPA is the designated agency in the Omaha-Council Bluffs metropolitan area for transportation data that are locally collected by participating governments in the metropolitan area, including the City of Omaha, Douglas County, and Sarpy County in Nebraska and the City of Council Bluffs and Pottawattamie County in the state of Iowa. MAPA is responsible for obtaining data from these government bodies to create a metropolitan transportation plan and for producing a comprehensive transportation improvement plan every 4 years.

Context and initial conditions

Based on the analysis of the documents and interview data, we provided a summary of findings in Table 1. This table includes data and relevant facts as well as the narrative on features of various components context and initial conditions.

Table 1. Conditions and context of the collaborative transportation data governance.

	Relevant rules/facts and characteristics
Structure: Network authority	• Overall enabling authority: Federal government mandate to enable MPO to be the lead organization for metropolitan area transportation planning; MAPA's Policy Board of Directors is the highest level decision body inside MAPA overseeing all decisions • Technical authority: TTAC advises the MAPA Policy Board of Directors about 'the Transportation Improvement Program, ongoing plans and studies, and provides valuable stakeholder feedback into the transportation planning process'
Structure: Network grouping	• Jurisdictional for traffic data provision: Anchor city in the metropolitan area, two counties in Nebraska, Iowa Department of Transportation covering Council Bluffs, Pottawattamie County, and other neighbouring small cities • Functional grouping: The information and technical group across organizational boundaries (information technology department, GIS people), operational group that includes traffic engineer and public work people, and policy group including heads of local governments and planning departments
Relationship: trust and resource interdependence	• Personal connections are the key rather than institutional ones • Level of trust depends on the grouping and individuals • MAPA depends on various local governments in the network to collect and share information • Financial incentives in the form of fund pass-through to pay for staff time and technology are the resource that MAPA can provide
Data and technology	• Traffic data collection (tube vs. manual counting with a device): difference is mainly between anchor city and the rest • Traffic data integration and analysis: much more under the control of MAPA but the biggest challenge is converting various data sources into geo-coded uniform data • Technology for data integration and analysis: Excel, GIS, mapping applications • Communication technology: communication among network member organizations: primary e-mail and file attachments, to external constituents and the public: website, Facebook, and Twitter

TTAC: Transportation Technical Advisory Committee; MAPA: Metropolitan Area Planning Agency.

Authority and grouping

The overall authority of MAPA originates from the Federal Government's mandate designating it the organization for metropolitan area-planning purposes. MAPA has authority over participating local and state governments to act as the coordinating agency to compile transportation data, conduct analysis, and prepare reports for the Federal Department of Transportation for its metropolitan area (MAPA 2014).

However, it does not have explicit authority to collect data on the ground. Nor does it have the authority to dictate transportation data collection methods.

Inside MAPA, the PBD is the top-level decision-making body that oversees all decisions made by MAPA, including transportation issues. The highest technical authority for transportation data and planning is the Transportation Technical Advisory Committee (TTAC). Both the PBD and TTAC have authority over the program office of MAPA with regard to transportation planning.

Two types of network grouping emerged from the analysis of documents and interview data. The first grouping is by jurisdiction. For the metropolitan area, the City of Omaha (hereafter, anchor city) is the largest city in the area that provides transportation information. Douglas and Sarpy Counties also provide transportation data covering other cities in the metropolitan area. For Council Bluffs in Iowa, as well as Pottawattamie County and other small cities in the same Metropolitan area, transportation data have been made available via the Iowa Department of Transportation website, with data collected locally. The vast majority of transportation data are from the anchor city as well as the Iowa Department of Transportation. The second grouping is by functions. The interview data reveal frequent correspondence and collaboration among IT and planning staff, particularly in the GIS area. Functional area employees who are directly responsible for traffic data, such as people in the engineering and public works departments, form another distinct group.

The primary grouping generally follows jurisdictional lines while operating in the network and inside their home organizations. For instance, interviewees reported that traffic engineers in the anchor city see their home city as their primary obligation and traffic data collection as their primary responsibility. The needs of the network and other jurisdictions seem to be secondary. The staff in the IT department have no jurisdiction over the traffic employees in a separate department. From the perspective of data collection and sharing, such a jurisdictional divide based on functional areas inside a government is even more pronounced than the divide across governments.

Relationships: trust and resource interdependence

The trust relationship across organizational boundaries is primarily based on personal ties and secondarily on institutional trust. The interview data show that the highest level of trust is evident among people who belong to the IT and GIS community. The trust level is relatively lower between the technical group and the functional groups with regard to data quality. A trust relationship that is based on personal ties also suggests that individuals matter. The individual who has been the main GIS coordinator at MAPA seems to have the trust of the information providers gauged by their willingness to work with the MAPA person on various initiatives. In contrast, a new staff member at MAPA faces the challenge of gaining the help and support of information providers in other jurisdictions.

MAPA depends on the participating governments for the collection and sharing of transportation information. MAPA needs traffic data on a regular basis from participating governments to develop a transportation improvement plan. Such information resource dependence ties MAPA and other participating government agencies together. Another side of resource interdependence is MAPA's provision of resources to local governments. MAPA obtains federal funding and passes on some of these funds to major local government agencies on the order of $20,000–40,000 specifically for transportation data collection in the form of paying for staff time and technology.

More broadly, MAPA provides resources in other areas such as community development to the same cooperating agencies. Such provision of resources has been recognized by the participating local government agencies as a major activity in trust-building.

Data and technology

Participating governments have a variety of data collection methods that create challenges for data integration. In the anchor city, traffic data are collected via manual input using hand-held devices. In other counties, the primary method is the use of tubes laid on the road to count the number of vehicles passing through. This difference in data collection methods requires calibration on the part of MAPA to harmonize the data and make sense of traffic counts.

The variety of data collection methods and lack of geo-coding require MAPA to make intensive efforts to integrate data from various sources. With the approval of the TTAC, MAPA has direct control over the method and technology for data integration and analysis. Its main task is to convert heterogeneous data formats into a standardized geo-coded one in a GIS database.

The technologies used for traffic data processing at the local governments vary significantly. The anchor city uses hand-held devices to enter traffic data and uploads them to a local computer. A specialized software, coupled with Excel, is used for traffic data processing. The counties use devices connected to traffic-counting tubes to gather the traffic data and upload them to the computers in their information system departments for data processing. At MAPA, the main software used to do initial processing is Excel, with the geographic information then added to be loaded into the ArcGIS software. The use of TransCAD coupled with ArcGIS helps produce the traffic-flow analysis.

Stages of information service production and managing collaborative governance activities

Workflow and the role of various groups

The first stage of producing transportation information service is traffic data collection and collaboration inside a local government. The functional department (i.e. Public Works) plays the dominant role in collecting traffic data at the first stage in that it makes decisions on the method and the timing and frequency of data collection. The interview data suggest, however, that the IT departments in various local governments typically play an assisting role. For the anchor city government, there is minimal involvement of the IT department in traffic data processing. In contrast, for county governments in the metropolitan area, the IT departments process the collected traffic data.

The second stage of traffic information production is data sharing across organizational boundaries. The main group is the data and technology staff in both MAPA and the participating local government. The IT department is the main point of contact for cross-boundary data sharing with the exception of the anchor city. MAPA makes the information requests and follows up with reminders. It can take between 2 and 6 months for MAPA to obtain traffic data from individual local governments.

The third stage is data integration that harmonizes traffic data collected through different methods and definitions. MAPA does all the work while consulting with the

Table 2. Collaborative network governance dynamics and management activities.

	Governance dynamics and management activities
Build trust and shared understanding	• Provide steady funding and assistance • Cultivate personal relationships via committed and principled interactions (repeated and timely communication) • Create shared understanding via communication mostly among the data people
Build institutions for joint action	• Have an agreement between the MPO and the state agencies • Some discussion among GIS folks and MAPA internal staff about common data standards
Build technical capacity for joint action	• Adopt GIS • Discuss a single portal and direct-data upload
Manage interdependence	• Secure grants and perform pass-through to provide incentives for participation • Strengthen ties by adding values beyond transportation data

TTAC on technical standards and with participating local governments on the technical details. The group leading this stage is the staff in MAPA's program office that is responsible for data integration. The last stage is data analysis and generation of maps/reports. The program office of MAPA is mainly responsible for preparation of presentation and reports.

Collaborative governance activities and their management

The first area of collaborative governance activities is building trust and shared understanding as shown in Table 2. Currently, the primary way for MAPA to win the trust and support of participating local governments is to provide financial support for activities related to regional planning and transportation. The main units of local governments benefitting from these funds include the public works departments, planning departments, and GIS units. Moreover, there are regular and ad hoc meetings between participating governments and MAPA to cultivate trust and create a shared understanding. There is frequent communication among GIS and data people on technology needs beyond the traffic count. The interviews with MAPA staff suggest the importance of personal relationships in securing cooperation from the relevant departments in these local governments to provide transportation data.

The second area is institution-building for joint actions. The main existing agreement for transportation planning is between MAPA and state agencies (MAPA 2014). The authority of direct data collection by MAPA, however, is rather limited. An explicit institutional agreement is lacking between MAPA and various local governments in terms of setting data standards. As an effort to build institutions for joint action, some GIS and data personnel in MAPA and other local governments have initiated a conversation about traffic data standards.

The third area is to build technical capability for joint actions. Currently, such activities focus on building GIS capabilities in terms of software and use. Most of the equipment money for MAPA and assistance to other local governments is applied to the GIS software license to acquire capabilities for better data quality and information interoperability with geo-coded data.

Lastly, MAPA plays a leadership role in managing resource interdependence. Although the most important task for MAPA is to manage interdependence while collecting and sharing transportation data, MAPA faces challenges when the anchor city and other participating local governments utilize their own traffic information for their planning purposes and thus are less dependent on MAPA. But MAPA provides values beyond transportation data when working with both public works and IT/IS units to strengthen resource interdependence. The interviews reveal that these department and local government units see MAPA providing coordinating service beyond transportation data and acting as a gateway to secure and manage federal grants that would otherwise be unavailable to these departments and units.

Driving the performance of the collaborative transportation data networks

The performance of this information and decision-support network administered by MAPA can be measured by the efficiency and effectiveness in various components of producing and providing relevant service. With regard to traffic data collection, data collection by individual jurisdictions has proven cost-effective as they have deployed the least-cost approach to data collection with use of either a traffic-counting tube or a hand-held counting device to collect traffic information. From the network-wide perspective, however, the variety of data collection methods used creates issue later on for data integration.

In terms of data integration, MAPA has only been able to generate high-quality data by investing significant time and resources. A considerable amount of time has been required for MAPA to model traffic flows of major roadways when the traffic count of one section of road is collected by one jurisdiction using one method and the other section of the road is collected using a different method. For data analysis and communication, the performance level is relatively high. Such performance is evident in the deployment of GIS and traffic-flow modules, as well as in MAPA's ability to integrate traffic-flow information from all directions of the interaction for the entire metropolitan area – as well as the traffic flow of highways cutting through the metropolitan area.

One of the challenges associated with improving network performance is the lack of collaboration between IT and functional units at the same local government. The IS/GIS interviewees – who understand the need for data standardization for improving data sharing, integration, and analysis – indicate their limited influence over the functional department people in the effort to standardize traffic data collection.

Incentives alone are not sufficient to improve the consistency and quality of data at the point of data collection in a network with distributed authority. The resource pass-through is sufficient to cover the cost of the majority of data collection activities in a particular department of the local government. However, as the limited success in establishing a uniform data collection suggests, such pass-through itself is not sufficient for the development and implementation of common data standards.

There has been strong cohesiveness and support from the GIS members of the collaborative data network. GIS interviewees have indicated their support for implementing guidance from MAPA with regard to data collection and standardization. These interviewees have also commented that the resource support from MAPA for their GIS operation is helpful. Moreover, interaction and communication reaches beyond just the traffic data. It covers regional planning that affords these GIS members of the network with regular contact and communication in regional planning activities, data forums, and a new aerial-mapping initiative.

Tracing the key events in the documents suggests that having the right talents who understand and properly utilize technology can significantly improve efficiency and effectiveness of information service. That is, one of the most significant contributions comes from the role of the GIS specialist at MAPA. Shortly after joining MAPA, the GIS coordinator migrated the traffic count data from an ACCESS relational database to a GIS (geo-coded) database to improve efficiency and effectiveness of data storage and analysis.

This case study suggests that technology can improve performance. For data integration and analysis, the enactment of appropriate technology by a key network staff member can significantly improve the efficiency and effectiveness. In addition, the potential of technical capabilities provides the needed vision and strategic goals for the network to further improve information service. For example, a cloud-based GIS portal, combined with appropriate technologies at the point of data collection, can significantly improve the workflow and process of data collection, analysis, and information dissemination. A hand-held device with wireless data services and accurate geo-coded traffic count could provide high-quality real-time traffic information to the portal.

Discussion and implications

The finding of a relatively significant jurisdictional divide between functional areas underscores the need to address the different priorities and interests between programme and IT people as articulated in the earlier literature (Kraemer et al.1989). Such a divide between functional areas is probably more salient in contexts where there is a lack of common standards for network member organizations in data collection and processing. The findings from this case study suggest a different emphasis when common standards are lacking and the network administrative organization does not have the standard-setting authority – which also underscores the importance of fitting strategy to a particular network structure rather than applying the same strategy to all structures (O'Toole 2015; Provan and Kenis 2008).

In terms of practice, the concern about divide between functional departments for improving cross-boundary data collection and data sharing would imply a different management strategy. The formulation of common standards may need to involve the heads of the functional departments that are directly responsible for data collection as well as the top executives of the examined governments. This recommendation provides the specifics of network management activities, especially the network member activation suggested by McGuire (2002). Moreover, for the building of institutions for joint action (Emerson, Nabatchi, and Balogh 2012), the findings suggest more attention should be given to the groups that align more with their functional responsibilities across the network rather than those departments within the same organization.

Second, the limited success employing only incentives to improve the standardization of data collection methods is probably more pronounced in an existing governance structure that does not provide MPOs the authority to mandate data-collection methods. The findings highlight the need to tie incentives to guidance/requirements for the purpose of improving data quality and information interoperability. The need for such coupling between incentives and requirements advances our knowledge about network management in terms of the need for coupling incentives with rules rather than offering financial or technical support alone. This need also suggests that some level of guidance and mandate is required.

Third, the success of building a subnetwork of GIS professionals underscores the importance of core areas of collaborative management activities, including regular communication to build trust, direct and ample incentives to win commitment to the network, and capacity-building for joint action. For practice, this study points to the need for information and decision-support networks to simultaneously pursue multiple areas of collaborative management activities to get results.

Fourth, the finding that a key network manager with expert knowledge on relevant technology contributes to service performance improvement underscores the performance impact of combining human capital and appropriate technology to advance information service. The relevance of knowledge about technology is probably more applicable for the class of information and decision-support service networks. The salient role that technology and technical knowledge play in these types of networks suggests that knowledge about and deployment of appropriate technology can significantly improve the quality of service (Yang and Maxwell 2011).

For the role of technology, this case study demonstrates that the appropriate use of relevant technology can significantly improve performance in data quality, data integration, data analysis, and visualization. Such a finding implies the need for elevating the importance of data and technology in driving performance. Moreover, discussion about the value of technology can inspire a network to set goals for the next level of performance. The motivating and goal-development aspects of technology for collaborative governance networks add nuances to our knowledge. Network managers can raise the importance of discussing technology and its potential as a way to discuss shared performance goals for the network. These management recommendations based on the case contribute to our understanding of the specifics of managing collaborative networks as related to technology. This study contributes to the existing network studies by directly addressing the role of IT in performance. For e-government studies, this finding provides insights into the interplay between technology and management when discussion about the performance-improvement potential of technology can be used as a network management strategy.

Conclusion and opportunity for future research

This article provides an integrated framework for managing the performance of information and decision-support networks. This framework integrates bodies of literature to enhance our understanding of the interplay among context, management, technology, and performance in a network setting. The proposed framework is one of the first efforts to integrate insights from several bodies of literature to advance the theory and practice of managing digital government in a cross-boundary setting. Moreover, this article conducts an exploratory case study, guided by the framework while allowing for the development of grounded theory, to explore the mechanisms by which the performance of an information and decision-support network can be improved.

The findings of this exploratory study offer several points for the advancement of theory and practice. First, managers and researchers need to pay attention to the divide between functional department staff and IS/IT staff both inside a jurisdiction and across the network. This case shows that, especially in the context of a lack of authority and common technical standards, this division can be one of the major barriers to major improvement in data integration and service quality. Second, there is a need to combine incentives with guidance and standards to drive results. The limited success in driving performance by the provision of incentives without strong guidance and standards suggests such a need. Collaborative network management needs to build institutional capacity for joint action (common standards and monitoring). Third, the combination of various collaborative network management strategies is effective, at least as evident in the GIS subnetwork. Such a finding suggests the need to combine communication, incentives, and technology for building a collaborative network.

Fourth, this case study suggests the performance-improvement potential of a network manager who understands and utilizes appropriate technology. For data-intensive information-service networks, having a tech-savvy network manager can be an asset to leverage technology for service improvement. Lastly, this study also points to the way in which technology can make a difference in service improvement. Conversation about the potential of technology can serve as a way to create shared goals and motivate network participants.

The utilization of the case study approach, while possessing the strength of generating new insights into collaborative data governance, does have its limitations. The findings of this study, although instructive in showing some potential pathways for network success or causal mechanisms, should not be treated as confirmative theory testing. Future research needs to examine other similar networks of information and decision-support service at various stages of development. Moreover, the statements made are specific to information and decision-support networks in which IT plays an important role in service production and delivery. Any generalization beyond this type of network should proceed with further empirical investigation of other types of networks.

Note

1. For the complete list of governmental units in the Council of Officials, visit http://www.mapacog.org/boards-a-committees.

Acknowledgements

This work is supported by the College of Public Affairs and Community Service, University of Nebraska at Omaha under the College's Urban Research Grant. We thank the staff at the Metropolitan Area Planning Agency and other people in the collaborative data network for their time and assistance. An earlier version of the paper was presented at the 2015 American Society for Public Administration conference in Seattle, WA.

Disclosure statement

No potential conflict of interest was reported by the authors.

Funding

This work is supported by the College of Public Affairs and Community Service, University of Nebraska at Omaha under the College's Urban Research Grant.

References

Agranoff, R. 2007. "Managing within Networks: Adding Value to Public Organizations." In *Public Management and Change Series*, edited by B. Radin. Washington, DC: Georgetown University Press.

Ansell, C., and A. Gash. 2008. "Collaborative Governance in Theory and Practice." *Journal of Public Administration Research and Theory* 18 (4): 543–571. doi:10.1093/jopart/mum032.

Bekkers, V. 2007. "The Governance of Back-Office Integration." *Public Management Review* 9 (3): 377–400. doi:10.1080/14719030701425761.

Bingham, L. B. 2008. "Legal Frameworks for Collaboration in Governance and Public Management." In *Big Ideas in Collaborative Public Management*, edited by L. B. Bingham and R. O'leary, 247–269. Armonk, NY: M.E. Sharpe.

Chen, B. 2008. "Assesing Interorganizational Networks for Public Service Delivery: A Process-Perceived Effectiveness Framework." *Public Performance & Management Review* 31 (3): 348–363. doi:10.2753/PMR1530-9576310302.

Comfort, L. K. 2007. "Crisis Management in Hindsight: Cognition, Communication, Coordination, and Control." *Public Administration Review* Supplement to Volume 67: 189–197. doi:10.1111/puar.2007.67.issue-s1.

Dawes, S. S. 1996. "Interagency Information Sharing: Expected Benefits, Manageable Risks." *Journal of Policy Analysis and Management* 15 (3): 377–394. doi:10.1002/(SICI)1520-6688(199622)15:3<>1.0.CO;2-T.

Dawes, S. S., A. M. Cresswell, and T. A. Pardo. 2009. "From "Need to Know" to "Need to Share": Tangled Problems, Information Boundaries, and the Building of Public Sector Knowledge Networks." *Public Administration Review* 69 (3): 392–402. doi:10.1111/puar.2009.69.issue-3.

Emerson, K., T. Nabatchi, and S. Balogh. 2012. "An Integrative Framework for Collaborative Governance." *Journal of Public Administration Research & Theory* 22 (1): 1–29. doi:10.1093/jopart/mur011.

George, A., and A. Bennett. 2005. *Case Studies and Theory Development in Social Sciences.* Cambridge, MA: MIT Press.

Hellberg, A.-S., and Å. Grönlund. 2013. "Conflicts in Implementing Interoperability: Re-Operationalizing Basic Values." *Government Information Quarterly* 30 (2): 154–162. doi:10.1016/j.giq.2012.10.006.

Kraemer, K. L., J. L. King, D. E. Dunkle, and J. P. Lane. 1989. *Managing Information Systems: Change and Control in Organizational Computing.* San Francisco, CA: Jossey-Bass Publishers.

MAPA. 2014. *Memorandum of Agreement for Transportation Planning and Programming by and between the Metropolitan Area Planning Agency, Metro Transit, Iowa Department of Transportation and the Nebraska Department of Roads.* Omaha, NE: MAPA.

McGuire, M. 2002. "Managing Networks: Propositions on What Managers Do and Why They Do It." *Public Administration Review* 62 (5): 599–609. doi:10.1111/puar.2002.62.issue-5.

McGuire, M. 2006. "Collaborative Public Management: Assessing What We Know and How We Know It." *Public Administration Review* 66 (s1): 33–43. doi:10.1111/puar.2006.66.issue-s1.

McGuire, M., and C. Silvia. 2010. "The Effect of Problem Severity, Managerial and Organizational Capacity, and Agency Structure on Intergovernmental Collaboration: Evidence from Local Emergency Management." *Public Administration Review* 70 (2): 279–288. doi:10.1111/puar.2010.70.issue-2.

Meier, K. J., and L. J. O'toole 2001. "Managerial Strategies and Behavior in Networks: A Model with Evidence from U.S. Public Education." *Journal of Public Administration Research and Theory* 11 (3): 271–294. doi:10.1093/oxfordjournals.jpart.a003503.

Miles, M. B., A. Michael Huberman, and J. Saldana. 2014. *Qualitative Data Analysis: A Methods Sourcebook.* 3rd ed. Los Angeles, CA: SAGE Publications.

O'Toole, L. J. 2015. "Networks and Networking: The Public Administrative Agendas." *Public Administration Review* 75 (3): 361–371. doi:10.1111/puar.12281.

Park, H. H., and K. Rethemeyer. 2014. "The Politics of Connections: Assessing the Determinants of Social Structure in Policy Networks." *Journal of Public Administration Research and Theory* 24 (2): 349–379. doi:10.1093/jopart/mus021.

Provan, K., and P. Kenis. 2008. "Modes of Network Governance: Structure, Management, and Effectiveness." *Journal of Public Administration Research and Theory* 18 (2): 229–252. doi:10.1093/jopart/mum015.

Provan, K. G., and R. H. Lemaire. 2012. "Core Concepts and Key Ideas for Understanding Public Sector Organizational Networks: Using Research to Inform Scholarship and Practice." *Public Administration Review* 72 (5): 638–648. doi:10.1111/puar.2012.72.issue-5.

Provan, K. G., and H. B. Milward. 2001. "Do Networks Really Work? A Framework for Evaluating Public-Sector Organizational Networks." *Public Administration Review* 61 (4): 414–423. doi:10.1111/puar.2001.61.issue-4.

Rethemeyer, K., and D. Hatmaker. 2008. "Network Management Reconsidered: An Inquiry into Management of Network Structures in Public Sector Service Provision." *Journal of Public Administration Research and Theory* 18 (4): 617–646. doi:10.1093/jopart/mum027.

Rethemeyer, R. K. 2009. "Making Sense of Collaboration and Governance." *Public Performance & Management Review* 32 (4): 565–573. doi:10.2753/PMR1530-9576320405.

Wood, D. J., and B. Gray. 1991. "Toward a Comprehensive Theory of Collaboration." *The Journal of Applied Behavioral Science* 27 (2): 139–162. doi:10.1177/0021886391272001.

Yang, T.-M., and T. A. Maxwell. 2011. "Information-Sharing in Public Organizations: A Literature Review of Interpersonal, Intra-Organizational and Inter-Organizational Success Factors." *Government Information Quarterly* 28: 164–175. doi:10.1016/j.giq.2010.06.008.

Yang, T.-M., L. Zheng, and T. Pardo. 2012. "The Boundaries of Information Sharing and Integration: A Case Study of Taiwan E-Government." *Government Information Quarterly* 29: S51–S60. doi:10.1016/j.giq.2011.08.014.

Yin, R. 2003. *Case Study Research: Design and Methods.* 3rd ed. Thousand Oaks, CA: SAGE Publications.

Appendix A. Interview questions

- When did you first become involved in reporting/using traffic counts?
- What is your relationship or experience with MAPA?
- Could you please describe your organization's process for reporting traffic information to MAPA? (Who is involved, how you go from getting the initial request from MAPA to sending them the information)
- How does your organization collect traffic count information?
- How do you store the data on traffic counts?
- Do you get the traffic count information from MAPA? If so, when and for what use?
- Do you think MAPA's unified traffic information useful for your organization? If so, in what way?
- Could you please describe your difficulties/challenges in working with MAPA on reporting traffic counts?
  o Your suggestions for improvement?
- How would you describe the role of your organization in the effort of the long-term traffic pattern programme?
- Which rules and/or regulations that you need to follow for the purpose of collecting traffic data?
- Do you receive any assistance from MAPA or other organization for the purpose of collecting traffic data?
- Besides MAPA, which organization do you work with to collect traffic data?
- Do you have any suggestions on the kind of technology, software programme, and/or website that would be useful for the purpose of traffic data?
- What do you think about a portal hosted by MAPA for you to use for submitting, storing, and retrieving traffic count data?
- What is the first idea that comes to your mind when you think about the traffic count project?
- What are the main goals and objectives of traffic count project in?
  o How have the goals evolved?
- Can you describe briefly the history of the traffic count project in your organization?
  o In what ways were important stakeholders involved?
  o What are some of the major milestones?
  o Any documents (e.g. annual report) you can share with us?
- How has the traffic count project changed the delivery of public services in your organization?
  o In what ways has the traffic count project changed the nature of work for your employees? How were employees involved in developing the traffic count project?
  o In what way, are have citizens benefited from your organization's implementation of the traffic count project? How were citizens involved in developing the traffic count project?
- What factors have enabled a smooth implementation of the traffic count project?
- What factors have impaired the smooth implementation of the traffic count project?
- In general, how is the technology side of the traffic count project managed?
- How do you evaluate the performance of the traffic count project in your organization?
- What is the relationship with federal, state, and other local governments in terms of implementing the traffic count project?
- With regard to the traffic count project, please tell us the agencies that have provided your agency with the traffic count data?
- With regard to the traffic count project, please tell us the agencies that your agency has provided the traffic count data?
- With regard to the traffic count project, please tell us the agencies that your agency has sought advice from?

Value of inter-organizational collaboration in digital government projects

Sergio Picazo-Vela, Isis Gutiérrez-Martínez, François Duhamel,
Dolores E. Luna and Luis F. Luna-Reyes

ABSTRACT
Collaborative approaches to public management are generally known to represent
sources of public value. However, certain theoretical and empirical gaps in understanding this process of value creation persist. We adopt a resource-based view to
analyse how public and private collaborations moderate relations among resources
and processes and creation of public value. Our results show that collaboration with
private organizations negatively moderates the effect of resources on public value
creation and positively moderates the effect of processes on public value creation.
Collaboration within the public sector positively moderates the effect of resources
but not the effect of processes.

Introduction

Public administrations in numerous countries have extended their boundaries to
collaborate with other public entities, NGOs or private organizations to conduct
information technology (IT) projects (Cordella and Bonina 2012; Luna-Reyes, Gil-
Garcia, et al. 2008). Such collaborations are motivated in part by the new opportunities
afforded by ITs (Cordella and Bonina 2012) and by organizational changes associated
with New Public Management (NPM) and public value management (PVM) (Bryson,
Crosby, and Bloomberg 2014; Pardo, Gil-García, and Luna-Reyes 2010; Stoker 2006).
The resulting organizational configurations have created more stakeholders and complexity in IT projects. This situation presents specific challenges for delivering consistent public value with respect to efficiency, transparency or accountability.

Collaboration should positively affect the value of IT projects in public administration (Luna-Reyes, Black, et al. 2008; Pardo, Gil-García, and Luna-Reyes 2010).
However, doubts exist about the impact on public value of public–private and
public–public collaborations (Cordella and Willcocks 2010; Stanimirovic and Vintar
2013). Some authors insist that such collaborations may diminish public value by

emphasizing efficiency, as stipulated by the NPM, at the expense of quality of service (Cordella and Bonina 2012; Cordella and Willcocks 2010). The literature presents no consensus regarding the role of collaboration in public value creation for IT projects in public administration. This lack of consensus stems from poorly developed theoretical approaches for analyzing the phenomenon (Thomson and Perry 2006). In addition, the literature has not convincingly validated the impact on performance of such collaboration quantitatively. The dominant empirical approach for analyzing collaboration remains focused on case studies (Ansell and Gash 2008; Emerson, Nabatchi, and Balogh 2012). The literature also suffers from a lack of consideration of internal resources and processes in IT project management to deliver value (Sako 2014). Practitioners face the dilemma of how to design projects using their own resources or through partnerships with the public sector (Public CIO 2013). This is why it is important to simultaneously consider internal resources and processes to assess public value delivered by IT projects in public administration.

Therefore, this research addresses three questions. What is the impact of inter-organizational collaboration (public and private) on public value obtained from public administrations' digital government projects? Are all types of collaboration equally valuable? How do interactions among types of collaboration on the one hand and internal resources and internal processes on the other hand affect public value obtained from those projects?

To address those issues, we use data obtained from a survey conducted from September 2013 to November 2013 with 152 state government employees in Mexico. The survey primarily sought to investigate the impact of resources and processes on perceptions of public value delivered through the development of digital government projects in public administration and the moderating effects of external collaboration on the relations between resources and processes with public value.

Our results show that internal processes of the public entity positively affect public value creation in their digital government projects, whereas internal resources have no effect. Collaboration with private organizations negatively moderates the effect of internal resources on public value creation and positively moderates the effect of internal processes on public value creation. Inter-organizational collaboration within public sector organizations, on the other hand, positively moderates the relation between internal resources and public value creation and has no effect on the relation between internal processes and public value creation.

This study is organized in five sections. The following section reviews the literature to derive a set of hypotheses about the role of resources, processes and inter-organizational collaborations on public value creation. The third section describes the research method. We then show the results of the statistical analysis. Next, we discuss the results. The study concludes with a series of managerial implications and proposals for future research.

Literature review

Value creation in public administrations

The conceptualization of value creation in government has evolved alongside three different approaches for managing government operations: traditional bureaucracy, NPM and the emerging paradigm of PVM (Bryson, Crosby, and Bloomberg 2014;

Stoker 2006). Under traditional bureaucracy, three primary sources of public value are fairness of processes, taking care of public resources and using them efficiently. Most NPM reforms place the citizen at the centre of the process as the 'customer' of government services. As a result, values related to programme effectiveness and customer satisfaction were added to the classic values of efficiency and fairness when assessing the work of government (Bryson, Crosby, and Bloomberg 2014; Stoker 2006). However, considering the citizen as a customer has been criticized because this conception, in many ways, limits government to the role of a service provider, ignoring other important aspects of government activity such as promoting democratic values among society (Fountain 2001). The emergent approach of PVM arose – at least in part – as a response to the individual customer represented in the NPM approach and considering the collective public as the real customer of government (Moore 2013). This emerging approach not only integrates the values of efficiency, fairness, effectiveness, customer satisfaction and democratic values, such as citizen participation, but also restores a set of broader objectives related to the economy and quality of life (Bryson, Crosby, and Bloomberg 2014; Cordella and Bonina 2012). An important criticism of the PVM approach is its lack of attention to an institutional design that promotes necessary incentives for collaborative governance (Shaw 2013). More detailed comparisons of the three approaches with respect to objectives and other managerial assumptions already exist in the literature (Stoker 2006). We limit our discussion specifying the type of value creation sought in those different streams as a basis for examining the impact of inter-organizational collaboration on public value. As we discuss later, the approaches also differ in how they deal with collaboration.

Collaboration and value creation in the public sector

Several streams of literature identify the importance of collaboration among government agencies and other partners (e.g. private and non-profit organizations), citing collaborative public management, multi-partner governance, joined-up government, PVM or networked government (Emerson, Nabatchi, and Balogh 2012; Luna-Reyes 2013; Shaw 2013).

Inter-organizational collaboration deals with the transfer, pooling and exchange of assets, knowledge, technology and business processes that help organizations obtain better results than when working by their own (Greasley, Watson, and Patel 2008). The literature has clarified the importance of collaboration to enhance public value (Cordella and Bonina 2012; Sako 2014). Decision makers in the public sector perceive ITs as platforms to promote collaboration and facilitate the creation of new forms of governance (Ansell and Gash 2008; Goldsmith and Eggers 2004).

NPM and PVM approaches consider the value of collaboration with both public and private organizations. Collaboration with private organizations, according to the NPM approach, should first respond to the need for lowering costs. It is also motivated by the belief that private organizations would be more efficient than government in developing similar tasks (Cordella and Willcocks 2010). In this sense, NPM approaches favour market-based systems involving private sector delivery of services (Stoker 2006). For the PVM approach, however, collaboration with both public and private organizations responds to perceived needs to deal with complex problems requiring coordination by a network of organizations (Pardo, Gil-García, and Luna-Reyes 2010; Stoker 2006). In PVM approaches, no sector has a monopoly on a public service ethos and collaboration between sectors becomes essential.

The literature does not yet demonstrate a full understanding of what determines successful collaboration in developing IT projects in public administrations (Dawes, Cresswell, and Pardo 2009). Moreover, there is a need to improve theoretical aspects of collaboration in this context (Ansell and Gash 2008; Emerson, Nabatchi, and Balogh 2012). Most studies disregard the choice of inter-organizational collaborations under different modalities and their impact on public value.

One notable exception is the model proposed by Ansell and Gash (2008) to guide collaboration across organizational boundaries. Five main components comprise the model: starting conditions, institutional design, facilitative leadership, collaborative processes and outcomes. This model acknowledges the importance of asymmetries in power, resources and knowledge, as well as the previous history of collaboration among partners (starting conditions). It recognizes the role of clear ground rules and transparency in institutional processes, clear decision-making rules, design policies, network structure and inter-organizational assessment mechanisms (institutional design) (Goldsmith and Eggers 2004). At the internal level, facilitative leadership involves designing a vision, policies and learning processes that enable knowledge utilization and promote insightful views of a current problem (Pardo, Gil-García, and Luna-Reyes 2010). Collaboration is supposed to engender participants' commitment and shared understanding about the problem area, improving results in a virtuous cycle (Vangen and Huxham 2011). This model has the advantage of combining antecedents and outcomes of collaboration. However, Ansell and Gash (2008) do not deal extensively with the role of resources nor do they specify differences between collaborating with private or public organizations. In addition, few quantitative studies provide evidence of value created through collaboration between public and private entities for public IT projects.

Research model and hypothesis

As explained in the introduction, our main research question deals with the role of different types of collaboration in transforming organizational capabilities into public value. Given the nature of our research questions, our study is grounded theoretically in the resource-based view (RBV) of the firm (Barney 2001; Ray, Barney, and Muhanna 2004). RBV distinguishes between resources and capabilities. Resources are inputs to which the organization has access, and capabilities refer to the organization's capacity to deploy resources to achieve outcomes (Piening 2013).

RBV addresses the issue of collaboration. According to Richardson (1972), closely complementary activities (that require ex ante coordination between partners) and dissimilar activities (that necessitate applying different sets of skills for each activity) will be conducted through collaboration. A public organization has the option of collaborating with another public organization or with a private organization. Analysis of resources and capabilities and the organizational design coordinating complementary resources in the context of public administration should determine how public agencies can maximize value from their activities and minimize costs of coordinating complementary resources.

New services require collaboration of entities with different capabilities. A single organization may lack the scale or capabilities to ensure all relevant services on its own, or the organization may not have time or interest to develop internal facilities or organization capabilities, human resources and specialized staff. Public administration agencies and bodies would then have to operate through a network of interdependent relations, linking integration and public value. Collaboration matters, as a collaborative advantage may be reached by developing and maintaining relation-specific assets, complementary resources and capabilities and effective governance, potentially enhancing public value (Dyer and Singh 1998).

Elaborating on the model proposed by Ansell and Gash (2008) and deriving additional insights from RBV, we explore how collaboration interacts with internal organizational resources and processes (or starting conditions) to create public value (Figure 1). In this model, we use internal processes as a proxy for organizational capabilities.

Public value, as discussed previously, involves many measures (Bryson, Crosby, and Bloomberg 2014; Cordella and Bonina 2012). We study two forms of public value. First, we consider the form of public value associated with efficiency and service delivery as determined by Karunasena and Deng (2012). We call this type of public value *internal efficiency and effectiveness*. In addition, public value has been recognized to have a broader impact on promoting democratic values (Cordella and Bonina 2012; Savoldelli, Codagnone, and Misuraca 2014). We call this second form of public value *external impact*.

Many studies assert a direct impact between resources and performance (Crook et al. 2008). Rare, difficult to imitate or substitute and organizationally embedded resources (Barney 1991), as inputs of productive processes, are linked to performance insofar as they represent value to customers or users. Such resources may include physical assets, such as IT systems, equipment, generic ITs and IT spending, as well as human resources, reputation, patents, IT technical

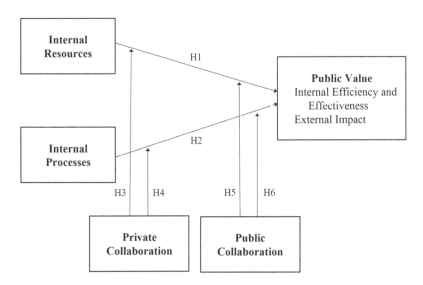

Figure 1. Research model and hypotheses.

skills or unique knowledge (Ray, Barney, and Muhanna 2004). The literature on digital government acknowledges the importance of organizational resources and processes as key success factors for projects (Gil-García 2012; Savoldelli, Codagnone, and Misuraca 2014); organizations with adequate resources have greater probability of creating public value. Hence, we formulate the following hypothesis:

H1. In digital government projects, internal resources positively influence public value through internal efficiency and effectiveness and external impact.

However, recent approaches in RBV indicate that business processes or capabilities mediate the relation between resources and value. The literature suggests that activities – what people do with resources – are what really matters (Ray, Barney, and Muhanna 2004). Certainly, private and public entities seek paths (processes) that led them to use resources more effectively in multiplying value for their customers. In accordance with previous research in digital government (Rinaldi, Montanari, and Bottani 2015), public organizations with well-established processes are likely to create public value (Gil-García 2012). Therefore, we formulate the following hypothesis:

H2. In digital government projects, internal processes positively influence public value through internal efficiency and effectiveness and external impact.

The literature on collaboration suggests that processes and internal resources are put to a productive use more effectively through collaboration rather than being managed in isolation (Ansell and Gash 2008). Collaboration allows participants to share risks and mobilize and synergize resources, reducing transaction and coordination costs (Steijn, Klijn, and Edelenbos 2011). Many government agencies already collaborate with private organizations (Ansell and Gash 2008; Hui and Hayllar 2010). For example, many US state governments collaborated with private organizations to develop e-government portals (Hui and Hayllar 2010). Although researchers believe that private organizations accomplish selected IT tasks and provide services more effectively, they express concerns that collaboration with private entities may be counterproductive to the external impact of digital government projects. That is, private sector ethos and practices may be at odds with the public mission and values (Siemiatycki and Farooqi 2012; Cordella and Willcocks 2010). Value created by public–private collaboration depends on the fit between objectives and attitudes of both partners and the organizational form chosen to govern their collaboration (Kivleniece and Quelin 2012). Despite potential negative effects from misalignment, we suggest that collaboration with public and/or private organizations positively moderate relations between resources and processes and the creation of public value, as collaborators may learn to adjust resources and processes to find synergies in the service of their public missions. Thus, we formulate the following hypotheses.

H3. In digital government projects, private collaboration positively moderates the relation between internal resources and public value through internal efficiency and effectiveness and external impact.

H4. In digital government projects, private collaboration positively moderates the relation between internal processes and public value through internal efficiency and effectiveness and external impact.

Theoretical and empirical evidence about differences between public–private partnerships and public–public partnerships remains scant. However, collaboration between public agencies seemingly differs from collaboration between public and private entities. Sharing social values and commitment to the public (a common 'public sector ethos') is supposed to assure better alignment between partners (Greasley, Watson, and Patel 2008), enhancing collaboration and reducing the occurrence of opportunistic actions and value appropriation by a single participant. However, even in public–public partnerships, strained relations can impede good performance. Public agents may compete for access to government funds or wish to appropriate partners' knowledge, thereby undermining trust. Public agents may also have weak incentives to collaborate in the absence of strong financial motives (Boag and McDonald 2010) or appropriate institutional design (Shaw 2013).

However, we expect performance linked with public–public collaborations to be positive, provided participants choose adequate sets of resources and processes to coordinate (Boag and McDonald 2010; Greasley, Watson, and Patel 2008). Complementary activities are those that represent the different phases in executing service processes, requiring high degrees of coordination in their implementation, whereas similar activities are distinct activities that share identical skills or capabilities (Richardson 1972). Similarity refers to the transfer of skills between activities, allowing savings through scope economies. Public–public collaborations should fit better closely to complementary activities exhibiting a higher degree of similarity than in public–private collaborations. Public–public collaborations may present the advantage of linking sets of similar resources to be pooled in the public interest, also lowering costs (Boag and McDonald 2010). Thus, we also expect that collaboration between public sector organizations moderates the relation between resources and capabilities and public value. Hence, we formulate the following hypotheses:

H5. In digital government projects, public collaboration positively moderates the relation between internal resources and public value through internal efficiency and effectiveness and external impact.

H6. In digital government projects, public collaboration positively moderates the relation between internal processes and public value through internal efficiency and effectiveness and external impact.

Method

Data were collected via a cross-sectional web-based survey conducted from September 2013 to November 2013. The population of the study was state government IT project managers working in IT departments in Mexico. Given that there was no directory for identifying members of this population, we created a list of all key IT project managers from directories of all thirty-two state government portals in the country. We gathered a total of 942 names and e-mail addresses. We used this list as the sample for this study, considering that these project managers were the best informed about IT projects in state government, public and private collaborations involved in the projects and their current results.

All 942 IT project managers in the list received an invitation to answer the survey via e-mail, informing them about its purpose and guaranteeing anonymity of their responses. To increase the response rate, we sent three reminders to those who had not responded. We received 307 responses and eliminated 155 incomplete responses. The 152 remaining usable responses represent a response rate of 16per cent. We used Qualtrics to gather responses, and average time to complete the survey was 15 min.

The questionnaire was developed based on the measurement instrument proposed by Fountain, McKinnon and Park (2003), translated and adapted to the Mexican context (Luna-Reyes, Gil-Garcia, and Estrada-Marroquín 2008). We adapted the survey instrument to render it more consistent with our purpose. We checked for content and face validity from a panel of three experts in digital government research in Mexico. The instrument had two sections. The first asked participants to provide information about their work experience, education and types of digital government projects in which they had collaborated. The second consisted of items related to organizational resources and processes, characteristics of the systems and their use, regulatory and legislative aspects related to the projects, collaborative aspects and inter-organizational relations. We asked participants to evaluate the results of their digital government projects to measure our study's dependent variables. Participants were asked about the measures of success used in the digital government projects in which they collaborated. Table 1 includes the survey questions used as operational definitions of each of the six constructs included in our model. We measured all questions on a 5-point Likert scale. The table includes Cronbach's alpha values for each construct as measures of their internal consistency. All values exceed .70, indicating items used to evaluate each variables were adequate (Hair et al. 2009).

Results

Survey respondents averaged almost 18 years of work experience and approximately 10 in the public sector. Ninety-seven per cent had at least a bachelor's degree, 2 per cent had some college and 1 per cent had a high school degree. Projects in the sample involved on average eight organizations in their development. The types of digital government projects in which respondents were involved are exhibited in Figure 2.

Table 2 shows descriptive statistics for all constructs of the model and all control variables. Control variables are the level of development of the institutional environment in the state, state economic development (states were categorized by income into three groups), the size of the projects (number of organizations involved) and the experience of respondents in years. Values in Table 2 show that survey respondents believe projects are delivering public value in an acceptable way. Means for the dependent variables approach 4 on a 5-point scale. Means for the independent variables are lower in both cases and closer to the midpoint of the Likert scale, reflecting that respondents perceive their projects lack the most appropriate resources and processes. The moderating variables display an important difference between public and private collaborations, with a higher level of involvement in public–public collaborations. The table also displays the main descriptive statistics for control

Table 1. Measurement instruments and internal reliability.

Internal resources Cronbach's alpha = .841	The e-government project in which I participate has the human resources required for successful completion. The team of people assigned to work on the e-government project in which I participate is qualified to complete it successfully. The e-government project in which I participate has adequate financial resources to be completed successfully. E-government applications in which I participate have adequate infrastructure for successful completion.
Internal processes Cronbach's alpha = .833	Well-defined processes facilitate the development of the e-government application in which I participate. Objectives and goals of the e-government project are well defined. Performance indicators of the e-government project in which I participate are well defined. There are external standards (ISO, ITIL, etc.) that clearly guide development of the e-government application in which I participate.
Private collaboration Cronbach's alpha = .735	Relations emerged with either an NGO or a company as a result of the e-government project in which I participate. It is common to hire private companies to develop some activities of e-government projects in which I participate. Results obtained by hiring private companies to develop some project' activities have been very positive.
Public collaboration: Cronbach's alpha = .891	It is common to work with other areas or offices of government in developing e-government projects in my organization. New relations with other(s) area(s) or office(s) of government have emerged as a result of the e-government project. There is suitable cooperation and/or collaboration in my area for the realization of e-government application(s). Working with other organizations in government enriches the project results. Working with other organizations in government creates synergies that facilitate the development of projects.
Internal efficiency and effectiveness Cronbach's alpha = .849	The success of this e-government project has increased the productivity of your organization. The success of this e-government project has reduced costs in your organization. The success of this e-government project has resulted in better quality of service.
External impact Cronbach's alpha = .834	The success of this e-government project has fostered more effective government policies and programmes. The success of this e-government project has led to more transparent government.t The success of this e-government project has fostered citizen participation. The success of this e-government project has created a favourable legal and regulatory environment for the use of information and communication technologies in government.

variables, showing an appropriately developed institutional environment albeit with high variations among states.

Table 3 shows Pearson's correlation coefficients for all constructs. Although correlations among the constructs are significant, values are smaller than Cronbach's alphas for the constructs. The highest significant correlation in Table 3 (.750) is between the study's two dependent variables, so no evidence suggests strong correlations affecting results.

To test our hypotheses, we used moderated multiple regression for each dependent variable. This method includes a hierarchical regression that first tests the relation of the independent variable and the mediator on the dependent variable and, second, tests the relation of a term that carries information about predictors

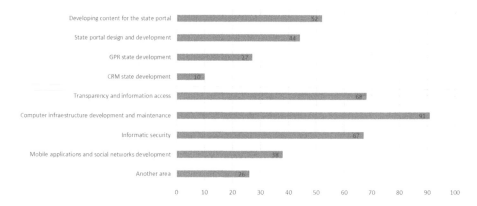

Figure 2. Categories of digital government projects. Note: respondents could choose more than one option.

Table 2. Descriptive statistics.

	Mean	SD
Dependent variables		
Internal efficiency and effectiveness	3.99	0.65
External impact	3.88	0.67
Independent variables		
Internal resources	3.31	0.85
Internal processes	3.67	0.73
Moderating variables		
Public–public collaborations	4.04	0.75
Public–private collaborations	3.15	0.86
Control variables		
Institutional environment	3.81	0.70
Less-developed state	.15	.36
Medium-developed state	.44	.50
Highly developed state	.41	.49
Years of experience in government	10.26	7.68
Years of working experience	17.62	7.96
Number of organizations involved	8.11	6.79

Table 3. Correlation matrix.

	1	2	3	4	5	6
1. Internal resources						
2. Internal processes	.589**					
3. Public collaboration	.476**	.530**				
4. Private collaboration	.368**	.345**	.518**			
5. Internal efficiency and effectiveness	.404**	.590**	.570**	.221**		
6. External impact	.498**	.669**	.601**	.350**	.750**	

$**p \leq .01.$

(interaction term). Tables 4 and 5 show results of the regression analysis. We tested all models for multicollinearity via tolerance and variance inflation factors and detected no problem.

Table 4 reveals that H1 is not supported. Internal resources are unrelated to internal efficiency and effectiveness ($b = -0.022$; $\beta = -.028$; $p = .724$). H2 is

Table 4. Regression results for dependent variable: internal efficiency and effectiveness.

Internal resources	−.006	−.017	−.028
Internal processes	.395***	.355***	.378***
Public collaboration	.438***	.601***	.570***
Private collaboration	−.121	−.120*	−.104
Interactions			
Internal resources × private collaboration		−.248**	−.244**
Internal processes × private collaboration		.213*	.235*
Internal resources × public collaboration		.380***	.383**
Internal processes × public collaboration		−.064	−.092
Control			
Less-developed state			.011
Highly developed state			−.083
Years of experience in government			.048
Years of working experience			−.050
Institutional environment			.003
Number of organizations involved			.045
Model statistics			
R^2	.454	.537	.547
Adjusted R^2	.438	.509	.498
Model F	28.633***	19.392***	11.061***

Values reported in the table are standardized coefficient values. *$p \leq .1$, **$p \leq .05$, ***$p \leq .001$.

Table 5. Regression results for the dependent variable: external impact.

Internal resources	.068	.061	.024
Internal processes	.437***	.423***	.392***
Public collaboration	.355***	.410***	.358***
Private collaboration	.011	.005	.006
Interactions			
Internal resources × private collaboration		−.328**	−.280**
Internal processes × private collaboration		.300**	.239*
Internal resources × public collaboration		.253**	.202*
Internal processes × public collaboration		−.115	−.072
Control			
Less-developed state			.074
Highly developed state			−.014
Years of experience in government			−.018
Years of working experience			−.053
Institutional environment			.172**
Number of organizations involved			.019
Model statistics			
R^2	.530	.574	.598
Adjusted R^2	.516	.549	.554
Model F	38.886***	22.566***	13.586***

Values reported are standardized coefficient values. *$p \leq .1$ **$p \leq .05$, ***$p \leq .001$.

supported. Internal processes positively affect internal efficiency and effectiveness ($b = 0.335$; $\beta = .378$; $p < .001$). H3 is not supported. Private collaboration moderated the effect of internal resources on internal efficiency and effectiveness, but negatively, contrary to expectations ($b = -0.166$; $\beta = -.244$; $p < .05$). H4 is supported. Private collaboration moderated the effect of internal processes on internal efficiency and effectiveness in the expected positive way ($b = 0.196$; $\beta = .235$; $p < .1$). H5 is supported. Public collaboration positively moderated the effect of internal resources on internal efficiency and effectiveness ($b = 0.277$; $\beta = .383$; $p < .05$). H6 is not supported. Public collaboration did not moderate the effect of internal processes on internal efficiency and effectiveness ($b = -0.075$; $\beta = -.092$; $p = .464$). It is interesting that the direct effect of public collaboration on internal efficiency and effectiveness is positive and that private collaboration exerts no significant effect on promoting efficiencies and effectiveness after including the control variables. No control variable affects value creation.

Table 5 shows regression results for the second dependent variable: external impact. Table 5 indicates that H1 is not supported. Internal resources are not related to external impact ($b = 0.019$; $\beta = .024$; $p = .749$). H2 is supported. Internal processes positively affected external impact ($b = 0.362$; $\beta = .392$; $p < .001$). H3 is not supported. Private collaboration moderated, but negatively, the effect of internal resources on external impact ($b = -0.199$; $\beta = -.280$; $p < .05$). H4 is supported. Private collaboration positively moderated the effect of internal processes on external impact ($b = 0.208$; $\beta = .239$; $p < .1$). H5 is supported. Public collaboration positively moderated the effect of internal resources on external impact ($b = 0.152$; $\beta = .202$; $p < .1$). H6 is not supported. Public collaboration did not positively moderate the effect of internal processes on external impact ($b = -0.061$; $\beta = -.072$; $p = .541$). It is interesting that only public collaboration directly affects the creation of external impact. Moreover, institutional environment relates positively and significantly with this type of public value.

Discussion

Table 6 shows a summary of the results of hypotheses testing. Three proposed hypotheses are supported (H2, H4 and H5), and hypothesis H1 is not supported. Contrary to the established literature (Gil-García 2012; Savoldelli, Codagnone, and Misuraca 2014), our regression results show that projects in organizations with more internal resources do not necessarily produce more public value. Previous research suggests that strategic resources explain performance only to the extent that organizations capture the economic value that they create (Barney and Clark 2007). If some stakeholders capture the value, then some benefits generated by strategic resources may not be revealed in performance measures (Collis and Montgomery 1995).

Our findings show that internal processes positively influence public value by enhancing internal efficiency and effectiveness and external impact (H2). Value creation is more easily achieved by public organizations through adequate implementation of internal processes. As a consequence, public value probably relates more to the quality of processes that mobilize resources than to the existence or availability of resources themselves. These findings are supported by the existing literature (Gil-García 2012; Savoldelli, Codagnone, and Misuraca 2014).

Table 6. Results of hypotheses testing.

Hypothesis	Internal efficiency and effectiveness	External impact
H1	Not supported	Not supported
H2	Supported (+)	Supported (+)
H3	Not supported (−)	Not supported (−)
H4	Supported (+)	Supported (+)
H5	Supported (+)	Supported (+)
H6	Not supported	Not supported

Our results suggest that the relation between government and private organizations can be counterproductive for value creation, a finding directionally coincident with Cordella and Willcocks (2010). Private collaboration in digital government projects moderated the relation between internal resources and public value with respect to internal efficiency and effectiveness and external impact (H3) but in a *negative* way. In other words, the relation between internal resources and value creation seems to be negative when a private organization is involved. The finding supports the perception that devoting greater quantities of internal resources to collaborations with private organizations may actually damage public value. Perhaps this result is explained by perceived corruption in the country and by the lack of continuity between government mandates. Large quantities of governmental internal resources combined with private organization resources could be perceived as a synonym for embezzlement or waste when a new governor reassigns government contracts. This result could also be explained by a mismatch between objectives, attitudes and organizational structures of public and private organizations (Cordella and Willcocks 2010; Kivleniece and Quelin 2012), leading to wasted time and money (internal resources) and subsequent loss in public value. Although some of these explanations may be valid for specific contexts, issues concerning government continuity and organizational mismatch represent more general situations (Wu and Zhang 2007).

Our results show that collaboration between government and private organizations can create value through internal processes, in line with existing studies (Ansell and Gash 2008; Cordella and Willcocks 2010). Private collaboration moderates the relation between internal processes and public value with respect to internal efficiency and effectiveness and external impact (H4). Results suggest that the more intense public–private collaboration, the better is the implementation of processes, leading to substantial improvement in public value with respect to internal efficiency and effectiveness and external impact. Sharing process standardization, methods and orientation towards task effectiveness, which are prevalent in private organizations, could explain those results. Measurability of performance may work better in collaboration with private organizations (Hefetz and Warner 2011) and offer better access to technology (Levina and Ross 2003). More formalized arrangements permit more decentralized decisions because formal procedures reduce the discretion of subordinates (Pfeffer and Leblebici 1977).

Regression results indicate that public–public collaboration in digital government projects positively moderated the relation between internal resources and public value with respect to internal efficiency and effectiveness and external impact (H5). The finding is consistent with previous research (Ansell and Gash 2008; Richardson 1972). This result suggests that public collaborations tend to pool sets of similar resources in the public interest rather than for financial gain. Collaboration by government with other public organizations may be perceived as a transparent application of resources enhancing external public value. That is, complementarity and similarity in sets of necessary internal resources improve internal efficiency and effectiveness. Shared common values and a strong commitment to the public seem to encourage public–public collaboration and increase public value (Boag and McDonald 2010).

Coordination costs correspond to the importance of information processing needs (Gulati, Lavie, and Singh 2009). In that sense, collaboration with public organizations may promote improved shared communication within the public administration that facilitates the pooling of key resources, sharing common traditions and language. Collaboration with public organizations may be more readily acceptable to public authorities and the public by gaining political legitimacy (Bryson, Crosby, and Stone 2006).

However, contrary to our expectations, public–public collaboration in digital government projects did not moderate the relation between internal processes and public value with respect to internal efficiency and effectiveness and external impact (H6), even though internal processes positively influenced value creation. Public–public partnerships brought nothing in that respect. This result could be explained by the similarity of organizational cultures and processes implemented which made no difference in the relation. This finding also confirms the result that process improvements must be expected through collaboration with the private sector than with the public sector.

Conclusion

The study's primary contribution is to present novel results in empirical examination of the impact of resources and processes of public administration on public value through the moderation of two types of external collaboration. Our study indicates that overall, processes matter more than resources in enhancing public value. However, collaboration with other public sector entities matters more for enhancing the impact of internal resources than for improving the impact of internal processes. Second, collaboration with other public entities seems to have more influence than collaboration with private entities in the two dimensions of public value analyzed. Private collaboration enhances the impact of processes on public value but not the impact of resources. Finally, our results contrast with results of other studies because they disregarded resources, processes and types of collaboration.

Our results give rise to several recommendations for public managers seeking to increase public value through digital government projects. Our research shows that investing solely in internal resources is not necessarily the key to value creation. The efficient use of such resources makes a difference. Instead of acquiring and accumulating internal resources, public managers should focus on improving internal processes and other activities, resulting in more efficient use of such resources. Continuous adoption and testing of new processes and standard operating procedures will create greater value internally and externally.

In the context of the collaboration processes described in the study and going back to Ansell and Gash's model (2008), our results also suggest that asymmetries in knowledge and resources play a positive role when they are complementary. In this sense, looking for appropriate partners to collaborate or paying attention to complementarities early in the process is another practical implication of our work. More specifically, collaborating with private entities may increase the impact of internal processes on public value, which may result from the fact that private organizations work differently, and then collaborating with them promotes learning from new processes. This requires public managers to develop a capacity to integrate those processes in their own organization. Collaborating with other public entities may increase the impact of internal resources on public value, which also may constitute a different kind of complementarity. That is to say, public agencies in this sample are joining complementary resources to do more. Again, public managers need to develop capabilities to share resources. Unfortunately, most of resource sharing in the public sector suffers from institutional constraints, which are not always under the control of the public manager. In this sense, managers with an interest in taking advantage of sharing resources will need to push for the development of the proper laws and regulations in this respect.

Maximizing public value thanks to collaboration requires the correct alignment of resources, experience, objectives, atmosphere and cultural norms, legal standards and tax issues. Our study suggests public managers should pay attention to the similarity and complementarity of activities to be coordinated to devise the right fit between those activities and types of collaboration adopted, with private entities or other public entities. They need to become facilitative leaders, capable of designing the vision and learning processes to work in each project.

As we described earlier, benefits from collaboration may be delayed because of the cost and effort needed to initiate the virtuous cycles described in the literature (Vangen and Huxham 2011). Our results also show that when better resource use is the goal, partnerships between public organizations may be the most beneficial vehicles. When improving processes is the goal, public managers may find more value in partnerships with the private sector. In any case, it is important to compare the skills and processes of all potential members in a partnership to access the best capabilities.

Future research could examine how public administration may use a variety of organizational forms simultaneously for different purposes or types of activities and with different levels of performance. The importance of legitimizing the mode of collaboration chosen would also merit further study. Institutional frameworks to promote collaborative governance and PVM are a work in progress (Shaw 2013). More research is needed into the development of absorptive and collaborative capabilities by public managers. We also need studies to show how direct collaboration with citizens may enhance public value and innovations in developing digital government projects.

Disclosure statement

No potential conflict of interest was reported by the authors.

References

Ansell, C., and A. Gash. 2008. "Collaborative Governance in Theory and Practice." *Journal of Public Administration Research & Theory* 18 (4): 543–571. doi:10.1093/jopart/mum032.
Barney, J. 1991. "Firm Resources and Sustained Competitive Advantage." *Journal of Management* 17 (1): 99. doi:10.1177/014920639101700108.
Barney, J. B. 2001. "Is the Resource-Based 'View' a Useful Perspective for Strategic Management Research? Yes." *Academy of Management Review* 26 (1): 41–56. doi:10.5465/AMR.2001.4011938.
Barney, J. B., and D. Clark. 2007. *Resource-Based Theory: Creating and Sustaining Competitive Advantage.* Oxford University Press Oxford. http://library.wur.nl/WebQuery/clc/1882076
Boag, G., and D. A. McDonald. 2010. "A Critical Review of Public-Public Partnerships in Water Services." *Water Alternatives* 3 (1): 1–25.
Bryson, J., B. Crosby, and M. M. Stone. 2006. "The Design and Implementation of Cross-Sector Collaborations: Propositions from the Literature." *Public Administration Review* 66 (November): 44–55. doi:10.1111/j.1540-6210.2006.00665.x.
Bryson, J. M., B. C. Crosby, and L. Bloomberg. 2014. "Public Value Governance: Moving beyond Traditional Public Administration and the New Public Management." *Public Administration Review*, June. n/a-n/a. doi:10.1111/puar.12238.
Collis, D., and C. Montgomery. 1995. "Competing on Resources: Strategy in the 1990s." *Harvard Business Review* 73 (4): 118–128.
Cordella, A., and C. Bonina. 2012. "A Public Value Perspective for ICT Enabled Public Sector Reforms: A Theoretical Reflection." *Government Information Quarterly* 29 (4): 512–520. doi:10.1016/j.giq.2012.03.004.
Cordella, A., and L. Willcocks. 2010. "Outsourcing, Bureaucracy and Public Value: Reappraising the Notion of the 'Contract State.'." *Government Information Quarterly* 27 (1): 82–88. doi:10.1016/j.giq.2009.08.004.
Crook, R., D. Ketchen Jr., J. Combs, and S. Todd. 2008. "Strategic Resources and Performance: A Meta-Analysis." *Strategic Management Journal* 29 (11): 1141–1154. doi:10.1002/smj.703.
Dawes, S., A. Cresswell, and T. Pardo. 2009. "From 'Need to Know' to 'Need to Share': Tangled Problems, Information Boundaries, and the Building of Public Sector Knowledge Networks." *Public Administration Review* 69 (3): 392–402. doi:10.1111/j.1540-6210.2009.01987_2.x.
Dyer, J., and H. Singh. 1998. "The Relational View: Cooperative Strategy and Sources of Interorganizational Competitive Advantage." *Academy of Management Review* 23 (4): 660–679. doi:10.5465/AMR.1998.1255632.
Emerson, K., T. Nabatchi, and S. Balogh. 2012. "An Integrative Framework for Collaborative Governance." *Journal of Public Administration Research & Theory* 22 (1): 1–29. doi:10.1093/jopart/mur011.
Fountain, J. 2001. "Paradoxes of Public Sector Customer Service." *Governance* 14 (1): 55. doi:10.1111/0952-1895.00151.
Fountain, J., R. McKinnon, and E. Park. 2003. *"E-Government Cross-Agency an D Intergovernmental Initiatives Research Project: Web Survey Results."* NCDG 03-011. Cambridge, MA: National Center

for Digital Government, Harvard University. http://www.umass.edu/digitalcenter/research/work
ing_papers/03_011FountainMcKinnonPark.pdf.

Gil-García, R. 2012. *Enacting Electronic Government Success: An Integrative Study of Government-
Wide Websites, Organizational Capabilities, and Institutions.* New York: Springer.

Goldsmith, S., and W. Eggers. 2004. *Governing by Network: The New Shape of the Public Sector.*
Washington, DC: Brookings Institution Press.

Greasley, K., P. Watson, and S. Patel. 2008. "The Formation of Public-Public Partnerships: A Case
Study Examination of Collaboration on A 'Back to Work' Initiative." *International Journal of
Public Sector Management* 21 (3): 305–313. doi:10.1108/09513550810863204.

Gulati, R., D. Lavie, and H. Singh. 2009. "The Nature of Partnering Experience and the Gains from
Alliances." *Strategic Management Journal* 30 (11): 1213–1233. doi:10.1002/smj.v30:11.

Hair, J., W. Black, B. Babin, and R. Anderson. 2009. *Multivariate Data Analysis.* 7 edition ed. Upper
Saddle River, NJ: Prentice Hall.

Hefetz, A., and M. Warner. 2011. "Contracting or Public Delivery? the Importance of Service,
Market and Management Characteristics, April 12." *Journal of Public Administration Research
and Theory* 22 (2): 289–317. doi:10.1093/jopart/mur006.

Hui, G., and M. Hayllar. 2010. "Creating Public Value in E-Government: A Public-Private-Citizen
Collaboration Framework in Web 2.0." *Australian Journal of Public Administration* 69 (March):
S120–31. doi:10.1111/j.1467-8500.2009.00662.x.

Karunasena, K., and H. Deng. 2012. "Critical Factors for Evaluating the Public Value of
E-Government in Sri Lanka." *Government Information Quarterly* 29 (1): 76–84. doi:10.1016/j.
giq.2011.04.005.

Kivleniece, I., and B. Quelin. 2012. "Creating and Capturing Value in Public-Private Ties: A Private
Actor's Perspective." *The Academy of Management Review* 37 (2): 272–299. doi:10.5465/
amr.2011.0004.

Levina, N., and J. Ross. 2003. "From the Vendor's Perspective: Exploring the Value Proposition in
Information Technology Outsourcing. MIS Quarterly, 331-364." *MIS Quarterly* 27 (3): 331–364.

Luna-Reyes, L. 2013. "Trust and Collaboration in Interorganizational Information Technology
Projects in the Public Sector." *Gestión Y Política Pública* 22: 173–211.

Luna-Reyes, L., L. Black, A. Cresswell, and T. Pardo. 2008. "Knowledge Sharing and Trust in
Collaborative Requirements Analysis." *System Dynamics Review (Wiley)* 24 (3): 265–297.
doi:10.1002/sdr.404.

Luna-Reyes, L. J., R. Gil-Garcia, and M. Estrada-Marroquín. 2008. "The Impact of Institutions on
Interorganizational IT Projects in the Mexican Federal Government." *International Journal of
Electronic Government Research* 4 (2): 27–42. doi:10.4018/jegr.2008040103.

Moore, M. 2013. *Recognizing Public Value.* Cambridge, Mass: Harvard University Press.

Pardo, T. A., R. Gil-García, and L. F. Luna-Reyes. 2010. "Collaborative Governance and Cross-
Boundary Information Sharing: Envisioning a Networked and IT-Enabled Public
Administration." In *The Future of Public Administration around the World: The Minnowbrook
Perspective.*, edited by R. O'Leary, S. Kim, and D. Van Slyke, 129–140. Washington, DC:
Georgetown University Press.

Pfeffer, J., and H. Leblebici. 1977. "Information Technology and Organizational Structure." *Pacific
Sociological Review* 20: 241–259. doi:10.2307/1388934.

Piening, E. 2013. "Dynamic Capabilities in Public Organizations." *Public Management Review* 15 (2):
209–245. doi:10.1080/14719037.2012.708358.

Public, C. I. O. 2013. "Public-Private Partnership or Government Owned." *Public CIO* 11 (4): 4–9.

Ray, G., J. Barney, and W. Muhanna. 2004. "Capabilities, Business Processes, and Competitive
Advantage: Choosing the Dependent Variable in Empirical Tests of the Resource-Based View."
Strategic Management Journal 25 (1): 23–37. doi:10.1002/smj.366.

Richardson, G. B. 1972. "The Organisation of Industry." *Economic Journal* 82 (327): 883–896.
doi:10.2307/2230256.

Rinaldi, M., R. Montanari, and E. Bottani. 2015. "Improving the Efficiency of Public Administrations
through Business Process Reengineering and Simulation." *Business Process Management Journal*
21 (2): 419–462. doi:10.1108/BPMJ-06-2014-0054.

Sako, M. 2014. "Technology Strategy and Management: The Business of the State." *Communications
of the ACM* 57 (7): 29–31. doi:10.1145/2618105.

Savoldelli, A., C. Codagnone, and G. Misuraca. 2014. "Understanding the E-Government Paradox: Learning from Literature and Practice on Barriers to Adoption." *Government Information Quarterly* 31 (Supplement 1 (June)): S63–71. ICEGOV 2012 Supplement. doi:10.1016/j. giq.2014.01.008.

Shaw, R. 2013. "Another Size Fits All? Public Value Management and Challenges for Institutional Design." *Public Management Review* 15 (4): 477–500. doi:10.1080/14719037.2012.664017.

Siemiatycki, M., and N. Farooqi. 2012. "Value for Money and Risk in Public-Private Partnerships." *Journal of the American Planning Association* 78 (3): 286. doi:10.1080/01944363.2012.715525.

Stanimirovic, D., and M. Vintar. 2013. "Conceptualization of an Integrated Indicator Model for the Evaluation of E-Government Policies." *Electronic Journal of E-Government* 11 (1): 292–306.

Steijn, B., E.-H. Klijn, and J. Edelenbos. 2011. "Public Private Partnerships: Added Value by Organizational Form or Management?" *Public Administration* 89 (4): 1235–1252. doi:10.1111/ j.1467-9299.2010.01877.x.

Stoker, G. 2006. "Public Value Management A New Narrative for Networked Governance?" *The American Review of Public Administration* 36 (1): 41–57. doi:10.1177/0275074005282583.

Thomson, A. M., and J. Perry. 2006. "Collaboration Processes: Inside the Black Box." *Public Administration Review*. doi:10.1111/j.1540-6210.2006.00663.x.

Vangen, S., and C. Huxham. 2011."The Tangled Web: Unraveling the Principle of Common Goals in Collaborations." *Journal of Public Administration Research and Theory*, December. doi:10.1093/ jopart/mur065.

Wu, F., and J. Zhang. 2007. "Planning the Competitive City-Region the Emergence of Strategic Development Plan in China." *Urban Affairs Review* 42 (5): 714–740. doi:10.1177/ 1078087406298119.

The digital government imperative: a context-aware perspective

Walter Castelnovo ⓘ and Maddalena Sorrentino

ABSTRACT
The paper applies a 'context-aware' research approach to explore Italy's digital government trajectory, using the information and communication technology -enabled programme that introduced the One-Stop Business Shop to exemplify its analytical potential. The interpretive lens captures the political, institutional and external forces at play to illustrate how the outcomes of public-sector reforms are shaped not by legislative strong-arming and ubiquitous technological enablement but by the environmental dynamics. To demonstrate the central role of contextual factors in achieving the desired change, the study conducts a qualitative exploratory analysis that opens doors left mostly closed by the deterministic view of the mainstream literature on digital reform.

1. Introduction

The many central and local government reforms introduced in the past 20 years aim to deliver efficient public services and relaunch the national economies in a world that continues to raise the competitiveness stakes (Michalopoulos 2003). Both the EU and the OECD prioritize simplified regulation and better preconditions to promote entrepreneurship and growth in a time of financial austerity and, although the advanced countries have imposed different measures to reform the public administration (PA) and improve administrative capacity since the mid-1990s, each has the same goal-setting agenda (OECD 1995, 25):

- More results-oriented;
- More value for money;
- Devolution of authority and more flexibility;
- Stronger accountability and control;
- Focus on client and service;
- Strengthened capacity for developing strategy and policy;
- Introduction of competition.

That goal-setting agenda sums up the key tenets of the New Public Management (NPM) wave that dominated public management practices for more than 20 years and that shined the light on information and communication technology (ICT) as a major agent of organizational change (Bellamy and Taylor 1998; Fountain 2002). This stance pushed the governments to use ICT as a fundamental lever to modernize and improve citizen services (Foley and Alfonso 2009) and achieve the desired outcomes (see the so-called ICT reform hypothesis discussed by Kraemer and King 2008). The major role of the internet and web-based technologies/applications is embodied by the provision of one-stop public services, a concept that comprises the one-stop shops in which the same co-located staff deliver multiple administrative services, the one-stop windows that integrate exclusively the customer interface, and web-integrated services where customer transparency and cross-services integration is primarily electronic (Barbosa, Pozzebon, and Diniz 2013; Dunleavy et al. 2006, 484).

This study takes an analytical approach that shifts the central focus from the *features* of the IT artefacts and solutions chosen by the one-stop shops to the *policies* that implicitly support e-government. Surprisingly underdeveloped by the research, the lens adopted reconstructs the implementation dynamics of the Italian One-Stop Business Shop, herein referred to also by its Italian title, the 'Sportelli Unici per le Attività Produttive' (SUAP), to help us better understand the logics and the role played by ICT in the course and outcome of a reform programme.

The SUAP law enacted by the Italian Government in 1998 compelled each local council to set up a new and distinct organizational unit to centralize the processes for opening, changing and closing a business activity. In general terms, the reform aimed to drive technological improvement in both the PA and the business spheres but, more specifically, the Italian policymakers saw it as a major enabler of administrative simplification and better access to business services that harnessed digital technology to standardize and streamline the bureaucratic procedures. However, the SUAP ran into so many implementation difficulties it failed to deliver the expected benefits and the Napoleonic administrative tradition by which Italy is ruled (Peters 2008) forced the legislator to make repeated adjustments to the laws that codify and trigger the SUAP reform. This legalistic approach stalled and deviated the programme's trajectory not only due to the confusion and uncertainty it sowed, especially among the councils that were handed the hot potato of coordinating the relevant procedures across independent organizations, but also because of opposing premises that threw in 'everything and the opposite of everything,' from NPM vs. joined-up government to front office vs. back office to disintermediation vs. re-intermediation.

The qualitative paper acknowledges the unpredictability of 'policy transformation' – intended as the original design of a policy translated *into IT artefact, work processes and stakeholder roles* (Goldkuhl 2016, 447) – and that it is less easy to control from a high altitude: 'sometimes successful (well-implemented policies) and sometimes unsuccessful (no implementation of policy elements and/or inappropriate side-effects occurring)' (ibidem). Moreover, 'there are negotiations of policy and other institutional aspects between different stakeholders that moderate original policy intentions' (ibidem).

The broader perspective adopted here combines the policy content, the implementation process and the backdrop against which the reform unfolds in a context-aware (configurational) methodological approach with a lens wide enough to capture the relevant 'structural-instrumental, cultural and environmental' aspects (Christensen et al. 2007;

Bezes et al. 2013). This theoretical path allows us to both *describe* how the SUAP programme evolved on the ground and *understand* the logics that shaped its outcomes.

The analysis suggests that hard-to-govern multiple factors, above all, the context in which implementation occurs, determine the success or failure of a multi-organizational programme, and that the implementer organizations face three particularly crucial issues: (i) the design of the coordination arrangements; (ii) the distribution of the competences and responsibilities across multiple actors and (iii) the capacity of each council to adopt appropriate change management strategies to translate the ICT resources into capabilities (Rose and Grant 2010).

Research considers one-stop shop provision the essential hub and spokes of any digital government system (Wimmer 2002; Glassey 2004; Bannister 2005; Gouscos et al. 2007; Verdegem and Hauttekeete 2008; Hogrebe, Kruse, and Nüttgens 2008; Howard 2014). The present study is timely and worthwhile on three counts: (i) to make sense of the inherent difficulties of public programmes by investigating the environment in which certain implementation decisions work and others don't; (ii) to reconstruct the SUAP case as an example of a major e-government initiative implemented in the past 20 years (OECD 2012) when Italy was in full NPM flow, clarifying how a 'softer' version of its principles took hold late in the day not only in Italy but also in other countries of the Napoleonic administrative tradition and (iii) to conduct a post-implementation assessment of the SUAP, which, to the best of our knowledge, has not yet been done, even though it was first written into law 18 years ago and last revised 6 years ago.

The contribution of the exploratory study is threefold. First, it evidences the effective capacity of digital government to achieve the expected benefits. Second, it extends prior research on e-government implementation, identifying the paradox of the secondary role played by ICT. Third, the configurational analysis sharpens our focus on the impacts of reforms on the administrative machinery.

The paper proceeds as follows. Section 2 reviews the relevant literature and describes the theoretical frame here applied to the SUAP programme. Section 3 outlines the research approach and questions that guide the paper. Section 4 illustrates the programme's evolution, using the organizational lens to analyse the dynamics between specialization and coordination. Section 5 discusses how the SUAP's trajectory has been shaped by country-specific contextual forces. The final section presents the authors' conclusions, the study's implications and the potential pay offs for the research and practice of PA reforms.

2. Theoretical frame and related works

Kraemer and King (2008, 5) offer four guiding principles to support the digital (or electronic) government (or e-government) 'reform hypothesis':

- The potential of ICT to reform the PAs and their relations with the satellite environments;
- The potential of ICT as a powerful reform tool that can catalyse change in organizational structures;
- The benefits of the proper use of ICT for the entire collective: administrators, staff, citizens, and PA;

– The under-realized potential benefits from ICT caused by a lack of managerial understanding of what the technology can do and an unwillingness of managers to pursue the potential of the technology when they do understand.

The wide discussion and criticism of these ideas has made the reform hypothesis described by Kraemer and King the more or less explicit subject of most e-government literature since the late 1990s (Kraemer and King 2008; Coursey and Norris 2008; Lips and Schuppan 2009; Bannister and Connolly 2011; Norris and Reddick 2013; Gil-Garcia, Vivanco, and Luna-Reyes 2014). However, while a vast store of up-to-date evidence supports the potential of digital public services, Gil-Garcia, Vivanco and Luna-Reyes (2014) argue that the mainstream debate tends to underestimate the interactive ability of ICT to transform public services and the organizational and institutional factors that influence their selection, design, implementation and specific use. Further, Baptista (2005, 167) observes that e-government is rarely taken for what it is, which is 'both a subset and a driver of government and public-sector reform.' The predominant use of the technocentric dimension to investigate e-government as a self-standing (or 'ghettoized' [Pollitt 2012, ix]) field of study ignores the fact that e-government raises or amplifies a number of political issues in a wide number of areas (Baptista 2005, 170). This misrepresentation of technology prevents a realistic assessment of the contextual forces that significantly influence the reform outcomes.

Hence e-government 'is not a model in itself' (Pollitt and Bouckaert 2011, 7) and many versions are observable in the empirical reality:

an e-Government that reinforces traditional bureaucratic hierarchies, an e-Government that facilitates the NPM, an e-Government that is designed to promote networking and wider concepts of governance. A great deal depends on the particular *context* in which a given e-technology is introduced, with what purposes, and so on (emphasis added).

The literature draws deeply on political science and public management to argue that ICT does not so much transform government as amplify existing or emerging political trends (Ostling 2010; Pollitt 2013), which, in turn, are influenced by country-specific contexts. Interestingly, the e-government research is beginning to adopt this view, recognizing the need to conceptually surpass the deterministic view of digital government in order to grasp its broader meaning.

The social sciences consider context a crucial key to unlock explanations and provide recommendations. For example, Pollitt (2013, xviii) defines context as 'a missing link,' that is, 'something that enables us to understand the different evolutions of public policy and management in different habitats.' He also notes that context enables us to clarify 'how particular species of reform are related to one another, and why the evolutionary tree branches at certain points' (ibidem).

Christensen and Lægreid (2013, 140) say that context is multiform and plays an active part in the processes of change in the public sector. In fact, context is 'a complex mixture of environmental pressure, historical institutional context and polity features' (p. 136) that shapes reforms and their effects. Therefore, Christensen and Lægreid (2007, 2013) suggest a context-aware approach to the analysis and interpretation of the 'course and outcome' of public decision-making, that is, an approach that uses a structural-instrumental, cultural and environmental lens to capture concrete aspects of reality. The scholars argue specifically that the reforms can be perceived from a *structural-instrumental* standpoint as conscious organizational design or re-engineering, given that the decision makers use the organizational structure and resources as instruments to achieve objectives. The emphasis on values and models borrowed from private firms and the critical roles of political leaders in organizational choices are the 'guiding lights' of the structural-instrumental perspective. The assumption is simple and linear: reformers change structures and the rest will follow (Pina E Cunha and Tsoukas 2015, 227).

The *cultural* perspective shows how reforms and change in public organizations trigger an institutionalization process that gradually introduces the 'core informal norms and values.' The fact that different countries and government institutions have different historical–cultural backgrounds means that their reforms follow a 'path-dependent' course that gives each national reform a distinct complexion. Moreover, public reforms must be put to the test of 'cultural compatibility' (Christensen et al. 2007, 132): 'initiatives that are incompatible with established norms and values in organizations will be rejected, while parts that are compatible will be implemented; controversial parts will be adapted so as to be made acceptable.' Hence, a reform is more likely to be successful when its underlying values are better aligned with the values embedded in the existing administrative system.

A further aspect is that public organizations are said to dwell in a dual *environment*: the technical part, mainly focused on efficiency, production and exchange; and the institutional part, which deals more with matters such as the appropriate organizational structure, internal culture and recruitment policy. The institutional environment is a breeding ground for the reform myths that spread to other public organizations, shape their isomorphic features (Christensen et al. 2007) and increase their legitimacy (ibidem, p. 132).

A recent comparative study of 10 years of administrative redesign in France and in Norway saw Bezes et al. (2013) use the three co-existing contexts identified by Christensen and Lægreid to gain insights into the complexity of delivering meaningful public reforms. The study is based on a configurational analytical approach that combines internal pressures, political factors and domestic historical–institutional legacies. Meyer, Tsui and Hinings (1993, 1175) broadly define a configuration as 'any multidimensional constellation of conceptually distinct characteristics that commonly occur together.' The main argument of the Bezes et al essay is that such an approach is necessary to understand and explain the change patterns, and to highlight the specific combinations of driving forces that conditioned the two nations' policymakers and public managers. Using concepts from organizational studies, Bezes et al. have developed a convincing approach to diachronically describe and compare the implementation of public reforms in highly diverse contexts.

Summing up, the above studies inform that the idea of a multilayered dynamic context is central to a range of theories that can strengthen our understanding of the determinants of organizational change. In fact, the studies that treat digital government as merely a technical matter, focusing on a single organization, do not capture the role of ICT 'in context' that is essential to gaining realistic insights. The literature review performed by the authors in September 2015 produced no e-government studies that apply the context-aware approach exemplified by Bezes and colleagues, leading the authors of the present work to test the effective heuristic capacity of this conceptualization.

3. Research approach and key questions

To better achieve the research purposes, the authors use an inductive method to define and connote the object of study but do not test predefined hypotheses. In other words, using the SUAP programme as an example of a major e-government intervention, the analysis seeks to identify the contextual factors that shaped its evolution from 1998 to 2015 but does not develop a general model of how ICT-enabled reform programmes 'work' on the ground. Basically, the research approach adopted can be considered as an exploratory, instrumental and embedded qualitative study (Yin 2003).

Here, to borrow the words of Goldkuhl (2016, 446), the interest is in whether and how the SUAP policies became institutionalized and thus carried by routinized activities, by public administrators' roles and knowledge and by IT artefacts. The benefits of an historical-institutionalist view (Christensen and Lægreid 2007; Peters 2008) is that it informs how existing institutions influence the perception of problems and limit the alternatives within the reorganization-making process, as well as how the choices are structured at the local level.

The Italian Government's SUAP programme made the approximately 8,000 (8,101 in 1998; 7,999 in 2016) local councils the mainstays and primary implementers of its Digital Agenda, a huge task given the significant differences in both their size and organizational capacities. Such a heterogeneous landscape therefore leads the present study to adopt a methodology that identifies specialization and coordination as the two key concepts of organization theory capable of providing a 'common grammar' (Bezes et al. 2013, 149) to describe and interpret the implementation and local variation of the One-Stop Business Shop reform path.

Italy is a good fit for a context-aware analysis. In the words of Bezes et al. (2013, 152), we are looking at an articulated situation in which multiple combinations of factors and explanatory logics 'work together and influence one another with a configurative perspective.' Applied to the meso-level, the analytical configurational approach treats organizations as clusters of interconnected structures and practices rather than as modular or loosely coupled entities whose components can be understood in isolation (Fiss 2007).

The study combines secondary data sources that range from earlier research to official government and non-governmental documents issued in the 1998–2015 review period and the personal knowledge bases of the two authors. The information was grouped and assessed thematically to gain a systemic view of the involvement and competences of the relevant actors and the hurdles erected by the institutional environment.

The qualitative exploration is guided by two key questions:

Q1. What contextual forces drive and/or constrain administrative reforms?

Q2. What role does ICT play in the course and outcomes of reform efforts?

These questions will be approached from two angles. First, the *descriptive*, which mainly illustrates the programme path, the responsibilities spread across the various administrative bodies, in particular, the decisions to attribute tasks to the numerous SUAP actors (specialization) and the mechanisms of inter-organizational coordination, and, second, the *explanatory*, which captures the political factors, the domestic historical-institutional legacies and the external pressures that are essential to understand and interpret the programme and its logics as a holistic constellation.

4. The SUAP reform programme

As part of the Italian Government's plan to simplify business–PA relations, the One-Stop Business Shop Act (Law 447/1998 or SUAP) compelled each of Italy's local councils to set up a single organizational unit for business owners to expedite all the requirements to open, change and/or close an activity. The SUAP could be set up either independently or jointly with other municipalities (inter-municipal cooperation) with the proviso that only one single organization handled the entire business service process and that a new figure of authority, the Head of Coordination, was appointed to manage and coordinate all the relevant public bodies in the SUAP sphere.

The government's stated objective was to modernize a legacy system whereby each Italian council was at liberty to decide and apply the procedures, forms and tariffs it saw fit, forcing business owners in especially complex and/or sensitive sectors to embark on a bureaucratic hike through numerous public offices to comply with a variegated menu of requirements and procedures. This not only added more layers of red tape but it also bumped up costs. Hence, the SUAP was tasked with streamlining the entire business authorization–licensing–permit process through the online coordination of all the public bodies involved (e.g. local healthcare authorities, fire brigade, provincial and regional governments, regional environment authorities) and ensuring the entrepreneurs a single point of contact (SPC) to obtain the necessary authorizations.

The programme's reliance on technology as the transformational tool to shape the SUAP into the desired digital government service centre (Hogrebe, Kruse, and Nüttgens 2008) has led the legislator to constantly tweak and re-costume the programme since its inception, subjecting Italy's One-Stop Business Shop to strong elements of discontinuity. That negative trend was arrested only in 2010 by Law 160, a watershed for the SUAP that leads us to better map its evolution by splitting the descriptive timeline into the two distinct phases of 1998–2009 and 2010–15.

4.1 *SUAP (1998–2009)*

The SUAP programme was seeded on the NPM bedrock of Italy's PA in a climate of continuous structural change, imposing radical changes that would completely change its make-up, in particular:

- Administrative decentralization and devolution of business-related services to the councils, considered the most appropriate institutional level to deal with local development;
- The separation of government from administrative functions, restricting the action of the political bodies to exclusively that of regulating the SUAP's functions and obliging the councils to appoint a new figure of authority to coordinate the relevant public bodies (Head of Coordination);

- The absence of the organizational direction typical of Napoleonic governance that left the councils without a basic SUAP model of operations;
- The use of ICT to achieve efficiency gains (reduction in business authorization processing time), improve efficacy (quality of business–PA relations), and ensure transparent procedures (online access to business owners/representatives to monitor application status).

In a nutshell, the Italian councils, very few of which had the necessary experience or capabilities, had to both define their SUAP structures and manage complex vertical and horizontal specialization and coordination issues.

Specialization – in general terms, the principles of decentralization and devolution call for splitting the various tasks across different administrative levels, that is, the vertical specialization of the SUAP business services. The central government established the general regulatory principles for the overall system; the regional governments had to issue certain sector laws and specific regulations for the functioning of the SUAP; and the councils, considered those more directly involved with the local citizens and businesses, had to organize and manage the SUAP's operations, implementing the directives issued by other government levels. The councils were purposely left free to define the SUAP's configuration but had to appoint a Head of Coordination to ensure the 'under-one-roof' management of all the coordination activities for opening, changing or closing a business.

Horizontal and vertical specialization was central to the local implementation of the SUAP programme. In fact, to more efficiently and efficaciously meet the needs of the business sector, the regulations indicated from the outset that it was necessary to channel the relevant competences (especially the construction and commercial authorizations traditionally handled by separate internal units) into a single specialized municipal organizational unit. However, the legislator left certain competences and discretionality to the specialized public bodies (e.g. local healthcare authorities, fire brigade, provincial and regional governments, regional environment authorities, etc.).

Coordination – is the linchpin of especially the internal and external horizontal aspects of the SUAP, which was given the immediate internal coordination challenge of ensuring the exchange of information between the business services organizational units and the operational coordination of the various competences. Internal coordination was particularly critical when the SUAP was implemented in a unit of the matrix kind, where the staff perceived the arrival of the Head of Coordination as 'interfering' with their autonomy and disrupting the status quo.

External coordination presented similar challenges, seeing that the Italian regulatory and institutional framework gives the jurisdiction of different business services to different public organizations. This fragmented scenario forces the SUAP to coordinate a plethora of public agencies over which it has no authority, making it and the Head of Coordination totally dependent on the good will and cooperation of all the relative governmental agencies to comply with its legal obligations.

Moreover, to implement the SUAP the Italian councils had to manage not only the internal and external coordination of the agents directly concerned with the business services procedures (positive coordination) but also the problems of negative coordination to prevent certain legally imposed restrictions (above all, authorization deadlines) from disrupting other organizational units not directly related to the SUAP.

The heavy demands of intra-organizational and inter-organizational coordination weakened the efforts of the Italian councils to help the SUAP programme achieve its goals and only 5,718 of Italy's 8,101 councils had implemented a One-Stop Business Shop by the end of 2007. This disappointing outcome, coupled with the pressing need to comply with the 'Bolkestein' Directive (2006/123/EC) applicable to all EU member states, forced the Italian legislator's hand again in 2010, resulting in a review of the One-Stop Business Shop's existing regulations and, ultimately, Law 160/2010.

4.2 SUAP (2010–15)

The major changes introduced to the SUAP programme by Law 160/2010 were primarily:

- The *www.impresainungiorno.gov.it* website (European Directive 2006/123/EC) to provide business owners with access to the Italian SUAP network via a single centralized online front office (SPC);
- Exclusively online delivery of business services and compulsory electronic communication with all SUAP-related actors;
- The need to possess basic technological requirements to qualify as full-fledged operators and gain accreditation with the Ministry for Economic Development (Ministero per lo Sviluppo Economico – MISE);
- The special agreement for councils opting to delegate SUAP management to their local chamber of commerce (CC);
- The default transfer of SUAP management to the local CC should the council fail to comply with the MISE accreditation requirements by 1 January 2011.

The new law had a significant impact on the dynamics of specialization and coordination.

Specialization – Law 160/2010 recognized the principle of both vertical and horizontal specialization but still introduced major vertical coordination factors that clashed with the specialization route charted since 1998, in particular: the centralization of the SUAP front office through the *impresainungiorno.gov.it* website; the government's definition of the qualifications for MISE accreditation and the compulsory transfer of the SUAP management to the local CC should it fail to meet those requirements.

Coordination – The stronger measures of Law 160/2010 aimed to hammer home the need to simplify the administrative processes, and several of them were also written into the national simplification agenda (Agenda per la Semplificazione 2015–17 (*www.italiasemplice.gov.it*)) to cover aspects such as standardized forms and the government-issued SUAP guidelines and standard operating procedures.

However, the inability of the different PA departments to work in organizational synergy was the biggest complaint recorded by the latest available data produced by a 2013 survey to measure the level of satisfaction with PA business services of the Italian small, medium and micro enterprises (SMME) (PromoPa 2013), which shows that neither Law 160/2010 nor the Agenda per la Semplificazione had done much to fix the matter of internal and external horizontal coordination. The failure of the first-generation of legal owners (the councils and their aggregations) to get the one-stop business shops up and running thus led the government to add yet another institutional actor to the SUAP cast, the CC, thereby absolving those councils who chose to transfer the SUAP management to these public bodies from the costly and complex redesign of their organizational geometry. Further, assigning the job of coordination to a reputable external player with recognized technological capabilities meant leapfrogging (or at least considerably lowering) the barriers to managing the internal relations of the council organization, effectively depriving the SUAP's Head of Coordination of managerial responsibilities. The management of external coordination followed a similar path given that, even though this task was not considered part of the formal relations subordinate to the hierarchy or other authority, the CC's *de facto* influence over the relevant institutions far outweighs that of a single council (especially the smaller) or council aggregations.

Hence, Law 160/2010 rebooted the under-subscribed SUAP system, raising the number of councils with a fully MISE-accredited SUAP from 4,999 in July 2011 to 7,649 in June 2013, 2,951 of which (mainly those of the smallest councils) CC managed (MISE 2013). Nevertheless, even though the One-Stop Business Shop is currently the most important fully online service delivered by Italy's local government (OECD 2012), the SUAP programme has yet to prove its effective capacity to generate the desired benefits.

In fact, despite the lawmaker's efforts to launch the SUAP 18 years ago and the continuous stream of legislation through 2010, not only are the policy objectives still out of reach, Italy has descended even further in the international competitiveness rankings (WEF 2014), which indicate no sign of improvement in the ease of doing business or those areas related to the activities of Local Government (EDB 2014), an almost imperceptible narrowing of the efficiency gap in the PA services (including those of the online SUAP) as perceived by the Italian SMME, and that the overweight bureaucratic and administrative system is a major risk factor that continues to threaten SMME survival (PromoPa 2013).

Hence, with the expected benefits still nowhere in sight, we can only conclude that the SUAP programme alone was not up to the job, which raises the hardly irrelevant questions of the *why* of these inadequate outcomes and how to get to the root of the problem. Two factors clear the technological side of any and all culpability for the lack of success: (i) most Italian councils, regardless of the type of organizational solution adopted, now have a MISE-accredited SUAP, which means they satisfy the technological requirements of Law 160/2010; and (ii) all the currently operating One-Stop Business Shops communicate electronically with both the businesses and the relevant public bodies, hence, we must look elsewhere for the causes.

Figure 1, below, frames the key policy measures of the SUAP programme's 1998–2015 timeline, the criticalities that emerged in phase one and the responses given in phase two.

5. Discussion

An exhaustive investigation into all the potentially relevant factors that sent the SUAP down such a long and winding road is beyond the remit of this paper, this section therefore scrutinizes exclusively the contextual conditions that most affected the dynamics of specialization and coordination, using the categories of political factors, historical and institutional legacy and external pressures identified by Bezes and colleagues (2013).

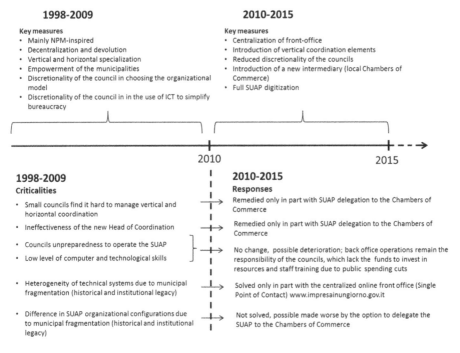

Figure 1. SUAP timeline (1998–2015).

The paper has illustrated how the unpreparedness of the Italian councils to manage the complex problems of intra-organizational and inter-organizational coordination between actors and processes was a strategic flaw that significantly eroded the expected benefits. Despite legal capacity as *process owner*, the SUAP's Head of Coordination never gained a foothold. In fact, each council would have had to re-engineer their internal organizational structure to strengthen the new role's influence, which, in turn, would ruffle feathers in the political domain and would not win support from the higher circles of government. Clearly, any attempt to transform the municipal machinery, coupled with the intrinsic weakness of the central and local government public bodies brought about by the collapse of Italy's political system, the fuse of which was lit in the early 1990s, has been severely hindered by fact that the functions of direction have been separated from those of administration (the reform legacy of the 1990s NPM doctrine).

Moreover, the global crisis and strong external pressures to cut public spending have depleted the economic resources needed to fund the much-needed strengthening of the councils' internal coordination managerial roles, while making ICT investments and new staff hires the first victims of austerity has prevented especially the smallest Italian councils from onboarding a new generation of public managers and from issuing internal managerial training and upskilling courses to promote the organic growth of the relevant capabilities.

The Italian PA's institutional and historical legacy of fragmentation stops the smaller councils from investing in managerial skills and further magnifies the negative impact of these contingent factors. Law 447/1998 initially addressed this problem by giving the councils the option to manage the SUAP in associated form, which led many regional governments to grant funding to the small municipalities to drive them off the original NPM path by incentivizing joined-up government (Conteh 2013). Interestingly, the Italian PA's firmly embedded legalistic culture has not stopped it from resisting the government's attempt to defragment by reform; in fact, the number of councils continues to hover at and around 8,000, 75 per cent of which have fewer than 5,000 residents, while 2,000 have less than 1,000, earning these tiny communities the sobriquet 'dust councils.'

Faced with the contextual constraints that only a profound upheaval of the entire Italian local government system could neutralize, Law 160/2010 introduced an alternative, outsourcing-based process management model that allowed the councils to delegate SUAP management to the local CC, sweeping away the obstacles that had defeated the new Head of Coordination. Nevertheless, the data reported in the previous section show that the CC-outsourcing route taken by a large number of Italian councils (2,951 at June 2013) does not seem to have helped the SUAP programme to hit target.

Delegating the SUAP to the CCs was dictated by several interrelated environmental factors: (i) the ongoing pressures exerted by the national business and industry associations and by the supranationals to accelerate the simplification process and to reduce the administrative burdens on enterprises and citizens; (ii) the business sector's growing dissatisfaction with the local councils (according to the PromoPa (2013) poll, the degree of satisfaction on a scale of 1–10 fell from 4.9 in 2006 to 4.3 in 2010); (iii) the constant struggle of the Italian councils to implement a fully operational One-Stop Business Shop (according to the government's *impresainungiorno.gov.it* website, a good 3,095 councils lacked the SUAP-MISE requisites at July 2010) and (iv) the political marketing goals set by the Berlusconi government to improve Italy's ranking in the international indices.

Such a complex narrative spotlighted the CC as the ideal candidates to manage the SUAP and to intermediate between the local councils and the business sector, not least because, public status notwithstanding, they are not seen in the same institutional bad light as their PA counterparts. Rather, the business sector perceives the CC as being free of the adversarial and overly bureaucratic demands of local government.

While the councils were offered alternatives (direct in-house implementation of the One-Stop Business Shop; associated management; delegation to the local CC) that may initially appear to have facilitated their work to the benefit of the entire system, this mixed bag of options and solutions merely veiled it in yet another layer of complexity (and potential weaknesses). Indeed, numerous councils took the easier path of placing the SUAP in the hands of the CC rather than face the inherent complexity of operating an associated form, thus undoing the inter-municipal cooperation incentivized by the special programmes of earlier years.

The paradox of Law 160/2010 was that it gave new life to the SUAP programme but reversed the direction of the 1998–2009 joined-up government policies, especially at the local level, which, among other things, were meant to deflect the SUAP programme from its original NPM launch pad. Hence, the 2010 legislative SUAP review, like many of the earlier legislative tweaks, suggests a reaction to external pressures more than the desire to undertake comprehensive and coherent reform.

The insights gleaned from the analysis conducted in Section 4 coupled with the above considerations enable us to formulate overall responses to the study's research questions:

Q1. What contextual forces drive and/or constrain administrative reforms?

The SUAP analysis confirms that the three categories of interlinked factors of environmental pressure, historical-institutional context and polity features framed by Christensen and Lægreid (2013) are essential to describe and explain the outcomes of nationwide administrative reforms, and that these multiple and intersecting factors are not a passive backdrop but actively work to delineate the implementers' scope of action.

The SUAP trajectory evidences how Italy's reform processes are typically over-layered and often subject to contradictory inputs that incorporate by 'accumulation' heterogeneous administrative principles, perspectives and practices (Christensen and Lægreid 2011). The administrative tradition's legalistic, top-down treatment of the SUAP programme's coordination and specialization issues has indubitably influenced this state of affairs by completely ignoring their primarily organizational and context-dependent nature. That a cross-cutting nationwide programme has failed to deliver the required support and direction to ensure coordination only corroborates the thorny point made by Sarapuu and colleagues (2014, 266) that coordination arrangements are not always logical, and 'are often biased towards certain values, interests and norms.'

Q2. What role does ICT play in the course and outcomes of reform efforts?

Even though, from the outset, the SUAP programme's standardization approach gave ICT the triple role of communication, coordination and integration at both the intra-organizational (in the operational units of the same local council) and the inter-organizational level (among various PAs within and across different responsibilities), the analysis absolves ICT of the blame for its mixed outcomes, placing more importance on the still unresolved organizational issues and less on the technical compatibility glitches usually made the scapegoats of the unsuccessful implementation of large public-sector IS projects (e.g. Margetts and Willcocks 1993; Taylor and Lips 2008).

Moreover, temporal advances in ICT (mainly web-based technologies) have greatly facilitated the deployment of platforms capable of solving the *technical* compatibility issues, with ongoing innovation producing increasingly performative and cost-effective ICT tools that support various one-stop provision formats. Nevertheless, the study shows that the availability of commodity-like IT assets alone was not enough to enable the administrative machinery's expected leap in quality. In particular, oblivious to the need to integrate and harmonize IT assets and organization routines, the councils continued to experience the age-old problems of *functional* compatibility (between the technical and the normative components) and *institutional* compatibility (between the multiple organizational and institutional bodies involved in the administrative processes) (Lanzara 2009). This is what has either stopped the SUAP from realizing its full potential or limited it solely to front-office operations.

6. Implications and conclusions

This paper combines the configurational approach and the 'common grammar' of Bezes et al. (2013) to describe the trajectory of Italy's One-Stop Business Shop (SUAP). Retracing the many stops and starts of the ICT-enabled administrative reform highlights not only the context-specific nature of public-sector transformation but also that success or failure is determined by multiple hard-to-govern factors. The study uses the critical lens of the configurational approach to more effectively capture, frame and assess the evidence as parts of the bigger picture, enabling us to connect the events and outcomes to the key factors of success typically cited in the e-government literature (Gil-Garcia and Pardo, 2005) and empirically ground this stream of research.

The analytical pay offs of a context-aware lens that integrates the country-specific factors and the organizational dynamics for both the theory and the practice of digital government are essential insights that: (i) make sense of the non-reducible complexity of public-sector transformations; (ii) correlate the implementation outcomes to a relatively small number of mixed contextual variables and (iii) cast light on the crucial role of the coordination and integration arrangements, identifying the macro- and micro-organizational implications. This is the understanding needed to inform future models and theories of change.

The configurational approach exemplified here has three practical benefits:

(i) Provides the public decision makers with a sturdier conceptual toolkit to calibrate the 'classical trade-off' between coordination across organizational boundaries and specialization (Askim et al. 2011, 1451) by demonstrating the substantial effort demanded of the implementers to design the coordination and integration arrangements. In particular, the SUAP case shows how the Napoleonic type of decentralized political-administrative environments strews the reform path with rocks and boulders;

(ii) Frames ICT as a resource that must be activated *prior* to the implementation effort and *only* afterwards transformed into capabilities by way of a contextual, path-dependent approach to adapt and integrate them with the extant routines and assets and

(iii) Suggests that to achieve the successful coordination of new programmes, the decision makers of the implementer organizations need extra resources in both the set-up phase and to keep the new routines up and running. A contextual approach is a vital piece of the reform puzzle without which neither the central nor the local decision makers can create the conditions for a successful government programme both *within* and *beyond* the public sector, for example, through the design of appropriate laws, regulations and evaluation procedures.

Our final argument is that this exploratory reconstruction of the SUAP reform path confirms the findings of previous studies that conclude that ignoring the historical institutional context tends 'to produce new reforms rather than increased performance' (Christensen and Lægreid 2013, 150). Unexpectedly, the analysis also clears ICT of all blame for the SUAP programme's mixed outcomes. Even though a configurational lens requires no causal explanation or general model to strengthen our understanding of the reform trajectories, the authors acknowledge that the example of this approach applied to the SUAP programme contains 'quite a lot of thin ice,' to use the words of Pollitt and Bouckaert (2011, 207). The most obvious limitation is that the adoption of an interpretative stance rules out a response to the 'why' question, which requires multiple and in-depth case studies to develop future conceptual efforts that analyse and operationalize the sum of the parts of the three categories identified by Bezes and colleagues.

Disclosure statement

No potential conflict of interest was reported by the authors.

ORCID

Walter Castelnovo ⓘ http://orcid.org/0000-0002-5741-5106

References

Askim, J., A. L. Fimreite, A. Moseley, and L. H. Pedersen. 2011. "One-Stop Shops for Social Welfare: The Adaptation of an Organizational Form in Three Countries." *Public Administration* 89 (4): 1451–1468. doi:10.1111/padm.2011.89.issue-4.

Bannister, F. 2005. "E-Government and Administrative Power: The One-Stop-Shop Meets the Turf War." *Electronic Government: An International Journal* 2 (2): 160–176. doi:10.1504/EG.2005.007092.

Bannister, F., and R. Connolly. 2011. "Trust and Transformational Government: A Proposed Framework for Research." *Government Information Quarterly* 28 (2): 137–147. doi:10.1016/j.giq.2010.06.010.

Baptista, M. 2005. "E-Government and State Reform: Policy Dilemmas for Europe." *Electronic Journal of E-Government* 3 (4): 167–174.

Barbosa, A. F., M. Pozzebon, and E. H. Diniz. 2013. "Rethinking E-Government Performance Assessment from a Citizen Perspective." *Public Administration* 91 (3): 744–762.

Bellamy, C., and J. Taylor. 1998. *Governing in the Information Age*. Buckingham: Open University Press.

Bezes, P., A. L. Fimreite, P. Le Lidec, and P. Lægreid. 2013. "Understanding Organizational Reforms in the Modern State: Specialization and Integration in Norway and France." *Governance* 26 (1): 147–175. doi:10.1111/j.1468-0491.2012.01608.x.

Christensen, T., and P. Lægreid. 2007. "The Whole-Of-Government Approach to Public Sector Reform." *Public Administration Review* 67 (6): 1059–1066. doi:10.1111/puar.2007.67.issue-6.

Christensen, T., and P. Lægreid. 2011. "Complexity and Hybrid Public Administration - Theoretical and Empirical Challenges." *Public Organization Review* 11 (4): 407–423. doi:10.1007/s11115-010-0141-4.

Christensen, T., and P. Lægreid. 2013. "Context and Administrative Reforms: A Transformative Approach." In *Context in Public Policy and Management*, edited by C. Pollitt, 131–156. Cheltenham: Edward Elgar.

Christensen, T., P. Lægreid, P. G. Roness, and K. A. Rovik. 2007. *Organization Theory and the Public Sector*. Abingdon: Routledge.

Conteh, C. 2013. "Strategic Inter-Organizational Cooperation in Complex Environments." *Public Management Review* 15 (4): 501–521. doi:10.1080/14719037.2012.674424.

Coursey, D., and D. F. Norris. 2008. "Models of E-Government: Are They Correct? an Empirical Assessment." *Public Administration Review* 68 (3): 523–536. doi:10.1111/j.1540-6210.2008.00888.x.

Dunleavy, P., H. Margetts, S. Bastow, and J. Tinkler. 2006. "New Public Management Is Dead. Long Live Digital-Era Governance." *Journal of Public Administration Research and Theory* 16 (3): 467–494. doi:10.1093/jopart/mui057.

EDB. 2014. *Doing Business 2015 - Going Beyond Efficiency*. Washington: The World Bank.

Fiss, P. C. 2007. "A Set Theoretic Approach to Organizational Configurations." *Academy of Management Review* 32 (4): 1180–1198. doi:10.5465/AMR.2007.26586092.

Foley, P., and X. Alfonso. 2009. "Egovernment and the Transformation Agenda." *Public Administration* 87 (2): 371–396. doi:10.1111/padm.2009.87.issue-2.

Fountain, J. E. 2002. *Information, Institutions and Governance*. Cambridge: J.F. Kennedy School of Government, Harvard University.

Gil-Garcia, J. R., and T. A. Pardo. 2005. "E-Government Success Factors: Mapping Practical Tools to Theoretical Foundations." *Government Information Quarterly* 22 (2): 187–216. doi:10.1016/j.giq.2005.02.001.

Gil-Garcia, J. R., L. F. Vivanco, and L. F. Luna-Reyes. 2014. "Revisiting the Problem of Technological and Social Determinism: Reflections for Digital Government Scholars." In *Electronic Government and Electronic Participation*, edited by Janssen, et al., 254–263. Amsterdam: IOS Press.

Glassey, O. 2004. "Developing a One-Stop Government Data Model." *Government Information Quarterly* 21 (2): 156–169. doi:10.1016/j.giq.2003.12.012.

Goldkuhl, G. 2016. "E-Government Design Research: Towards the Policy-Ingrained IT Artifact." *Government Information Quarterly* 33 (3): 444–452. doi: 10.1016/j.giq.2016.05.006.

Gouscos, D., M. Kalikakis, M. Legal, and S. Papadopoulou. 2007. "A General Model of Performance and Quality for One-Stop E-Government Service Offerings." *Government Information Quarterly* 24 (4): 860–885. doi:10.1016/j.giq.2006.07.016.

Hogrebe, F., W. Kruse, and M. Nüttgens (2008). One-Stop Egovernment for Small and Medium-Sized Enterprises (SME): A Strategic Approach and Case Study to Implement the EU Services Directive. Bled 2008 Conference. Bled, Slovenia.

Howard, C. 2014. "Rethinking Post-NPM Governance: The Bureaucratic Struggle to Implement One-Stop-Shopping for Government Services in Alberta." *Public Organization Review* 15 (2): 1–18.

Kraemer, K., and J. L. King. 2008. "Information Technology and Administrative Reform: Will E-Government Be Different?" In *E-Government Research. Policy and Mangement*, edited by D. Norris, 1–20. Hershey, PA: IGI Global.

Lanzara, G. F. 2009. "Building Digital Institutions: ICT and the Rise of Assemblages in Government." In *ICT and Innovation in the Public Sector*, edited by F. Contini and G. F. Lanzara, 9–48. London: Palgrave Macmillan.

Lips, M. B., and T. Schuppan. 2009. "Editorial - Transforming E-Government Knowledge through Public Management Research." *Public Management Review* 11 (6): 739–749. doi:10.1080/14719030903318921.

Margetts, H., and L. Willcocks. 1993. "Information Technology in Public Services: Disaster Faster?" *Public Money & Management* 13 (2): 49–56. doi:10.1080/09540969309387763.

Meyer, A. D., A. S. Tsui, and C. R. Hinings. 1993. "Configurational Approaches to Organizational Analysis." *Academy of Management Journal* 36: 1175–1195. doi:10.2307/256809.

Michalopoulos, N. 2003. "Administrative Reform in Europe: The Dialectical Coexistence between Convergence and Diversity". UNTC Occasional Papers Series, No 3/2003. Thessaloniki: United Nations Thessaloniki Centre for Public Service Professionalism.

MISE. 2013. *Sportello Unico Attività Produttive - Iniziative Di Monitoraggio Dell'attuazione Della Riforma*. Roma: Ministero dello Sviluppo Economico.

Norris, D. F., and C. G. Reddick. 2013. "Local E-Government in the United States: Transformation or Incremental Change?" *Public Administration Review* 73 (1): 165–175. doi:10.1111/puar.2013.73.issue-1.

OECD. 1995. *Governance in Transition: Public Management Reforms in OECD Countries*. Paris: OECD.

OECD. 2012. *Italy: Reviving Growth and Productivity*. Paris: OECD.

Ostling, A. 2010. "ICT in Politics: From Peaks of Inflated Expectations to Voids of Disillusionment." *European Journal of Epractice* 9: 1–8.

Peters, B. G. 2008. "The Napoleonic Tradition." *International Journal of Public Sector Management* 21 (2): 118–132. doi:10.1108/09513550810855627.

Pina E Cunha, M., and H. Tsoukas. 2015. "Reforming the State: Understanding the Vicious Circles of Reform." *European Management Journal* 33 (4): 225–229. doi:10.1016/j.emj.2015.05.001.

Pollitt, C. 2012. *New Perspectives on Public Services. Place and Technology*. Oxford: Oxford University Press.

Pollitt, C., ed., 2013. *Context in Public Policy and Management*. Cheltenham: Edward Elgar Publishing.

Pollitt, C., and G. Bouckaert (2011). *Public Management Reform. A Comparative Analysis: New Public Management, Governance, and the Neo-Weberian State*. 3rd ed. Oxford: Oxford University Press.

PromoPa. 2013. *Imprese E Burocrazia - Come Le Piccole E Micro Imprese Giudicano La Pubblica Amministrazione*. Milano: Franco Angeli.

Rose, W. R., and G. G. Grant. 2010. "Critical Issues Pertaining to the Planning and Implementation of E-Government Initiatives." *Government Information Quarterly* 27 (1): 26–33. doi:10.1016/j.giq.2009.06.002.

Sarapuu, K., P. Lægreid, T. Randma-Liiv, and L. H. Rykkja. 2014. "Lessons Learned and Policy Implications." In *Organizing for Coordination in the Public Sector*, edited by P. Lægreid, K. Sarapuu, L. H. Rykkja, and T. Randma-Liiv, 263–277. Basingstoke: Palgrave Macmillan.

Taylor, J. A., and A. M. B. Lips. 2008. "The Citizen in the Information Polity: Exposing the Limits of the E-Government Paradigm." *Information Polity* 13 (3/4): 139–152.

Verdegem, P., and L. Hauttekeete. 2008. "The User at the Centre of the Development of One-Stop Government." *International Journal of Electronic Governance* 1 (3): 258–274. doi:10.1504/IJEG.2008.020449.

WEF. 2014. *The Global Competitiveness Report 2014–2015*. Geneva: World Economic Forum.

Wimmer, M. 2002. "A European Perspective Towards Online One-Stop Government, the Egov Project." *Electronic Commerce Research and Applications* 1: 92–103. doi:10.1016/S1567-4223(02)00008-X.

Yin, R. K. 2003. *Case Study Research: Design and Methods*. 3rd ed. Thousand Oaks: Sage.

Open innovation in the public sector: drivers and barriers for the adoption of Challenge.gov

Ines Mergel ⓘD

ABSTRACT
Online Open Innovation (OI) platforms like Challenge.gov are used to post public sector problem statements, collect and evaluate ideas submitted by citizens with the goal to increase government innovation. Using quantitative data extracted from contests posted to Challenge.gov and qualitative interviews with thirty-six public managers in fourteen federal departments contribute to the discovery and analysis of intra-, inter, and extra-organizational factors that drive or hinder the implementation of OI in the public sector. The analysis shows that system-inherent barriers hinder public sector organizations to adopt this procedural and technological innovation. However, when the mandate of the innovation policy aligns with the mission of the organization, it opens opportunities for change in innovation acquisition and standard operating procedures.

Introduction

Open innovation (OI) is the process of crowdsourcing solutions to organizational problems to ensure organizational survival or renewal (Chesbrough 2003). Online platforms are used to announce product design contests, such as Lego's design of new sceneries, or Netflix's search for a new algorithm to suggest movies to its users. The knowledge of traditional innovators like R&D departments in private sector organizations is supplemented by including external amateurs who are not part of the organization into the product design process using monetary incentives to encourage participation (Chesbrough and Crowther 2006).

Similarly, public sector organizations are using OI approaches to access knowledge from citizens. For that purpose and as part of the Digital Government Strategy, the US federal government established a new policy instrument to access knowledge of external problem solvers, such as citizen scientists or citizen hackers (The White House 2009). The policy and follow-up executive mandates (The White House 2010) support the America Competes Act (2007) designed to increase economic development and the effectiveness and efficiency of public service delivery. US federal government agencies are using a shared online platform called Challenge.gov to post their problem statements and collect ideas from citizens.

However, OI approaches are challenging for public sector organizations: the traditional innovation acquisition process is highly regulated and follows strict rules and regulations, while OI processes are by design open and have few rules. Arundel et al. provide a three-prong model: bottom-up, policy-dependent, or knowledge-scanning innovation methods of public sector agencies in their analysis of over 3,000 European government agencies (2015). Government organizations are either working with a group of pre-approved vendors and contractors who are responding to requests for proposals, which are then internally vetted before a solution proposed by a vendor is implemented. Or, innovations are driven by policy mandates as a source of innovation in the public sector. The Affordable Care Act in the United States for example led to the creation of a new online marketplace, HealthCare.gov, a technological as well as procedural innovation that was not available in government before. Selected government agencies, such as the Defense Advanced Research Projects Agency (DARPA), are designed to create research collaborations with outsiders, including University partners to increase their access to innovations (Colatat 2015). These forms of internal innovation creation following the standards of the bureaucratic governance process is called 'closed innovation' (Felina and Zenger 2014). Stepping outside of the formalized innovation acquisition process with contractual relationships and opening up the innovation process to amateur problem solver is therefore a challenge for public sector organizations.

This article builds upon the existing OI literature in the private sector by adding a new empirical context to enhance our understanding of barriers to innovative e-governance practices. E-governance in this case is analysed to understand a technological innovation – the Challenge.gov platform – and a managerial innovation – a change from traditional contract- and grant-based innovation acquisition to crowdsourcing of innovative problem solutions. The longitudinal study spans the time from 2010 to 2014 to understand how public managers perceive factors that hinder or support the implementation process. The result is a multilevel analytical framework of barriers that work against and drivers that foster the implementation of a technological and managerial innovation.

The key contributions of this article are to add a new empirical case that has not been developed in the literature: OI in the context of government; and a multidimensional analytical approach that not only takes in-house barriers of e-government in a single organization into account, but also reviews drivers and barriers at the intra-, inter-, and extra-organizational levels of analysis focusing on all federal agencies engaged in OI practices.

The current OI literature focusses almost exclusively on private sector organizations. However, as Meijer (2015) states, the literature on public innovation and e-governance needs to go hand-in-hand. Both bodies of literature aim to understand how government organizations can respond to societal challenges, changing demands by citizens, and the need to provide services in a more efficient and effective manner.

The research questions include: What are the empirical factors that hinder the implementation of OI practices in public sector organizations? And, What are the empirical factors that drive the implementation of OI practices in public sector organizations? To answer these questions, the article first provides a review of the current state of the OI literature and then applies the OI concept to the public sector context. The research design outlines the data collection and analysis steps combining data from the online platform Challenge.gov and interviews with public managers.

The findings are organized along three levels of analysis and provide insights into intra-, inter-, and extra-organizational factors for OI.

Literature review: OI in the public sector

OI is an umbrella term that describes processes, outcomes, and business models of a new form of innovation creation. OI approaches appeared first in the private sector allowing organizations to explore new clientele, market segments, or the invention of new products and designs. Current OI studies focus predominantly on research and development-intensive industry organizations (Murray et al. 2012; Villarroel 2013). Practices and research have only minimally been expanded to the public sector.

The OI process

Chesbrough defined the OI process as a new form of purposive inflows and outflows of knowledge to accelerate internal innovation and expand the markets for the external use of innovation (2003). OI approaches are using crowdsourcing and peer production processes to invite the public to co-create solutions for organizational problems (Benkler 2006). Using Howe's 'wisdom of the crowds' notion to add citizen's knowledge in incremental pieces to the overall solution, crowdsourcing processes need to be supported by an online platform to advertise and collect solutions from a geographically distributed crowd (Howe 2006; Surowiecki 2004). Some contest processes expand the innovation collection phase and include crowd judging or crowd improvement of the selected solutions (Mergel 2015).

Factors influencing the adoption of OI processes

Factors influencing the adoption of OI processes in the private sector include the role of individuals and teams in designing and managing contests (Du, Leten, and Vanhaverbeke 2014; Ettlie and Elsenbach 2007). While in the private sector, employees sometimes aim to protect their current inventions, public sector employees are not hired to constantly search for new markets, ideas for new products, or even to actively seek out return customers to ensure the survival of the organization.

The openness versus closeness characteristics of the search process oftentimes influences the outcomes or the extent of OI adoption. Salge et al. found that too little and too much openness in the search process is related curvilinear to the outcomes of OI processes and the definition of the goal of the contest is oftentimes problematic for organizations (2013). If problem solvers do not feel that they can contribute a meaningful solution, or the solution is too simple to attract the right problem solvers, the contest might not lead to the expected outcomes (Jeppesen and Lakhani 2010; Lakhani and Jeppesen 2007; Dahlandera and Piezunkab 2014). In public sector organizations, this might not even be a problem of designing a sophisticated and appropriate search process, instead regulatory government organizations in the United States are prohibited by law to actively seek citizen input and are limited to certain types of regulated interactions. This can in turn reduce the adoption and implementation of OI processes in some government agencies.

At the organizational or system level, existing research has focussed on the general cultural climate that supports innovation acquisition. Opening the organizational boundaries and subsequently agreeing to support the initial costs to design and (re) organize the organizational procedures to allow an OI approach requires a paradigm shift of top management as well as organizational units involved in the implementation process (Murray et al. 2012). In the public sector, changes in standard operating procedures need to be vetted, tested, and approved by top management and flexibility in adjusting organizational rules rarely exists (DeHart-Davis, Chen, and Little 2013).

Similarly, the existing OI literature looks at these issues from an inter-organizational perspective in which OI occurs, such as policy development and the need for implementation of new governance approaches to OI – deciding whether the system as a whole allows an open or closed innovation approach (Felina and Zenger 2014). These decisions are rarely made bottom-up in the public sector. Instead all processes and interfaces with the public or other organizations are designed to ensure accountability. In government, public managers perceive the existing red tape – a set of rules and regulations governing an organization's behaviour – as hindrances for the adoption of innovations (Rainey, Pandey, and Bozeman 1995). However, acquisition procedure following a request for proposals process and formal contracts with contractors and vendors lead to a maximum of accountability and reduce risk for contract managers.

Extra-organizational factors focus on the role of stakeholders located outside the organization and include the role of users and consumers of OI processes, the changing needs of society, and recent technological developments. For example, are there external problem solvers that are willing to participate in the process or is there an existing OI network and community that might be interested in taking on problem solving for the organization (West and Lakhani 2008; Piezunka and Dahlander 2015). Ropera et al. have shown that opening the organization for knowledge in-flows can in turn have positive externalities and influence a positive climate and image of the organization (2013). As a result, openness incentivizes problem solvers to provide their knowledge and help create a solution (Fu 2012). However, the relationship between the solution seeker and solvers can result in an unbalanced power relationship with different incentives for each participating party (Gambardella and Panico 2014).

Other extra-organizational factors – outside the direct influence sphere of the focal organization – include larger societal factors, such as the trend of using crowdsourcing and crowdfunding approaches as an acceptable interaction mechanism between organizations and stakeholders (Howe 2006; Shirky 2008). This aspect is closely coupled with the development of public participation platforms and increases the general digital literacy that allows stakeholders to participate in the process. In addition, societal aspects can also be considered as new forms of industry or contractor relationships.

Previous research on OI in the public sector found several important benefits for public sector organizations. Mergel and Desouza found that OI approaches are used to increase awareness of changes in policy or aim to recruit eligible parties to gain their attention to programmes (2013). The main goal is to reach otherwise disconnected parts of the population who are never in contact with government but might have valuable insights on how public service delivery should be designed to reach them.

Contests submitted by public managers on Challenge.gov mostly focus on awareness raising for societal problems and the availability of public services and programmes, public service improvement to create citizen satisfaction, in form of speed or reliability of public services, as well as knowledge-seeking initiatives or the call for technical solutions (Mergel et al. 2014). Rarely do OI processes lead to radical or disruptive innovations in the public sector. The most innovative outcomes are realized in science and technology-oriented agencies, including NASA which ran a contest to capture meteors or change their trajectory to avoid collision with earth (NASA n.d.).

Other related engagement concepts in the public sector focus on co-production of public services (Joshi and Moore 2004), co-development of public policy in form of e-rulemaking processes (Coglianese 2004), or collaborations with the public in budgeting processes (de Sousa Santos 1998). These procedures invite citizens to create a public good and with their early participation in governance processes increase trust, accountability, and ultimately higher degrees of buy-in for the final budget, policy, or service. However, OI processes by design go beyond localized communities who are directly affected by a policy, instead the recruitment of problem solvers is designed to access knowledge from mostly nonprofessional problem solvers who are usually not part of the participation processes. In addition, OI projects incentivize participation with monetary prizes that can be of smaller denomination but oftentimes reflect the value an organization would pay for a contractor or vendor to provide the solution through a contract or grant.

As Lee et al. state, national-level policies for the implementation of OI approaches have just recently been designed in the public sector and government organizations are in the very early stages of the implementation process (2012). In an environment without prior experience of opening up the formal innovation creation process, with multidimensional innovative practices that include technological innovations, process innovations, and outcome innovations, it is therefore important to understand how government organizations perceive the challenges of a new governance instrument.

Equally important for the development of a theory of OI is an understanding of the factors that foster the implementation. The research framework presented in this article explores these factors at three different levels of analysis: (a) extra-organizational and societal factors; (b) inter-organizational or system-wide factors that influence government organizations as a whole and in their interactions with each other; and (c) intra-organizational factors that are individual to each agency, its specific political context, mission, and organizational culture.

Research design: data collection and analysis

The sample for studying OI in the public sector includes all US federal government agencies using the crowdsourcing platform Challenge.gov from 2010 to 2014, the first 5 years of its existence. Agencies in this sample are comparable because they all received the same Presidential mandate, operate in comparable political environments, and simultaneously have to find ways to implement the mandate. This full-census approach not only allows the inclusion of the whole population of adopters but also focusses the data analysis efforts on similar cases that are facing the same technological, cultural, and organizational circumstances when they are adopting and implementing a new policy. The range of participating agencies is wide enough to understand systematic differences between agencies with a variety of missions and diverse sets of stakeholders. The sample might have limitations, because it does not include non-adopters.

The data collection was designed in two phases: in the first phase, contests posted by federal agencies and departments during the first 5 years of existence of Challenge.gov were extracted from the platform. A research team reviewed problem statements, target problem solvers, monetary and non-monetary incentives, duration of the contests, possible indications of different contest phases, and expected outcomes. In iterative discussions with two research assistants, each contest was analysed, compared, and categorized according to the researchers' judgments. Challenges were coded based on similarities of problem statements and categorized into awareness, service, knowledge, and technical solutions. The contests were sorted by agency and year posted. The result of this exploration is that a total of thirty-six agencies used Challenge.gov to post their public management problems representing fourteen of the fifteen departments of the US federal government. The site itself allowed for limited data collection that represented the data points listed above and did not reveal any information about internal decision-making or strategic thinking behind the use of the site.

To compensate for the limited availability of public data, in a second data collection phase, the agencies that posted contests on Challenge.gov were invited to participate in a qualitative interview study to elicit the perceptions of public managers in charge of designing and managing prizes and contests for their agencies. Thirty-six public managers participated in semi-structured interviews that lasted between 60 and 90 min.

The interview outline was informed by the analysis of the contests and the existing literature on OI. The questions focus on organizational factors influencing the decision to follow the Presidential mandate, the internal strategic and managerial decision-making processes that preceded posting of challenges online, marketing strategies to reach the desired audience of problem solvers, intended and actual outcomes, implementation of the contest outcomes, as well as lessons drawn from the process. Each interview was recorded with the permission of the subjects, transcribed verbatim, and hand-coded line-by-line.

The narrative analysis was designed to develop a case-oriented understanding of the phenomenon itself, but from the viewpoint of public managers who are participants in the social phenomenon. This type of interpretative approach helps to gain a deeper understanding of intra-organizational decision-making processes, strategic conversations behind closed doors, managerial implementation problems, and trial and errors that occur. These data are not publicly observable through an online ethnographic approach and cannot be experimentally examined or measured using quantitative metrics, such as intensity, amount, or frequency measures (Denzin and Lincoln 2011). The goal is not to derive causal relationships; instead the narrative analysis of the interviews with programme managers helps to identify common themes among the agencies included in the study (Miles, Huberman, and Saldana 2014).

Findings

The findings of how the US federal government agencies adopted the use of Challenge. gov to post OI contests can be divided into two main factors: (a) drivers for the adoption of OI approaches; and (b) barriers for the adoption of OI approaches. Each set of factors is divided into intra-, inter-, and extra-organizational factors.

Finding 1: drivers for OI

Except for NASA and DOD's DARPA, none of the agencies posting challenges to Challenge.gov expressed an initial internal need to solve certain types of problems. As a matter of fact, all agencies said that they have in-house experts and in cases they cannot find a solution, they hire contractors. Needs were created through OSTP staff who went through the secretaries of departments or administrators of agencies to convince top leadership to test the new policy instrument. The national priorities of the White House's Open Government initiative have driven initial tests, such as mobile application challenges to encourage the use of datasets posted to Data.gov:

> We worked with the Executive Office of the President, which got us involved in the challenges, and then Safety.data.gov. We are trying to build those bridges within our organization and outside of our organization, to ideally help the field. It came about in a very straightforward manner. We are meeting regularly with the CTO's office of the President. The then Technology Officer, Anish Chopra, told us that he wanted us to do a challenge and he wanted it out in two weeks.

Findings show that the main driver for the adoption of OI approaches is top-down mandates, which then lead to early experimentations with contests and prizes. Rarely do agencies go beyond the formal mandate to adopt OI, except for science and technology agencies like NASA, which had gained experiences inviting professional coders to solve technology problems using the OI platform TopCoder. All other agencies jumped on the bandwagon as a result of several follow-up executive orders and memos, such as the Innovator's Toolkit (The White House 2010). However, before any of them was able to post and promote their contests on Challenge.gov, they had to overcome institutional, legal, managerial, and cultural barriers. This process can take up to 2 years, before an agency is finally able to post an OI contest.

Intra-organizational factors

The intra-organizational drivers emerge at two different stages of the process: (1) before the policy was officially published, and (2) after the policy instrument was available to agencies. Pre-implementation, few agencies used OI approaches proactively to initiate external searches for problem solvers outside the traditional grants and contracts instruments. Only one agency was already interested in exploring opportunities to invite problem solvers into the organization:

> We wanted to use innovations, or use the tools and resources available to us to do things that are innovative to solve some of the [problems], meet some of our strategic goals, that we may not be able to get at conveniently or expeditiously through more traditional mechanisms.

As a matter of fact, most government employees experienced the need to access external knowledge free from the constraining context of the existing rules and regulations.

Top-down management decision

In most of the agencies, the pressure to adopt OI approaches was pushed down from the top of the agency to the implementers. Even the simple request to populate the

Challenge.gov platform came from top management, as one public manager points out

> I'm not sure if it came from our immediate supervisor, or the supervisor's supervisor: but it came down that Challenge.gov is launching; we need to have challenges to be there when it launches, because we were one of the first challenges on Challenge.gov. So it was told us that we needed to do a challenge, and to think of a challenge.

This shows that adoption was not an emergent bottom-up, experimental process, instead public managers were told to align their procedures with the policy requests.

The extent to which agencies then started to internally experiment with a crowd-sourcing process is driven by the mission – the core task of an agency. As an example, a public management problem occurs that influences all subagencies and teams within a large department and still cannot be solved internally. As a result, an idea emerges, needs top-down approval to be posted on Challenge.gov, and then manifests itself in an actual contest. One public manager describes the process in a public health agency:

> Actually the assistant secretary was the one who initiated both of them. She is the sole approval authority within [our agency], so she is the only one who can sign off on anybody doing a prize challenge in [our agency]. The most recent Twitter challenge, the now trending challenge hashtag 'Health in My Community', was proposed by our operational data analytics team that's called 'The Fusion Cell.' They had spoken with state, local regional, tribal and territorial representatives over the course of several months, investigating ways to utilize the different data sources that were available via various social networking mechanisms.

Another public manager added: 'I mean the impetus came from the White House to our administrator to us. Our administrator was very supportive of us using [Challenge.gov].'

Strategic alignment with the organizational mission

For most agencies, the support of the organizational mission and alignment with their own innovation strategy are key drivers to use an OI approach instrument. Mission alignment ranges from reputational gains, for example being seen as an innovator, to creating awareness and educating the public about available public programmes. One manager explains: '[Our agency] benefits just in general from running competitions and getting our name out there and [being] associated with things that are innovative and working with startups and early stage companies.' Agencies did not have opportunities to fulfil this part of their strategic innovation plans using the existing instruments. The Prizes and Contests policy allowed them to reach out in innovative ways.

Connect to new communities of problem solvers

The traditional innovation acquisition instruments limit government's access to problem solver communities that are not already pre-approved on acquisition schedules or solutions to problems cannot simply be solved by an existing long-term contract. Agencies stated that they were in a holding pattern: knowing that they had to reach out to emergent communities of problem solvers to get access to potentially non-standard ideas, they did not have an instrument that allowed them to interact with these problem solvers. One public manager stated the need to improve the current innovation practices:

> I think there is just an overall embrace in general about looking at new ways of doing work and having outside people help us with the work that we do.

OI approaches provide government with innovative ways to reach out to the academic community and especially student problem solvers who might have already been working on similar projects. The other larger stakeholder group includes software developers who were encouraged to collaborate with government to create mobile applications using open data.

Inter-organizational drivers

The General Service Administration (GSA), the agency in charge of providing the Challenge.gov platform, recognized early that the Presidential mandate was not immediately implemented. GSA initiated roadshows, phone conferences, and webinars to provide trainings and best practices that helped to initiate intra-organizational conversations about prizes and challenges. In collaboration with OSTP, federal agencies were trained to adopt contests, as one programme manager explained:

> OSTP set up a center of excellence at [agency] for challenges and prizes and we worked with [name] in particular for the Big Data ideation challenge. It is a government-wide opportunity that I see OSTP has taken the lead in making that all of the agencies understand that it's legal to do competition and prizes, where probably before we would have felt we didn't have the right or the authority to do such a thing. They clarified the rulings, the legalities of all of that, and then they gathered best practices. This was trying to educate the folks at the agencies about competitions and prizes.

Existing technological platform Challenge.gov

In addition to providing procedural guidance, GSA was also in charge of setting up the shared online platform Challenge.gov. A central approach to solving the technological problems for all participants has encouraged agencies to use the platform knowing that legal barriers regarding the review of the Paperwork Reduction Act were already prescreened and preapproved. One public manager explained that 'we have resources now and connectivity that we could not have envisioned five years ago.' The platform is made available at no-cost to the agencies.

Organizational mimicry

Agencies that are adopting prizes and challenges slower than others reported that they tend to mimic already existing behaviour from agencies that were able to jump onto the bandwagon earlier:

> Outside of [the interviewee's agency], NASA has done some fairly innovative things, and GSA. Other government agencies that I have seen as being innovative, or doing [open] innovation, or using [open] innovation to solve their problems: the office of the National Coordinator is very forward leading in that area.

Mimicry does not only flow from the outside in (mimicking NASA's or GSA's innovative behaviour), but also within a larger department, public managers copy each other's behaviour and learning from each other.

Extra-organizational and societal drivers

Extra-organizational or societal drivers include factors that occur outside government as an institution. Public managers are picking up general technological or behavioural trends that allow them to rethink their internal needs or existing mechanisms, which might lack opportunities to initiate innovations, or even to reach out to those parts of their stakeholders they usually cannot reach through the existing channels. With the previous wave of e-government, using social media to reach out to citizens, public managers have already made positive experiences collaborating with citizens and feel comfortable to structure these outreach mechanisms through a central platform. A public manager explained his agency's positive experiences that drove the Challenge. gov approach:

> We ran probably the largest and one of the earliest sort of video contests, during the H1N1 flu issue. We ran a contest where we solicited videos from the public to talk about prevention of H1N1. A significant amount take on that and participation of the public.

Another public manager explained the cultural shift he observed and how his organization picked up the general trends:

> This is a new construct: the whole idea of ideation and innovation as a practice or a cultural norm is. There may be elements of it within our culture, we don't formally recognize, or don't formally encourage, but we're moving [into OI], since now that there is awareness, there's the move to formally embrace it, encourage it and 'inculturate' it.

The more experience agencies gain with crowdsourcing mechanisms to engage large amounts of problem solvers, the more they recognize the shift among citizens who want to be in contact with the government. One public manager explains:

> We saw that there was a demand and a desire for students to engage with the State Department, but we weren't able to meet that demand through the virtual internship program. We thought let's look at other ways that we can have a lot of the college students engaging with the State Department. Looking at Challenge.gov and other sites, we thought hey, using a challenge type thing is a way to have even more students be involved, and aware of the work that we're doing.

Other agencies explained that the broad participation of problem solvers who were never in touch with government showed them the potential of existing slack capacity among external problem solvers as an indicator for broad societal acceptance of free or low-prized contributions beyond citizens' help to solve government problems.

Finding 2: barriers for OI

Barriers for the adoption of online OI approaches include legal barriers, uncertainty about the process and its outcomes, technological barriers to design crowdsourcing processes, and most importantly cultural factors that prevent or delay the adoption decisions. Agencies were instructed to find money in their existing budgets to conduct prize contests. The monetary requirements include dedicated personnel, such as department-level point of contacts, and prize money to pay for the winning solutions. In order to get to the point where agency representatives interviewed for this research project launched contests, the institutional barriers had to be addressed. Some of the barriers are rooted in the specific context of government organizations; other barriers are inherently connected to the perceptions and tasks of individuals involved in the OI process. Working through these barriers delayed the process for years as one interview explains:

> We had to figure out an internal mechanism for making [challenges] happen. That's taken over a year. But, I think it's a year well spent. The America Competes Act supposedly authorizes federal agencies to give prizes. But many agencies don't feel confident in it that actually does provide the right coverage for agencies. Our legal staff definitely did not feel that it was appropriate.

Intra-organizational barriers

Intra-organizational barriers refer to factors that occur inside each organization and can be solved by the organization itself. These factors include legal, cultural, technical, and institutional barriers.

Legal barriers

Public managers perceived the absence of a legal framework as risky. One manager mentioned that prizes and contests 'gave everything kind of an air of uncertainty' and that the America Competes Act only provides a vague umbrella framework that is still open for interpretation. Agencies coped with the vagueness and absence of existing rules by borrowing rule structures from agencies that had already implemented prizes and contests and had set a precedent. The existing rules were then adapted to the local contexts.

Examples of legal uncertainty focus on management and targeting of external audiences. These processes are closely regulated through the existing 'cookie' policy (tracking of online user behaviour), measurement, and surveys. Especially, when it comes to personally identifiable information collected by a government agency, section 208 privacy provisions of the e-government act require agencies to conduct a privacy impact assessment (2002). These provisions needed to be adapted to allow new technologies and citizen interactions. However, agencies that target specific audiences struggle with the implementation. One public manager explains:

> We had to figure out how kids could be involved. Could they submit something? Do they have to get parental permission? At what age? The second part of that was, we had to customize the entry form on Challenge.gov to ask questions about age to be able to support that, because Challenge.gov, assumes that you are of a certain age.

The second aspect of legal considerations includes intellectual property (IP) rights. While IP issues are arranged by contract in the traditional innovation acquisition processes, these issues had to be re-evaluated for the use of voluntary submissions of knowledge by citizens. In the private sector, several models of co-ownership of submitted solutions or shared patents have evolved (see for example: Belderbosa et al. 2014). In the public sector, however, one public manager explained:

> There is a debate going on right now about whether or not, and if someone wins a prize and the government pays them however much money for their best technology solution, if that's a direct pathway for that person to be able to work with government. Can that be used for a sole source justification, can we just get the technology to use as a license, or do we actually have to release another contract and compete for the solution that the government actually buys? There's a lot of disagreement about what the government can do with the technology, especially if we don't write in the rules that there's a government right to the intellectual

property. But often times, if it's bigger market simulation prizes, people won't participate if the government is going to own their IP.

These legal barriers prevent government organizations to proactively seek out more complex solutions, especially if they are not able to actually implement the results of the contest.

Cultural factors

The organizational culture factors include several different aspects of the OI process: (a) type of agency and political context, (b) acceptance of external innovations, and (c) the lack of top-management support and buy-in.

Individual-level factors depend on the type of agency, as an example, science and technology agencies are more likely to abandon the idea to invite external non-professional problem solvers into their innovation process. The R&D-oriented teams are trained (and hired) to develop answers in-house and might feel that it is their core job to know it all. The result is oftentimes that solutions from non-professional problem solvers are not accepted (Katz and Allen 1982). One public manager in a science agency described the general rejection of the new process:

> We're an R&D and technology development organization. People here believe that they are the best engineers in the world, and so if they can't solve it, nobody can.

Another public manager adds that it is difficult for government employees not to be able to fulfil the requirements of their job: This significant cultural change in the way innovations are acquired challenges employee attitudes:

> It is a big shift, because in some ways it is admitting and acknowledging maybe that we the government don't have all the answers and that we can benefit from other people's perspective. It is a cultural shift for people to think that way.

One public manager explained how his agency worked to explore the cultural barriers. Instead of changing the mindsets of those people who were against the implementation of prizes and contests, he says:

> Actually, we didn't really work around the culture. We basically found the people who were leading the way, and promoted their data the most and encouraged others to follow the same path.

Technological barriers

Public managers pointed to the fact that an innovative approach comes with initial resistance due to the newness of the technology itself, and new ways of defining and soliciting input for public sector problems: 'So they look easy, but they are not simple.' The standard way to communicate the need for solutions is directly tied to the existing RFP (request for proposals) process, using language that is industry standard or terms only known to professionals. However, problem statements in the OI process need to be written in plain language – not only closed ended enough to make them understandable to amateur problem solvers, but also open ended enough to allow for innovations the agency has not thought about itself. OI provides a new infrastructure and reverses the highly structured contract process:

> The more fuzzier aspect, the fungible aspect of prize challenges that isn't addressed in the [department's' guidance] is what goes into developing a problem statement, and what goes into developing a successful challenge. That's far more challenging.

Previous research on OI processes in the private sector has shown that the degree of openness in defining problems is crucial for the success of a contest. Salge et al. showed that too much openness does not support the process and that a guided approach is oftentimes better (2013). The technology itself was not flexible enough to support these steps:

> One of the unexpected things is the Challenge.gov site itself is very rigid, in terms of what you can put in there. I thought we were going to be able to have a system where people actually entered their plans online. Instead, what we ended up with was a system where we have a Microsoft Word document as a template. They complete their template separately, and then they upload that. So that was a surprise to me, for the way the Challenge.gov worked. The technical limitations, word limits, letter limits.

Uncertainty about innovation outcomes

Public managers confronted with the use of contests and challenges need to adapt to a new organizing process that challenges their current standard operating structure, such as contract management. In the standard acquisition process, expectations, framing, contractual and legal statements are clearly designed and have been codified as organizational knowledge in handbooks and operating manuals.

In addition to the concerns about the design elements of an OI process, public managers are reluctant about innovation outcomes. Public managers, trained to explicitly define the deliverables for a contract or grant, now have to accept that OI is designed to find answers for problems that do not have a predefined solution. In combination with uncertainty about the boundaries and capabilities of the solver community, public managers therefore expressed high degrees of uncertainty about the innovation outcomes:

> We didn't know how to solve the problem. Not that we could have created an RFP, where we were confident would have been the right way to solve the problem. We knew the problem that needed to be solved was proliferating the use and availability of Blue Button Personal Health Records. What we didn't know was what the best way to go about doing that. We wouldn't have been able to say to industry: Here's what we're looking for: This particular way to proliferate the availability of use.

Institutionalization barriers

After agencies overcame policy, process, and legal barriers, organizational responsibilities needed to be redefined to institutionalize OI in the existing organizational structure. One public manager explains how difficult it was for his agency to start to incorporate contests into the standard operating procedures:

> This is because the concept is not to set up an office of innovation, and not have a place that does innovation, and do this with more of an [institutionalization], and making it part of the [department's] culture. There is no office, and there's also no chief innovator, and there's no one who hashes it out. There is no concrete structure that people can go to and say oh good, the Office of Innovation helped me with this.

This ad hoc process shows how agencies are struggling with the institutionalization and the lack of organizational structure in early phases of the adoption process. Previous research has shown that organizational structure will eventually follow strategies (or policies in the government context) (Burgelman 1983). The initial lack of organizational structure has led to dedicated organizational roles in other parts of the government system. As an example, the City of Boston and the City of Philadelphia have institutionalized an Office of Innovation and a Chief Innovation Officer role.

Similar to institutionalization of organizational roles, the organizational culture is slowly changing from a closed innovation paradigm to an open paradigm where experimentation is part of a trial and error process. One public manager explains that while there is top management support, lower ranks might not be on board and hinder institutionalization:

> The top levels of leadership that would be the assistant secretary and the deputy assistant secretary; there is support, and enthusiasm. The senior leadership below them and then some of the leadership in the different management levels however getting them to embrace this construct and this culture of innovation, which is a little different than some of them may be used to. They, being innovative and doing innovative things implies a certain amount of inherent risk, and they are by definition risk adverse. That is counter intuitive to the way their structure operates.

As a result, public managers avoid experimentation. Government's existing culture does not allow what one interview partner called a safe environment 'to take smart risks' and he called for 'a place to take risks, a place where failing is ok. Don't punish people for failing if you told them you wanted them to take a risk. You can't encourage smart risk taking and then punish failure.'

Inter-organizational barriers

Hurdles that cross different government organizations occur only when two or more agencies have to actively collaborate and interview partners reported mostly barriers in the initial set-up. Legal barriers expand beyond intra-organizational needs to start to use OI and have to be resolved in a time consuming manner. Collaborative contests with shared promotion and outcomes include for example the First Lady's collaboration with the Department of Agriculture to run the Apps for Healthy Kids challenge, or the Department of Health and Human Services' collaboration with the Environmental Protection Agency and their My Air, My Health challenge. One public manager explained the process:

> Interagency bureaucratic challenges of doing an Interagency Memorandum of Understanding, an MOU, have proven to be quite challenging. Each agency gets its own funds; it is charged with investing in the program sand projects that will help it achieve its mission. Everyone believes that if we could work better across agencies that we would be better coordinated and we might more quickly overcome some of the challenges that we have in terms of clean energy and wellbeing and so forth. But there are still a lot of bureaucratic hurdles that are just there. I want to simplify the process so that any agency that is interested in doing a Big Data challenge can. I could make the process as simple as possible for them to engage, rather than it being a horrendous process. So every time we want to do a new contest, we have to set up a whole new MOU framework.

These inter-organizational barriers highlight the need for directions from the Office of Management & Budget as agencies gain more experience and recognize opportunities for inter-organizational collaboration.

Extra-organizational and societal factors

Extra-organizational barriers are far less prevalent than extra-organizational drivers. Barriers in this context mostly focus on mindfulness of how changes in
internal processes and government experimentation with innovative policies
might be perceived by the public. In traditional procurement processes, accountability is built into the process with exact guidelines, reporting structures, and
accountability measures that are designed to keep a close watch of appropriateness
of managerial actions:

> We as federal employees are good stewards of the taxpayers' money that we're entrusted with
> using; especially if we're using it in a contract mechanism to procure goods and services from
> outside the federal government. That being said, it's not a clean line of sight. It's not a straight
> line between Point A and Point B as far as how we do [OI].

Furthermore, monetary incentives and the publicness of the selection and judging
process provide ground for concern:

> How we manage money is [regulated in the America Competes Act], specifically how we can
> use appropriated funds as a cash prize in a contest. It also says we can work with other
> agencies and departments to do this, and it says we can partner not just within the federal
> government, but with nonfederal partners to do that. So that makes it more clear cut for us. It
> helps make the line a little straighter between Point A and Point B. Competes actually made
> challenges easier to use because it more clearly defined the rules for us as federal employees
> using you know, taxpayer money.

Discussion and conclusions

This article provides empirical evidence for factors driving and hindering government organizations to adopt and implement a new policy instrument called Prizes
and Challenges in the US federal government. To gain a deeper understanding of
how the internal strategic and managerial decision-making processes are influenced
by these factor and ultimately lead to the outcomes observable on Challenge.gov, this
article provides a framework on three dimensions: intra-, inter-, and extra-organizational factors. The data include agencies involved in this form of innovation acquisition and adds to our understanding of how OI online practices diffuse in the public
sector.

OI was introduced as a new umbrella concept for inviting external, non-professional problem solvers to help government find solutions for problems they weren't
able to solve internally or with the help of the standard innovation instruments grants
and contracts. The current OI literature focusses on private sector organizations (for
a review, see West and Bogers 2014). Based on one embedded case study – the use of
the online platform Challenge.gov – and a policy instrument 'Prizes and Contests' of
the US federal government, the barriers and drivers for the implementation and use
of the platform are analysed. This article shows the complexity of issues that public
sector organizations have to deal with when they are confronted with a political
mandate to innovate as opposed to private sector organizations. In addition, OI
approaches don't only need a crowdsourcing platform, but public managers need
to be empowered to take risks and step outside the risk-free request for proposal
process in traditional acquisition routines.

Barriers occur on the inter- and extra-organizational levels making it increasingly complex for government organizations to adopt a new technology. The summary overview in Table 1 shows the need to study the resulting implementation strategies of those agencies that did not reject the adoption of OI. The drivers provide insights about the changing needs of government organizations for a pathway to access innovative ideas from outside of government. Existing innovation acquisition instruments as part of the innovation paradigm limit government organizations to involve those problem solvers who are not part of the formal acquisition process. Open advertising possibilities and collection of the crowdsourced innovations allow government to use e-governance mechanisms that were not previously available.

This article also adds to the literature on co-production and co-design of public services (Joshi and Moore 2004; Osborne, Radnor, and Strokosch 2016; Boivard 2007). While previous research on co-production has mostly focussed on inclusion of citizens in form of public participation processes to gain their support, trust, and insights in structured decision-making processes, OI opens a new conduit to include external knowledge into the problem-solving processes. OI is however significantly different from previous waves of co-production and leads to innovative ideas and solutions by providing monetary incentives and using online platforms to broaden the inclusion of ideas and not only local participation.

In addition to the existing OI literature, previous research on e-government has mostly focussed on internal barriers or drivers. This article shows that external barriers and drivers are out of the control of a single agency and equally important in adoption and implementation decisions of an e-government innovation.

The findings highlight the opportunity to review what the innovations outcomes are and what their potential impact is on the innovation process itself and the broader innovation culture in government. Most of the current e-government and OI research focusses on the diffusion and adoption decision; however, there is no research that looks at short-term innovation products and long-term changes in the organization. It is important to study the outcomes of the OI process beyond the number of solutions submitted from citizens during the crowdsourcing process, which can only indicate interest in a given topic, but says little about the value of the innovation. Indirect outcomes, such as legitimization of an innovative acquisition process, public value creation, or the changing climate towards external innovations in government, can be studied to understand the extent of the impact on government.

Limitations

This research is clearly limited by its focus on a specific layer of the US federal government's executive branch situated in a specific political climate: President Obama's administration's push for an agile government with the use of new technologies. As one of the first studies on OI in the public sector, the framework developed here can help researchers design their own OI inquiries or conduct comparative public administration research. The inclusion of a variety of government agencies with diverse sets of missions and mandates contributes to our understanding of how government agencies implement OI given their own political context, differences in top-management sentiments towards innovation, and diverse organizational cultures.

The interview partners selected for this study do not only focus on successful cases. The nature of the study helps to understand what makes OI approaches

Table 1. Summary of findings: drivers and barriers of open innovation in the public sector.

Level	Drivers	Barriers
Intra-organizational	Pre-policy time frame: • Internal experimentation Post-policy time frame: • Top-down management decision • Strategic alignment with mission • Necessity to change existing innovation acquisition framework • Recognizing unsolvable internal public management problems • Opportunity to connect with new community of problem solvers	Type of agency: • Adoption speed • Regulatory barriers (extent to which agencies are allowed direct citizen interaction) Legal aspects: • Properties of submitted solutions • Collection of PII through contests • Time lag from decision to implementation: (a) Working through organizational barriers: 2 years (b) Simple → complex public management problems Cultural aspects: • NIH syndrome • Inertia: waiting out policy waves, leadership changes ('trickle down') Procedural aspects: • Understanding crowdsourcing processes • Defining public management problems • Designing contest phases • Recruit judges • Monetary/Non-monetary contests
Inter-organizational factors	• GSA & OSTP guidance, best practices, innovators toolkit, roadshows, webinars • Organizational mimicry of existing practices • Existing technological platform to promote challenge and collect ideas	• Legal: MOUs
Extra-organizational factors	• Introduction of new policy instrument through Presidential mandate National Priorities (e.g. economic development) • Digital Government Strategy • Societal acceptance of crowdsourcing processes	• Recruiting of 'unreachables': weak ties to otherwise disconnected citizens • Expectations of professional problem solvers vs. general citizenry • Power distance/cultural distance: we vs. them mentality

NIH: Not invented here; PII: personally identifiable information.

unsuccessful for some government actors, as opposed to others who given the alignment of OI policy instrument and e-government platform with their organizational mission made it very successful.

In conclusion, OI – even several years after it was officially introduced through a Presidential mandate in the US federal government – is still in its early stages. Each agency has to work through not only legal barriers, but also cultural internal barriers.

Only in cases where there is clear alignment with the organizational mission and openness of the organizational culture, agencies attempt to adopt (oftentimes low risk) prizes and contests. While some agencies have waited for a Presidential mandate like to allow them to innovate in an open format, clearly for other agencies, the mandate is a burden and they reject a sustainable implementation of OI.

Disclosure statement

No potential conflict of interest was reported by the author.

ORCID

Ines Mergel ⓘ *http://orcid.org/0000-0003-0285-4758*

References

Arundel, A., L. Casali, and H. Hollanders. 2015. "How European Public Sector Agencies Innovate: The Use of Bottom-Up, Policy-Dependent and Knowledge-Scanning Innovation Methods." *Research Policy* 44 (7): 1271–1282. doi:10.1016/j.respol.2015.04.007.

Belderbosa, R., B. Cassimana, D. Faemsa, B. Letena, and B. Van Looy 2014. "Co-Ownership of Intellectual Property: Exploring the Value-Appropriation and Value-Creation Implications of Co-Patenting with Different Partners." *Research Policy* 43 (5): 841–852. doi:10.1016/j.respol.2013.08.013.

Benkler, Y. 2006. *The Wealth of Networks: How Social Production Transforms Markets and Freedom.* New Haven, CT: Yale University Press.

Boivard, T. 2007. "Beyond Engagement and Participation: User and Community Coproduction of Public Services." *Public Administration Review* 67 (5): 846–860. doi:10.1111/j.1540-6210.2007.00773.x.

Burgelman, R. A. 1983. "A Model of the Interaction of Strategic Behavior, Corporate Context, and the Concept of Strategy." *Academy of Management Journal* 8 (1): 61–70.

Chesbrough, H. 2003. *Open Innovation: The New Imperative for Creating and Profiting from Technology.* Cambridge, MA: Harvard Business Press.

Chesbrough, H., and A. K. Crowther. 2006. "Beyond High Tech: Early Adopters of Open Innovation in Other Industries." *R&D Management* 36 (3): 229–236. doi:10.1111/j.1467-9310.2006.00428.x.

Coglianese, C. 2004. "E-Rulemaking: Information Technology and the Regulatory Process." *Administrative Law Review* 56 (2): 353–402.

Colatat, P. 2015. "An Organizational Perspective to Funding Science: Collaborator Novelty at DARPA." *Research Policy* 44 (4): 874–887. doi:10.1016/j.respol.2015.01.005.

Congress, 110th. 2007. "America COMPETES Act." In *H.R.2272*, edited by 110th Congress. Washington, DC: Library of Congress.

Dahlandera, L., and H. Piezunkab. 2014. "Open to Suggestions: How Organizations Elicit Suggestions through Proactive and Reactive Attention." *Research Policy* 43 (5): 812–827. doi:10.1016/j.respol.2013.06.006.

de Sousa Santos, B. 1998. "Participatory Budgeting in Porto Alegre: Toward a Redistributive Democracy." *Politics & Society* 26 (4): 461–510. doi:10.1177/0032329298026004003.

DeHart-Davis, L., J. Chen, and T. D. Little. 2013. "Written versus Unwritten Rules: The Role of Rule Formalization in Green Tape." *International Public Management Journal* 16 (3): 331–356. doi:10.1080/10967494.2013.825193.

Denzin, N. K., and Y. S. Lincoln. 2011. "Introduction: The Discipline and Practice of Qualitative Research." In *The Sage Handbook of Qualitative Research*, edited by N. K. Denzin and Y. S. Lincoln, 1–19. Thousand Oaks, CA: Sage.

Du, J., B. Leten, and W. Vanhaverbeke. 2014. "Managing Open Innovation Projects with Science-Based and Market-Based Partners." *Research Policy* 43 (5): 828–840. doi:10.1016/j. respol.2013.12.008.

E-Government Act of 2002, Public Law 107–347—DEC. 17 2002, Issuing Organization: 107th U.S. Congress, Washington, DC.

Ettlie, J. E., and J. M. Elsenbach. 2007. "The Changing Role of R&D Gatekeepers." *Research-Technology Management* 50 (5): 59–66.

Felina, T., and T. R. Zenger. 2014. "Closed or Open Innovation? Problem Solving and the Governance Choice." *Reearch Policy* 43 (5): 914–925. doi:10.1016/j.respol.2013.09.006.

Fu, X. 2012. "How Does Openness Affect the Importance of Incentives for Innovation?" *Research Policy* 41 (3): 512–523. doi:10.1016/j.respol.2011.12.011.

Gambardella, A., and C. Panico. 2014. "On the Management of Open Innovation." *Research Policy* 43 (5): 903–913. doi:10.1016/j.respol.2013.12.002.

Howe, J. P. 2006. "The Rise of Crowdsourcing." *Wired Magazine Online* 14 (6). https://www.wired.com/2006/06/crowds/

Jeppesen, L. B., and K. R. Lakhani. 2010. "Marginality and Problem-Solving Effectiveness in Broadcast Search." *Organization Science* 21 (5): 1016–1033. doi:10.1287/orsc.1090.0491.

Joshi, A., and M. H. Moore. 2004. "Institutionalised Co-Production: Unorthodox Public Service Delivery in Challenging Environments." *Journal of Development Studies* 40 (4): 31–49. doi:10.1080/00220380410001673184.

Katz, R., and T. J. Allen. 1982. "Investigating the Not Invented Here (NIH) Syndrome: A Look at the Performance, Tenure, and Communication Patterns of 50 R & D Project Groups." *R&D Management* 12 (1): 7–20. doi:10.1111/radm.1982.12.issue-1.

Lakhani, K. R., and L. B. Jeppesen. 2007. "Getting Unusual Suspects to Solve R&D Puzzles." *Harvard Business Review* 85: 5.

Lee, S. M., T. Hwang, and D. Choi. 2012. "Open Innovation in the Public Sector of Leading Countries." *Management Decision* 50 (1): 147–162. doi:10.1108/00251741211194921.

Meijer, A. 2015. "E-Governance Innovation: Barriers and Strategies." *Government Information Quarterly* 32 (2): 198–206. doi:10.1016/j.giq.2015.01.001.

Mergel, I. 2015. "Opening government: Designing Open Innovation Processes to Collaborate with External Problem Solvers." *Social Science Computer Review* 33 (5): 599-612.

Mergel, I., and K. Desouza. 2013. "Implementing Open Innovation in the Public Sector: The Case of Challenge.Gov." *Public Administration Review* 73 (6): 882–890. doi:10.1111/puar.2013.73. issue-6.

Mergel, I., S. I. Bretschneider, C. Louis, and J. Smith. 2014. "The Challenges of Challenge.Gov: Adopting Private Sector Business Innovations in the Federal Government." In *Proceedings of the 2014 47th Hawaii International Conference on System Sciences (HICSS)*, 2073–2082. Washington, DC: IEEE.

Miles, M. B., A. M. Huberman, and J. Saldana. 2014. *Qualitative Data Analysis: A Methods Sourcebook*. 3rd ed. Thousand Oaks, CA: Sage.

Murray, F., S. Stern, G. Campbell, and A. MacCormack. 2012. "Grand Innovation Prizes: A Theoretical, Normative, and Empirical Evaluation." *Research Policy* 41 (10): 1779–1792. doi:10.1016/j.respol.2012.06.013.

NASA. n.d. "Asteroid Initiative: NASA's Asteroid Redirect Mission and Grand Challenge." http://www.nasa.gov/mission_pages/asteroids/initiative/-.U-T1bPldXTo

Osborne, S. P., Z. Radnor, and K. Strokosch. 2016. "Co-Production and the Co-Creation of Value in Public Services: A Suitable Case for Treatment?" *Public Management Review* 18 (5): 639–653. doi:10.1080/14719037.2015.1111927.

Piezunka, H., and L. Dahlander. 2015. "Distant Search, Narrow Attention: How Crowding Alters Organizations' Filtering of Suggestions in Crowdsourcing." *Academy of Management Journal* 58 (3): 856-880.

Rainey, H. G., S. Pandey, and B. Bozeman. 1995. "Research Note: Public and Private Managers' Perceptions of Red Tape." *Public Administration Review* 55 (6): 567–574. doi:10.2307/3110348.

Ropera, S., P. Vahterb, and J. H. Lovec. 2013. "Externalities of Openness in Innovation." *Research Policy* 42: 1544–1554. doi:10.1016/j.respol.2013.05.006.

Salge, T. O., T. Farchi, M. I. Barrett, and S. Dopson. 2013. "When Does Search Openness Really Matter? A Contingency Study of Health-Care Innovation Projects." *Journal of Product Innovation Management* 30 (4): 659–676. doi:10.1111/jpim.12015.

Shirky, C. 2008. *Here Comes Everybody: The Power of Organizing without Organizations*. New York: Penguin.

Surowiecki, J. 2004. *The Wisdom of Crowds*. New York, NY: Knopf Doubleday.

The White House. 2009. *The Open Government Initiative*. edited by Executive Office of the President. Washington, DC: White House.

The White House. 2010. *Guidance on the Use of Challenges and Prizes to Promote Open Government Edited by Office of Management and Budget*. Washington, DC: Exectuvie Office of the President.

Villarroel, J. A. 2013. "Strategic Crowdsourcing: The Emergence of Online Distributed Innovation." In *Leading Open Innovation*, edited by A. S. Huff, K. M. Moeslein, and R. Reichwald, 171–200. Cambridge, MA: The MIT Press.

West, J., and K. R. Lakhani. 2008. "Getting Clear about Communities in Open Innovation." *Industry & Innovation* 15: 223–231. doi:10.1080/13662710802033734.

West, J., and M. Bogers. 2014. "Leveraging External Sources of Innovation: A Review of Research on Open Innovation." *Journal of Product Innovation Management* 31 (4): 814–831. doi:10.1111/jpim.2014.31.issue-4.

Toward precision governance: infusing data into public management of environmental hazards

David M. Hondula, Evan R. Kuras, Justin Longo and Erik W. Johnston

ABSTRACT
Precision governance is an administrative capacity in which policy decisions are enhanced with information about individual and collective preferences and contexts. We introduce the prospects for precision governance of natural hazards through the use of both big and individual data technologies, describing what is enabled and what concerns arise with their use. We ground our perspective with a topical focus on mitigating the health risks of high temperatures in the chronically hot setting of Phoenix, Arizona, USA. A study examining individually experienced temperature data provides compelling evidence that the transition towards data-driven precision governance will enhance hazard preparedness and response efforts.

1. Introduction

One of the essential functions of government is to protect public safety. Government and the public at large are now paying more attention to the health impacts of natural hazards. Government agencies often play a central role in helping communities prepare for, respond to, and recover from events like tornadoes, floods, and snowstorms. The growth of the digital era, and all of its technological and computational affordances, make it possible for public agencies and other actors to employ *precision governance* in their efforts to protect communities when such hazards occur. Johnston et al. (2013) defined precision governance as 'the ability to design governance infrastructure – the collection of technologies and systems – to represent individual and collective choices and policy preference into augmented societal policy decisions.' Here, we add to the notion that the individual and collective policy preferences that would ideally be incorporated into a precision governance approach also include latent preferences and needs of individuals and groups based on fine-scale differences in circumstances and experiences.

Those involved in protecting the public when hazards occur, from officials to non-profits to individuals, are increasingly able to customize preparation and response efforts based on historical and real-time data. The incorporation of a variety of data sets and streams can improve community and individual readiness for natural hazards as well as decision-making when events are imminent or occurring. Furthermore, the public is increasingly demanding improvements in these efforts from government agencies (Kapucu 2009). Thus, improvements in hazard-related interventions might not only limit unwanted consequences of these events but also improve the relationship between the public and government. Moreover, the network of individuals and organizations involved in hazard preparedness and response is both large and complex (Robinson et al. 2013), and the benefits of precision govern- ance-oriented strategies could aid in the coordination of the many actors that play a role in protecting communities.

To discuss the prospects for data-driven, evidence-based public management of the risks associated with hazards, we draw examples from our local experiences in Maricopa County, Arizona, the anchor of the hottest large metropolitan area in the United States. In this locale, a hazard of concern for public health agencies is extreme heat. The growing availability of health and exposure data and our ability to analyse and interpret these data in meaningful ways has the potential to transform the manner in which local agencies respond to the serious threat of this hazard.

We are interested in two aspects of the use of data in governance: first the preparation and then the decision-making. Regarding preparation, the operational question is how to thoughtfully and intentionally build a governance infrastructure that collects the appropriate data, analyses it to be useful, and then communicates it to those who need to make decisions. Regarding decision-making, the question of interest is how the behaviour of government agencies, collaborators, and the public adjusts when information is readily available that can influence how they organize or act. From a public health perspective, developing a robust evidence base that informs the design and deployment of effective intervention measures that protect the public when hazards occur continues to be a priority of researchers and practitioners alike. Yet, the key evidence to foster effective evidence-based public health management of environmental hazards, particularly those related to weather and climate, is largely absent (Hess et al. 2014).

2. Case study context: extreme heat in Maricopa County, Arizona

High ambient temperature is an environmental health hazard that has received increasing attention from researchers and policymakers in recent years given the prospects of increasing global and urban temperatures (Luber and McGeehin 2008; Hondula, Georgescu, and Balling 2014; Winkler et al. 2015). An association between temperature and a wide range of adverse human health outcomes including mortality has been documented across many geographic settings (McMichael et al. 2008). Notable extreme heat events in the past few decades have resulted in hundreds (Chicago, 1995) to tens of thousands (Europe, 2003) of deaths over time periods spanning days to weeks (Semenza et al. 1996, Conti et al. 2005). Direct financial impacts on the healthcare system from an individual heat event in a single geographic location can exceed tens of millions of dollars (Knowlton et al. 2011; Lin et al. 2012).

In the United States, extreme heat ranks among the leading weather-related causes of death, responsible for more fatalities each year than most other natural hazards combined (Berko et al. 2014). Few localities in the United States face higher tem- peratures each year than the Phoenix, Arizona metropolitan area, a region that is home to more than 4 million people and that faces summertime daily maximum temperatures regularly exceeding 40°C (104°F). Heat continues to exert a considerable public health toll among residents of greater Phoenix: the Maricopa County Department of Public Health reported 433 heat-related deaths over the period 2010–2014 and Petitti et al. (2015) reported a total of more than 8,500 heat-related hospitalizations and emergency department visits over the period 2008–2012. Extreme heat disproportionately impacts certain communities and populations in Maricopa County including those with low incomes and ethnic minorities, outdoor workers, homeless, those without home air conditioning, and individuals using drugs or alcohol (Harlan et al. 2012; MCDPH 2014).

Returning to the definition of precision governance, in the context of extreme heat, the *individual and collective choices* of interest are (1) the behaviour changes that reduce the risk of adverse health outcomes and (2) the occurrence (or lack thereof) of adverse health outcomes. The *societal policy decisions* of interest are the plans and programmes that agencies implement with the goal of limiting unwanted consequences. In central Arizona, these societal policy decisions include the Extreme Heat Emergency Response Plan of the Arizona Department of Health Services, the coordination and activation of the Phoenix Heat Relief Network of cooling centres and water distribution facilities by the City of Phoenix and the Maricopa Association of Governments, the operation of a surveillance programme by the Maricopa County Department of Public Health and the issuance of extreme heat warnings to the general public by the Phoenix forecast office of the National Weather Service. At longer time scales, educational campaigns and infrastructure modifications (e.g. increasing tree/shade cover, implementing white and cool roof technology) are the major efforts described in policy and planning documents that are intended to reduce impacts (e.g. Chow, Brennan, and Brazel 2012).

3. Constraints on hazard management

Many of the public management strategies for extreme heat already operate under the paradigm of increasing the precision of governance (albeit at a coarser scale than the one we imagine in this manuscript), leveraging a large literature that has accumulated over the past several decades. For example, public warning systems for heat are often designed based on city-specific threshold temperatures derived from epidemiological analysis (e.g. Pascal et al. 2006) and educational campaigns employ messaging built from the same evidence base (e.g. White-Newsome et al. 2014). The risk-assessment studies that contribute to this evidence base are often performed at a regional or citywide scale, which matches the scale at which heat occurs (e.g. the meteorological features associated with heat are hundreds or more kilometres in their spatial extent) but does not match the scales relevant for heat exposure such as individual households, parcels, or even smaller spatial units (Ruddell et al. 2009). Communication of the threat of heat also tends to be based at the regional scale: warning messages are often targeted to entire counties or groups of counties and disseminated to broad areas (e.g. the entire viewing audience of a local television or radio news outlet).

As a consequence, we contend that the preparation for – and response to – hazards is limited by information that is often too coarse to guide the most efficient deployment of resources to those in need despite the positive intention of hazard management plans and response actions. The fact that heat continues to exert a considerable public health burden in our geographic focus area of central Arizona, as well as many other municipalities around the world, indicates that there are still ample opportunities to improve our approach to dealing with high temperatures in terms of preparedness and response efforts. We hypothesize that a transition to a governance framework centred on greater precision would be an effective strategy for reducing impacts moving forward. In such a framework where individual preferences and contexts are the basis for preparation and decision-making, new design possibilities can emerge. Targeting, customization, and personalization of response efforts could be especially beneficial in the light of time and resource constraints that are common in government agencies involved in hazard management (e.g. Hu and Kapucu 2016).

A prime example of the shortcomings of current societal policy decisions for heat and their influence on individual collective choices is early warning systems, which are a centrepiece of heat preparedness strategies in many localities (Lowe, Ebi, and Forsberg 2011). In the current approach, where (typically) one broad warning message is communicated to the entire population of a city or other large region, the conditions do not exist for a message recipient to easily understand or explore what specifically the warning may mean in the context of their individual life, needs, and preferences. We believe that this lack of precision at least partially explains why evidence of behavioural changes in response to heat warnings has been scant despite generally high awareness of warnings (e.g. Kalkstein and Sheridan 2007; Bassil and Cole 2010).

Perhaps more concerning is the perception reported in some of these studies that many individuals believe that they are not at risk from heat and/or the warning message is not intended for them. While the physiological evidence is quite clear – individuals exposed to high temperatures for a prolonged period of time are at risk of illness or death – individuals who do receive warning messages about heat are, in fact, quite *unlikely* to experience any harm from heat: the average American, for example, spends approximately 90 per cent of his or her time indoors (Leech et al. 2002), much of which may be spent in climate-controlled settings (at work, at home, or in transit). The delivery of repeated heat warnings to a significant portion of the population that is not physically 'experiencing' heat during much of their daily activity could build latent complacency regarding the seriousness of the hazard that may leave them unprepared when they partake in activities that expose them to high temperatures. This latent complacency builds as a result of repeated false alarms from weather warnings (Barnes et al. 2007).

Most of the research related to false alarms for natural hazards concern high-visibility events like tornadoes and floods: a false alarm in these cases is defined as the hazard not materializing (e.g. a tornado did not happen or occurred in a different location than was forecast/warned). In the case of heat, we suggest that a different type of false alarm occurs. Weather forecasts for heat are highly accurate; a true 'false alarm' almost never occurs. Instead, the false alarm occurs at the *individual* level – an extreme heat event occurs but does not result in any notable impacts for certain people. In a 2009 study of heat-vulnerable communities in Maricopa County, 63 per cent of survey respondents indicated having zero heat-related symptoms of any kind (Hayden, Brenkert-Smith, and Wilhelmi 2011). When considering the scale at which extreme heat events occur (multiple cities or regions), the *individual* false alarms are more likely to be the norm than the exception. Although debate continues regarding the validity of a false alarm-complacency mechanism in real-world hazard situations (Barnes et al. 2007), it seems more likely than not that some portion of the many individuals who do not believe that heat is a risk to them are of this mindset because they have repeatedly experienced heat and heat warnings in the past with no adverse health effects.

As a result of coarse information about the public health impacts of extreme heat, misguided or inefficient planning, policy-making, and decision-making can also occur at the agency level. Concerns about the health impacts of heat motivate local, national, and international policy aimed at reducing outdoor temperatures, whether through efforts to reduce the urban heat island effect in cities or decelerate emission of greenhouse gases worldwide (e.g. Solecki et al. 2005; Patz et al. 2005). Given that there is a clear association between high outdoor temperatures and adverse human health outcomes, the notion that reducing outdoor temperatures (or limiting future increases) will have benefits for health seems logical. The scientific literature is only recently, however, beginning to examine how outdoor temperatures relate to the entirety of a person's heat exposure (Kuras et al. 2017). Without a rich understanding of the relationship between outdoor temperatures and experienced temperatures, some public policies concerning the health impacts of heat may be misdirected. In urban areas, for example, focusing urban heat island mitigation strategies on central business districts (where the heat island effect is most intense) may not be the optimal strategy for reducing adverse heat-health outcomes because those may not be the places where the most vulnerable individuals tend to experience high temperatures through the course of their daily lives (because that is not where they live, work, or recreate). The resources invested in such programmes could yield greater benefits for health if they were invested in energy affordability or home weatherization programmes for those who are unable to use air conditioning on a regular basis. The reverse may also be true, but the coarseness of the information currently available in most settings makes it impossible to fully evaluate the trade-offs between certain strategies and properly account for health benefits versus other important dimensions of urban heat like energy and water use, real estate, tourism, and other commercial activity.

4. Data-driven governance

Advances in data collection and accessibility as well as computational power and resources have dramatically accelerated our ability to understand environmental hazards like heat in the nuanced, specific manner that is necessary for effective precision governance. These advances can direct transformational changes in the public management of hazards within the next 10–20 years.

Epidemiological and geographical analyses of the social and environmental risk factors for adverse health outcomes related to heat exposure have benefitted tremendously from improvements in computational power and data accessibility. It is not uncommon for heat-health studies published in recent years to incorporate data sets involving tens of millions of health records, satellite imagery with spatial resolution of tens of metres or better, and/or social and infrastructure data sets at the household and parcel level for entire metropolitan areas (e.g. Rosenthal, Kinney, and Metzger 2014; Morabito et al. 2015). The studies provide the evidence base that makes it possible to target intervention measures for heat to the communities where the benefits will be disproportionately highest as well as shape those intervention measures to the specific needs of at-risk populations. There is already evidence that some jurisdictions are utilizing the output of this research in their hazard management plans (e.g. the San Francisco Department of Public Health: https://www.sfdph.org/dph/EH/climatechange/ and Minnesota Department of Health: http://www.health.state.mn.us/divs/climatechange/extremeheat.html).

Computational advances continue to improve our ability to understanding the physical dimensions of environmental hazards as well. For example, complex models that require significant computing infrastructure are being used to simulate how changes to infrastructure, the land surface, and the atmosphere (e.g. building design, land use change, increasing greenhouse gas concentrations) will impact thermal environments at scales ranging from individual buildings to the entire globe (e.g. Ohashi et al. 2015; Zhao et al. 2015). One emerging theme from this research is that, with respect to urban heat island mitigation, there is not a 'one-size-fits-all' approach – mitigation strategies that are effective in some locations, like green roofs, are likely to be ineffective or inefficient in others (e.g. Georgescu et al. 2014).

A technological advance that has captured the interests of researchers and decision makers is the increasing accessibility (and decreasing cost) of small but reliable electronic devices that are suitable for recording environmental data such as air quality and temperature. These devices have the potential to provide foundational data sets and feed into real-time information management systems for hazard responders that provide the level of detail imagined in our conceptualization of precision governance. Examples of these devices range from mobile sensors that can be attached to clothing or the exterior of a bag, smartphone technology that is carried in purses or in individuals' pockets or hands, and stationary sensors embedded and camouflaged into societal or natural infrastructure such as lamp posts and trees (Khan, Imon, and Das 2015; Hart and Martinez 2006). Yet, another data source includes smart home temperature monitoring technologies such as the Nest thermostat. Data from these types of sources can be crowd-sourced or pooled to better understand at-home thermal conditions and potentially hazardous heat exposure (Chan et al. 2008; Muller et al. 2015). The emergence of these technologies has allowed researchers to collect large amounts of data for which, previously, only crude estimates or models were available.

Information about heat exposure at the human scale has become attainable due to the increasing capacity for researchers to harness the sensing potential of the public, and reciprocally, public interest (or at least cooperation) in participatory or research-oriented monitoring efforts. Engagement in such efforts has multiple motivations. For one, research and governmental institutions may ask members of the public to help collect environmental data by distributing sensors and/or asking individuals to record systematic observations (Conrad and Hilchey 2011). Second, members of the public or community groups may initiate an environmental monitoring effort to advocate for better management of health hazards or environmental conditions (Minkler et al. 2008). Similarly, citizens may voluntarily input observations into mobile smartphone applications to share information about traffic congestion or weather hazards, or in contrast, passively contribute data through smart devices that track environmental and meteorological conditions along with location information (Kamel Boulos et al. 2011). Finally, some individuals are motivated to collect their personal environmental data so as to have a better understanding of their own activities and exposures. This type of monitoring aligns with the 'quantified self' movement that also includes activities like tracking one's weight, measuring exposure to harmful chemicals, or recording the number of steps walked each day (Swan 2009).

An important dichotomy can and should be drawn between spatially explicit and personally explicit environmental data collected by and/or about the public. Spatially explicit data are place dependent and can be gathered passively by smartphones (e.g. Overeem et al. 2013), home-monitoring devices, or by citizen volunteers that regularly record data or make observations in a certain place or along a transect (e.g. Muller et al. 2015). These data are useful for environmental justice efforts that can target excessively hot and marginalized areas of a city (Declet-Barreto et al. 2013) or for higher resolution weather forecasting (Muller et al. 2015). Personally explicit data are person dependent and are recorded wherever the individual happens to be at the time of measurement. For example, an individual may record a car accident, incident of cardiac arrest, or fine particulate matter levels wherever he or she is located at a given time (Kamel Boulos et al. 2011; Minkler et al. 2008). Personally explicit data allows researchers and decision makers to know precisely what conditions members of the public are actually experiencing as they go about their daily lives.

In the context of extreme heat and individual-level intervention, data of interest for researchers and decision makers include the personally explicit ambient air temperatures that individuals experience as they go about their daily lives (hereafter referred to as individually experienced temperatures, or IETs; Kuras, Hondula, and Brown-Saracino 2015). Already, a small number of research teams have utilized small, portable, personal-sensing technology to more precisely and intentionally collect heat exposure and vulnerability data from members of the public (see Basu and Samet 2002; Bernhard et al. 2015; Kuras, Hondula, and Brown-Saracino 2015). Other research groups have creatively used temperature data to identify periods of time when participants were moving between indoor and outdoor settings and therefore exposed to different amounts of air pollution (Nethery et al. 2014) or to assess the relationship between indoor and outdoor temperature and distress calls by attaching temperature monitors to paramedics' bags (Uejio et al. 2016). These efforts have yielded critical insights into hidden vulnerabilities that may otherwise be misclassified through more blunt and conventional monitoring technologies. In the future, these approaches will likely be expanded to include a wider range of variables that are important to consider for human heat stress, including sunlight, wind, humidity, and activity level, but already lay the groundwork for considerable advancements in the type of information that can improve preparation and response.

5. A study of IETs

5.1. *Methods*

To explore how personally explicit environmental data could be used for precision governance interventions, we conducted a study of IETs in the Phoenix area following Kuras, Hondula, and Brown-Saracino (2015). Currently, the framing of many extreme heat intervention measures does not directly take into account individual-level differences in exposure. We sought to determine if individuals living in the same city experience the same heat events differently. The study took place from 20:00 13 September to 20:00 20 September 2014 to capture IETs under warm season conditions. With the exception of 2 days during the study period with unseasonably low temperatures related to the remnants of Hurricane Odile, mean daily temperatures in Phoenix ranged from 30.5°C (87°F) to 35.1°C (95°F) during the study week as measured at Sky Harbor Airport (KPHX). Five greater Phoenix neighbourhoods were selected to provide contrasts in geography, vegetative landscape, demographics, and socioeconomics. From among those neighbourhoods, eighty residents were recruited to participate in the study through information bulletins posted in local businesses, flyers distributed on the street, and emails sent through Homeowner associations and neighbourhood groups. Research participants were equipped with Thermochron iButtons (DS1921G-F5#) that measured and recorded instantaneous air temperatures at 5-min intervals during the study week. Participants were asked to clip their iButtons to a belt loop or bag such that the device was continuously exposed to the surrounding air, thus recording the time series of ambient air temperatures that were also physically 'experienced' by participants as they went about their daily lives, regardless of time spent indoors or outdoors, clothing, or recreational activity. In addition, participants were asked to record any period of time in which they were not carrying their iButtons (these data removed prior to analysis). IET data were later averaged to 15-min intervals for reporting purposes and pseudonyms were used to protect participant confidentiality. All times are reported in Local Daylight Time.

5.2. *Results*

In line with the findings of other personal heat exposure assessments, temperatures recorded at KPHX overestimated IETs of research participants, especially on hot days (Figure 1, Kuras, Hondula, and Brown-Saracino 2015; Bernhard et al. 2015, Basu and Samet 2002). However, the highest IET measurement from among any participant

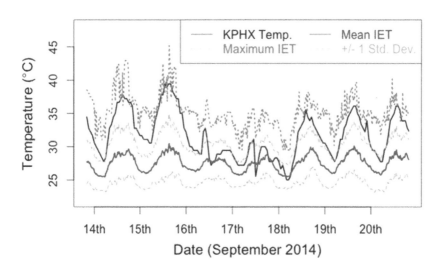

Figure 1. Temperatures recorded at Phoenix Sky Harbor International Airport (KPHX, solid black line) and mean individually experienced temperatures (IETs, solid blue line) from 13 to 20 September 2014. One positive and negative standard deviation from the mean (dashed grey lines) and maximum IET (dotted red line) are presented as well.

was consistently recorded at or above KPHX temperatures (maximum IET in Figure 1).

To illustrate the utility of IET data in providing precise information about who is experiencing high temperatures and when, we focus on IET data for Monday, 15 September, on which temperatures recorded at KPHX ranged from 30.6°C (87°F) to 39.4°C (103°F) (Figure 2). Again, the majority of participants recorded IETs multiple degrees lower than outdoor temperatures while the hot outliers were exposed to temperatures mostly in excess of conditions at KPHX, especially during the night-time hours.

For each hour on Monday, IETs in the top 5 per cent from among all participants were examined to identify the individuals who experienced the highest temperatures. We focus on three individuals, Dolores, Hunter, and Iris, with contrasting time periods of high exposure to demonstrate how IETs can help refine our intervention strategies (Figure 3). Dolores had among the highest percentage of IETs in the top 5 per cent (36.4 per cent of all her Monday measurements), followed by Hunter (29.2 per cent of Monday measurements) and Iris (20.8 per cent). A number of observations concerning patterns of exposure can be made by comparing the IETs of Dolores, Hunter, and Iris on Monday. First, high IETs during the night-time period suggest that some participants did not use or have access to home cooling devices. This observation applies to Dolores, whose morning IET tracked KPHX temperatures more closely than Hunter and Iris. Dolores recorded similarly high night-time IETs, which further supports the suggestion that she did not use a home cooling strategy. Second, occasional and short spikes in IETs suggest that some participants were exposed to heat for only small durations at a time. Around 3 P.M., Dolores experienced one of these peaks, as did Iris from 6 to 7 P.M. Third, some participants experienced high temperatures for sustained periods of time during the daytime

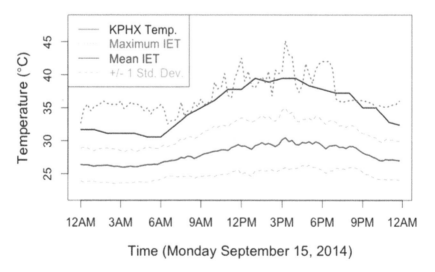

Figure 2. Temperatures recorded at Phoenix Sky Harbor International Airport (KPHX, solid black line) and mean individually experienced temperatures (IETs, solid blue line) on Monday, 15 September 2014. One positive and negative standard deviation from the mean (dashed grey lines) and maximum IET (dotted red line) are presented as well.

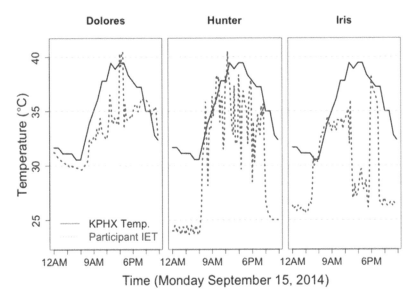

Figure 3. Individually experienced temperatures (IETs, dotted blue lines) of three selected participants as well as temperatures recorded at Phoenix Sky Harbor International Airport (KPHX, solid black line) on Monday, 15 September 2014.

hours. Hunter broadly recorded high IETs from 7 A.M. to 8 P.M., although the variability in his IETs suggests that his thermal conditions changed frequently throughout the day. Iris more consistently recorded high IETs from 4 A.M. to 12 P.M. although it was the IETs from 4 to 8 A.M. that were among the top 5 per cent from all participants in that time range. Both cases of more sustained heat exposure may have been due to occupational or lifestyle factors. For example, Hunter or Iris may have worked in a hot restaurant kitchen or taken long walks outside.

5.3. *Discussion*

On an individual scale, IET data can enable interventions in which members of the public that opt to passively record their experienced temperatures receive tailored information about heat-health risks and resources. For individuals like Dolores who have high IETs during the overnight hours, information that enables the individual to have expanded access to home cooling devices would lower the risk of heat-related illness. Such interventions may include assistance with cooling bill payments, weatherization, and air conditioning repair. For individuals such as Dolores and Iris that are exposed to high temperatures sporadically and for a short amount of time, personalized heat-health warning messages may avert a heat emergency distress call. These messages could be triggered when individuals have exceeded a predetermined and personalized threshold for heat-health risk and could inform individuals of their current risk and provide useful suggestions such as nearby cooling and hydrating resources (e.g. cooling centres, air-conditioned public spaces with water fountains, cafes, convenience stores) and heat-health advice (how to stay hydrated, how to identify symptoms of heat stress, and how to seek medical attention). For those like Hunter and Iris who experience sustained high temperatures for a longer period of time, similarly tailored messages may have a positive impact, especially if they also provide information about heat-health risks and resources associated with occupation or lifestyle.

On a collective scale, IET data can assist health agencies and emergency managers to better identify and engage at-risk populations at critical intervention points by revealing temporal and spatial patterns of exposure and vulnerability. With more precise information about who experiences high night-time temperatures, short peaks, or sustained periods of high temperatures, decision makers can more effectively target a heat-exposed population or place with the appropriate short-term information resources or longer term cooling, hydrating, educational and economic resources meant to proactively prevent heat stress.

On a hot day such as Monday, 15 September 2014, a blanket heat warning would not necessarily provide useful, or meaningful information to Dolores, Hunter, Iris, or, as we can infer from heterogeneous IETs reported elsewhere (Kuras, Hondula, and Brown-Saracino 2015), many residents of the Phoenix metropolitan area. Such contrasting experiences in heat exposure necessitate a transition towards precision governance in which we more effectively target the people, times, and places of highest vulnerability with evidence-based, tailored, and useful interventions and management of this public hazard.

6. Ethical considerations for precision governance

Evidence-informed policy should be better positioned to address public problems than policy based on anecdotal experience or informal beliefs (Quade 1975). Yet, governance relies on a combination of truthful claims and the representation of values, with participants engaged in rational discourse aimed at reaching universally acceptable decisions (Habermas 1996). More data should mean less arguing about 'facts,' with greater energy devoted to discussing values and the interpretation of uncertainty. A more colloquial expression of the relationship between facts and values in political discourse has been expressed as 'everyone is entitled to his own opinion, but not to his own facts,' a quotation often attributed to the late US Senator Daniel Patrick Moynihan. As a sentiment emerging from the golden age of policy debate during which Senator Moynihan was a key player, the quote efficiently parses the politics/administration dichotomy and the relationship between values and evidence, between beliefs and facts: we may differ on what the best course of action ought to be, but we can surely agree on what *is* is. The attraction of this idea has recently been revived in the context of political controversies such as 'climate science denial,' in which disagreements about values (e.g. Are humans responsible for future generations and other species? What is a tolerable rate of climate change for the planet's ecosystems and people? Should individual freedom of choice be subservient to collective well-being?) are often being shielded behind disputes about the fact of anthropogenic influence on climate. In this environment, disagreements between facts and opinions become conflated and resolution becomes seemingly impossible.

It is in such an arena that we can understand the appeal of greater precision in governance through more data, more detailed analytics and increasing certainty over 'the facts.' We now have the ability to measure phenomena like heat exposure more precisely, continuously over time and space, to assemble data that dwarfs the data limits of previous generations. Scientists and analysts are regularly improving their methods for interpreting these data and extracting actionable information from them. Despite these advances, there are several ethical reflections that practitioners, governance participants, and decision makers should consider when seeking to advance the greater use of data in support of governance.

First is to understand the limitations of what data and analysis can reveal about truth, regardless of the volume of data accumulated. It is tempting to believe that, with massive volumes of data from very large numbers of individuals, big data provide an increasingly clear picture of all relevant entities. However, depending on the methods for data collection, some people will fail to be represented in big data regardless of the volume collected. In this setting, prior concerns over the digital divide take on a new dimension where the experiences of some people are not captured in current data collection methods. In proposing a concept of the 'digitally invisible,' Longo et al. (2017) suggest that big data analysis based on smartphone use, Internet of Everything devices, and electronic payment transactions will be biased against those in societies who do not regularly use those devices and cards. Benoit (2015, np) has called this problem 'the myth of $N = $ All' and argues that it presents a particular challenge in the context of growing use of data for policy-making.

Second, data-driven governance should acknowledge the post-positivist observation that there is no airtight distinction between facts and values, and that data collection and analysis is a product of the biases and subjective worldview of the researcher (Fischer 2003). What to study, how to study it and what is seen when it is studied are all influenced by the researcher's values. Also, data can only be translated into actionable information through judgments made by analysts or decision makers (Majone 1989). There is no algorithm or artificial intelligence that can substitute for the presence and necessity of values-based decision-making.

Privacy and security are also crucial concerns. One challenge involves the difficulty of protecting personally identifiable information in anonymized population data sets, a computational process alternatively referred to as re-identification or de-anonymization. A different privacy issue emerges in the context of informed consent. Debates continue as to whether it is ethical to conduct research on people without their expressed consent – a subject normally the domain of research ethics committees – because the data in question involve public statements on social media sites. De-anonymization is one challenge (Zimmer 2008), as is the taking-out-of-context of public statements made by identifiable individuals (Boyd and Crawford 2012). Manipulation of variables that affect 'research subjects' became an area of concern in 2014 when the news feeds of over 600,000 Facebook users were modified to test the theory of emotional contagion (Kramer, Guillory, and Hancock 2014). Concerns were raised following the publication of the study that the research involved 'practices that were not fully consistent with the principles of obtaining fully informed consent and allowing participants to opt out' (Verma 2014).

The use of large data sets to identify correlations as an aid to predict future events (or how to react to them) has emerged in domains ranging from policing to lending. Predictive policing involves analysing high volume and continuous data flows, including social media and telephone metadata, to predict where future crimes are more likely to occur, so that police forces can allocate resources accordingly. Concerns have been raised about over-prediction of crime, police bias, a lack of evidence that such systems actually reduce crime, and the abdication of decision-making to opaque algorithms promoted by for-profit firms (Joh 2014). New firms have emerged that provide credit-worthiness evaluations of potential borrowers based on their social media presence. 'Digital redlining' is the process of identifying locations or networks to exclude individual or groups from things like access to credit (White House 2014). In both cases, previous protections – e.g. against unlawful search, or fairness in credit evaluations – are being challenged by the use of data and advances in technology. Ultimately, precision governance should not be seen as a substitute for human decision-making that replaces or limits discretion by either the bureaucrat or the citizen. Rather it can serve to augment informed decision-making. Towards that end the question becomes first whether or not these information interventions are useful at achieving each party's desired outcome, and second, what training or additional context is needed to increase the likelihood that both groups will understand the strengths and limitations of the precision governance approach.

Finally, the call for precision governance acknowledges prior experience with personalization in public management and service delivery (Needham 2011). Identified largely with the Blair government in the United Kingdom, personalization was applied to a range of policy areas including social services, healthcare, and education. Through personalization, citizens were given greater control over the delivery of public services with the intention of improving people's lives, increasing efficiency, and focusing on the needs of the client from their individual perspective. Despite its strong support across the political spectrum, Ferguson (2007) notes that 'some of its implications may be less than benign both for those who provide social work services and even more so for those who use them.' Personalization derives from the earlier concept of 'street-level bureaucrats' (Lipsky 1980), identifying the public servants who deal directly with the clients and targets of service delivery and who often exercise discretion in service delivery by being its closest connection to their needs. But where street-level bureaucracy envisions the embodiment of discretion within the purview of the public servant, dealing one-on-one with a client across the desk, personalization at the scale of whole societies risks stereotyping individuals based on data correlates. While precision governance can serve to make policy interventions more relevant to the individual, it must guard against stigmatizing them as 'at-risk' or 'in-need.'

7. Discussion and opportunities for precision governance

The role of information in the design of good governance infrastructures is increasingly important, as data are a public good that can be used to serve a public purpose (see Johnston et al. 2013). An informed public has always been seen as central to realizing the potential of democratic governance but *it has always been treated as an assumption, not as an intervention.*

In the preceding sections, we have described how the coarseness of existing interventions for natural hazards, and specifically extreme heat, leaves us short of the notion of precision governance we can imagine with the rich data sources and data-driven tools becoming available today and in the near future. We have also presented the results of a case study based on individual experiences demonstrating that there may be a strong opportunity gap in the management of health risks associated with high temperature exposure that could be addressed with innovative governance infrastructures. To conclude, we present hypothetical use cases for individual-based data about heat exposure as a means of illustrating the possibilities of precision governance. The types of improvements that are possible include over-arching elements like better communication, tailored messaging, proactive engage-ment of at-risk populations at critical intervention points, and generation of feedback loops that promote learning and improve decision making. We do not intend to prescribe specific preparation or intervention strategies, as their design requires a much wider array of perspectives and expertise. Instead, our goal in imagining the cases below is to demonstrate how the movement towards precision governance creates opportunity spaces to ask new and important questions about connecting people, government, and technology for public protection from hazards.

Our first case imagines individualized information about heat delivered through mobile platforms. Such an intervention based on information enables the self-regula-tion of individuals to avoid extreme heat by using emerging sensor technologies. In the context of extreme heat, the data of interest are the temperatures that people experience and their resulting physiological state as they go about their daily lives. In cases of overheating, individuals should minimize their exposure well before any adverse physiological symptoms are noticeable. Certain smartphones are already able to alert users when they – the phones themselves – become too hot for safe operation of the internal hardware. But soon analogous technology could be available to alert phone *owners* when they – the people – are in danger far earlier than the onset of physiological symptoms.

Indeed, mobile technology already serves as the basis for enhanced communica-tion of warnings related to weather, geologic, and terrorism-related hazards through the Wireless Emergency Alert (WEA) system managed by the Federal Emergency Management Agency and other federal organizations (see Casteel and Downing 2013). Currently, WEAs are not issued for extreme heat. This may be an appropriate policy decision as the nature of the hazard posed by heat is different than that posed by an oncoming severe thunderstorm or tsunami – unusual sheltering or evacuation procedures are not needed by a majority of the population. But could WEAs related to heat be effective for a small portion of the population who are likely to, or do experience, severe heat conditions for a prolonged period of time? If those individuals could be detected and alerted, what type of information could be delivered to them that would facilitate their decision-making process for seeking relief? We find it easy to imagine that it will soon be possible to use information about heat exposure that could be streamed in real time, to communicate directly with those at risk or others who could intervene. The information could very well improve the effectiveness of strategies for lowering risk ranging from better timing of taking breaks and drinking water to accessing nearby cooling and medical resources. We suggest that these improvements would occur because contextualized information would be more likely to compel behaviour change than a broad message.

A second use case where we envision that change in governance of hazards could occur concerns the ability of organizations to evaluate their performance in hazard preparedness and response. While there is little doubt that the short- and long-term initiatives for heat risk reduction currently in place in jurisdictions across the world have had substantial benefits, there is as of yet no means for systematic documentation of the collective benefits of these initiatives for public health. Evaluating programmes strictly based on records of health outcomes can only provide correlative evidence of success, and disentangling the benefits of the interventions from other factors that may influence health outcomes has proven to be a methodological challenge for the field thus far (Toloo et al. 2013; Boeckmann and Rohn 2014). This severely inhibits the ability of organizations – including government agencies – to know which strategies are most helpful and cost-effective as well as to accurately forecast what the future public health burden of heat may be in a given area. In our local setting, an important operational decision for protecting vulnerable populations from extreme heat is establishing the opening and closing hours for cooling centres. With data about thermal exposure at the individual level becoming available, it may be possible to provide more precise scheduling guidance. Individual-level data also make it possible to directly study or monitor in real time the changing thermal conditions of populations of interest when certain intervention measures are enacted. Compared to the current baseline of having no, or only very coarse and unreliable, indicators to evaluate heat intervention measures, this would seem to be a vast improvement. Further, because quantifying the impact of heat adaptation strategies is absent from much of the literature aimed at projecting the public health burden associated with climate change (Deschenes 2014; Hondula et al. 2015), developing these types of evaluation metrics can also inform efforts to construct long-term adaptation and mitigation plans and policies.

In summary, our observations of the state of modern hazards governance, and the results from our studies and others with personal ambient temperature sensors, suggested that generalized approaches to heat preparedness and response are not as efficient as the precision approaches possible with information interventions because many people experience heat differently on the same day. The design of this type of information intervention for precision governance that includes data preparation, analysis, targeted communication, and then local responses can serve as a model for many other governance challenges that will likewise benefit from the increased availability of data that can be used for public good. To do so effectively will require that governments invest in building capacity in precision governance as a best practice and essential competency. Governments have historically faced the challenge of viewing information technology projects as 'special circumstances' instead of a necessary capacity, leading to the propensity to view contracting-out for IT services as the most efficient mechanism. The developing field of data analytics risks tumbling down the same slope, where external experts hold the reins of the new powerful technologies, with those inside government left to ponder the meaning of these new analytic techniques. Seeing information technology or precision governance as external to the primary functions of government is short-sighted. Building information and data capacities within government must be seen as a generational challenge in training and practice (Johnston 2015).

Acknowledgements

The authors thank Keren Hirsch at the Center for Policy Informatics at Arizona State University for editing the manuscript, as well as Sharon Harlan at Northeastern University and Ben Ruddell at Arizona State University for their support of research projects discussed herein.

Disclosure statement

No potential conflict of interest was reported by the authors.

Funding

This work was supported by the Virginia G. Piper Health Policy Informatics Initiative at Arizona State University and by the National Science Foundation under grant number BCS-1026865, Central Arizona-Phoenix Long-Term Ecological Research (CAP LTER).

References

Barnes, L. R., E. C. Gruntfest, M. H. Hayden, D. M. Schultz, and C. Benight. 2007. "False Alarms and Close Calls: A Conceptual Model of Warning Accuracy." *Weather And Forecasting* 22 (5): 1140-1147. doi:10.1175/WAF1031.1.

Bassil, K. L., and D. C. Cole. 2010. "Effectiveness of Public Health Interventions in Reducing Morbidity and Mortality during Heat Episodes: A Structured Review." *International Journal of Environmental Research and Public Health* 7 (3): 991-1001. doi:10.3390/ijerph7030991.

Basu, R., and J. M. Samet. 2002. "An Exposure Assessment Study of Ambient Heat Exposure in an Elderly Population in Baltimore, Maryland." *Environ Health Perspect* 110 (12): 1219-1224. doi:10.1289/ehp.021101219.

Benoit, K. 2015. "Ten Challenges of Big Data for Social Science." Presented at the conference Policy Making in the Big Data Era: Opportunities and Challenges, June 15-17. University of Cambridge, Cambridge, UK.

Berko, J., D. D. Ingram, S. Saha, and J. D. Parker. 2014. "Deaths Attributed to Heat, Cold, and Other Weather Events in the United States, 2006-2010." *National Health Statistics Reports* 76: 1-15.

Bernhard, M. C., S. T. Kent, M. E. Sloan, M. B. Evans, L. A. Mcclure, and J. M. Gohlke. 2015. "Measuring Personal Heat Exposure in an Urban and Rural Environment." *Environmental Research* 137: 410-418. doi:10.1016/j.envres.2014.11.002.

Boeckmann, M., and I. Rohn. 2014. "Is Planned Adaptation to Heat Reducing Heat-Related Mortality and Illness? A Systematic Review." *BMC Public Health* 14 (1): 1112. doi:10.1186/1471-2458-14-1112.

Boyd, D., and K. Crawford. 2012. "Critical Questions for Big Data: Provocations for a Cultural, Technological, and Scholarly Phenomenon." *Information, Communication & Society* 15 (5): 662–679, doi:10.1080/1369118X.2012.678878.

Casteel, M. A., and J. R. Downing. 2013. "How Individuals Process NWS Weather Warning Messages on Their Cell Phones." *Weather, Climate, and Society* 5 (3): 254–265. doi:10.1175/WCAS-D-12-00031.1.

Chan, M., D. Estève, C. Escriba, and E. Campo. 2008. "A Review of Smart Homes- Present State and Future Challenges." *Computer Methods and Programs in Biomedicine* 91 (1): 55–81. doi:10.1016/j.cmpb.2008.02.001.

Chow, W. T., D. Brennan, and A. J. Brazel. 2012. "Urban Heat Island Research in Phoenix, Arizona: Theoretical Contributions and Policy Applications." *Bulletin of the American Meteorological Society* 93 (4): 517–530. doi:10.1175/BAMS-D-11-00011.1.

Conrad, C. C., and K. G. Hilchey. 2011. "A Review of Citizen Science and Community-Based Environmental Monitoring: Issues and Opportunities." *Environmental Monitoring and Assessment* 176 (1–4): 273–291. doi:10.1007/s10661-010-1582-5.

Conti, S., P. Meli, G. Minelli, R. Solimini, V. Toccaceli, M. Vichi, ... L. Perini. 2005. "Epidemiologic Study of Mortality during the Summer 2003 Heat Wave in Italy." *Environmental Research* 98 (3): 390–399. doi:10.1016/j.envres.2004.10.009.

Declet-Barreto, J., A. J. Brazel, C. A. Martin, W. T. L. Chow, and S. L. Harlan. 2013. "Creating the Park Cool Island in an Inner-City Neighborhood: Heat Mitigation Strategy for Phoenix, AZ." *Urban Ecosystems* 16 (3): 617–635. doi:10.1007/s11252-012-0278-8.

Deschenes, O. 2014. "Temperature, Human Health, and Adaptation: A Review of the Empirical Literature." *Energy Economics* 46: 606–619. doi:10.1016/j.eneco.2013.10.013.

Ferguson, I. 2007. "Increasing User Choice or Privatizing Risk? the Antinomies of Personalization." *British Journal of Social Work* 37 (3): 387–403. doi:10.1093/bjsw/bcm016.

Fischer, F. 2003. *Reframing Public Policy: Discursive Politics and Deliberative Practices.* New York: Oxford University Press.

Georgescu, M., P. E. Morefield, B. G. Bierwagen, and C. P. Weaver. 2014. "Urban Adaptation Can Roll Back Warming of Emerging Megapolitan Regions." *Proceedings of the National Academy of Sciences* 111 (8): 2909–2914. doi:10.1073/pnas.1322280111.

Habermas, J. 1996. *Between Facts and Norms.* Translated by W. Rehg. Cambridge: MIT Press.

Harlan, S. L., J. H. Declet-Barreto, W. L. Stefanov, and D. B. Petitti. 2012. "Neighborhood Effects on Heat Deaths: Social and Environmental Predictors of Vulnerability in Maricopa County, Arizona." *Environmental Health Perspectives* 121 (2): 197–204. doi:10.1289/ehp.1104625.

Hart, J. K., and K. Martinez. 2006. "Environmental Sensor Networks: A Revolution in the Earth System Science?" *Earth-Science Reviews* 78 (3–4): 177–191. doi:10.1016/j.earscirev.2006.05.001.

Hayden, M. H., H. Brenkert-Smith, and O. V. Wilhelmi. 2011. "Differential Adaptive Capacity to Extreme Heat: A Phoenix, Arizona, Case Study." *Weather, Climate, and Society* 3 (4): 269–280. doi:10.1175/WCAS-D-11-00010.1.

Hess, J. J., M. Eidson, J. E. Tlumak, K. K. Raab, and G. Luber. 2014. "An Evidence-Based Public Health Approach to Climate Change Adaptation." *Environmental Health Perspectives* 122 (11): 1177–1186.

Hondula, D. M., M. Georgescu, and R. C. Balling. 2014. "Challenges Associated with Projecting Urbanization-Induced Heat-Related Mortality." *Science of the Total Environment* 490: 538–544. doi:10.1016/j.scitotenv.2014.04.130.

Hondula, D. M., R. C. Balling Jr, J. K. Vanos, and M. Georgescu. 2015. "Rising Temperatures, Human Health, and the Role of Adaptation." *Current Climate Change Reports* 1 (3): 144–154. doi:10.1007/s40641-015-0016-4.

Hu, Q., and N. Kapucu. 2016. "Information Communication Technology Utilization for Effective Emergency Management Networks." *Public Management Review* 18 (3): 323-348. doi:10.1080/14719037.2014.969762

Joh, E. E. 2014. "Policing by Numbers: Big Data and the Fourth Amendment." *Washington Law Review* 89: 35–68.

Johnston, E., R. Krishnamurthy, T. Musgrave, and A. Vinze. 2013. *How Open Data Moves Us Closer to "Precision Governance"*. Washington, DC: International City/County Management Association.

Johnston, E. W. (Ed.) (2015). *Governance in the Information Era: Theory and Practice of Policy Informatics*. New York, NY: Routledge Press.

Kalkstein, A. J., and S. C. Sheridan. 2007. "The Social Impacts of the Heat–Health Watch/Warning System in Phoenix, Arizona: Assessing the Perceived Risk and Response of the Public." *International Journal of Biometeorology* 52 (1): 43–55. doi:10.1007/s00484-006-0073-4.

Kamel Boulos, M. N., B. Resch, D. N. Crowley, J. G. Breslin, G. Sohn, R. Burtner, ... K.-Y. Chuang. 2011. "Crowdsourcing, Citizen Sensing and Sensor Web Technologies for Public and Environmental Health Surveillance and Crisis Management: Trends, OGC Standards and Application Examples." *International Journal of Health Geographics* 10 (1): 67. doi:10.1186/1476-072X-10-67.

Kapucu, N. 2009. "Performance under Stress: Managing Emergencies and Disasters: Introduction." *Public Performance & Management Review* 32 (3): 339–344. doi:10.2753/PMR1530-9576320300.

Khan, A., S. K. A. Imon, and S. K. Das. 2015. "A Novel Localization and Coverage Framework for Real-Time Participatory Urban Monitoring." *Pervasive and Mobile Computing* 1–17. doi:10.1016/j.pmcj.2015.07.001.

Knowlton, K., M. Rotkin-Ellman, L. Geballe, W. Max, and G. M. Solomon. 2011. "Six Climate Change–Related Events in the United States Accounted for about $14 Billion in Lost Lives and Health Costs." *Health Affairs* 30 (11): 2167–2176. doi:10.1377/hlthaff.2011.0229.

Kramer, A. D., J. E. Guillory, and J. T. Hancock. 2014. "Experimental Evidence of Massive-Scale Emotional Contagion through Social Networks." *Proceedings of the National Academy of Sciences* 111 (24): 8788–8790. doi:10.1073/pnas.1320040111.

Kuras, E. R., D. M. Hondula, and J. Brown-Saracino. 2015. "Heterogeneity in Individually Experienced Temperatures (Iets) within an Urban Neighborhood: Insights from a New Approach to Measuring Heat Exposure." *International Journal of Biometeorology* 59: 1363–1372. doi:10.1007/s00484-014-0946-x.

Kuras, E.R., Bernhard, M. C., Calkins, M.M., Ebi, K.L., Hess, J.J., Middel, A., et al. 2017. "Opportunites and Challenges for Personal Heat Exposure Research". *Environmental Health Perspectives*. doi:10.1289/EHP556.

Leech, J. A., W. C. Nelson, R. T. Burnett, S. Aaron, and M. E. Raizenne. 2002. "It's about Time: A Comparison of Canadian and American Time-Activity Patterns." *Journal of Exposure Analysis and Environmental Epidemiology* 12 (6): 427–432. doi:10.1038/sj.jea.7500244.

Lin, S., W. H. Hsu, A. R. Van Zutphen, S. Saha, G. Luber, and S. A. Hwang. 2012. "Excessive Heat and Respiratory Hospitalizations in New York State: Estimating Current and Future Public Health Burden Related to Climate Change." *Environmental Health Perspectives* 120 (1): 1571–1577. doi:10.1289/ehp.1104728.

Lipsky, M. 1980. *Street-Level Bureaucracy: Dilemmas of the Individual in Public Service*. New York: Russell Sage Foundation.

Longo, J., E. Kuras, H. Smith, D. M. Hondula, and E. Johnston. 2017. "Technology Use, Exposure to Natural Hazards, and Being Digitally Invisible: Implications for Policy Analytics." *Policy & Internet* 9 (1): 76-108. doi:10.1002/poi3.144.

Lowe, D., K. L. Ebi, and B. Forsberg. 2011. "Heatwave Early Warning Systems and Adaptation Advice to Reduce Human Health Consequences of Heatwaves." *International Journal of Environmental Research and Public Health* 8 (12): 4623–4648. doi:10.3390/ijerph8124623.

Luber, G., and M. McGeehin. 2008. "Climate Change and Extreme Heat Events." *American Journal of Preventive Medicine* 35 (5): 429–435. doi:10.1016/j.amepre.2008.08.021.

Majone, G. 1989. *Evidence, Argument and Persuasion in the Policy Process*. New Haven, CT: Yale University Press.

MCDPH (Maricopa County Department of Public Health). 2014. "Heat-Associated Deaths in Maricopa County, AZ." Final Report for 2014. http://www.maricopa.gov/publichealth/Services/EPI/pdf/heat/2014annualreport.pdf.

McMichael, A. J., P. Wilkinson, R. S. Kovats, S. Pattenden, S. Hajat, B. Armstrong, ... B. Nikiforov. 2008. "International Study of Temperature, Heat and Urban Mortality: The 'Isothurm'project." *International Journal of Epidemiology* 37 (5): 1121–1131. doi:10.1093/ije/dyn086.

Minkler, M., V. B. Vásquez, M. Tajik, and D. Petersen. 2008. "Promoting Environmental Justice through Community-Based Participatory Research: The Role of Community and Partnership Capacity." *Health Education & Behavior* 35 (1): 119–137. doi:10.1177/1090198106287692.

Morabito, M., A. Crisci, B. Gioli, G. Gualtieri, P. Toscano, V. Di Stefano, G. F. Gensini, and K. Dalal. 2015. "Urban-Hazard Risk Analysis: Mapping of Heat-Related Risks in the Elderly in Major Italian Cities." *Plos One*. doi:10.1371/journal.pone.0127277.

Muller, C. L., L. Chapman, S. Johnston, C. Kidd, S. Illingworth, G. Foody, and R. R. Leigh. 2015. "Crowdsourcing for Climate and Atmospheric Sciences: Current Status and Future Potential." *International Journal of Climatology* 35: 3185–3203. doi:10.1002/joc.4210.

Needham, C. 2011. *Personalising Public Services: Understanding the Personalisation Narrative.* London: Policy Press.

Nethery, E., G. Mallach, D. Rainham, M. S. Goldberg, and A. J. Wheeler. 2014. "Using Global Positioning Systems (GPS) and Temperature Data to Generate Time-Activity Classifications for Estimating Personal Exposure in Air Monitoring Studies: An Automated Method." *Environmental Health : A Global Access Science Source* 13 (1): 33. doi:10.1186/1476-069X-13-33.

Ohashi, Y., T. Ihara, Y. Kikegawa, and N. Sugiyama. 2015. "Numerical Simulations of Influence of Heat Island Countermeasures on Outdoor Human Heat Stress in the 23 Wards of Tokyo, Japan." *Energy and Buildings* 114: 104–111. doi:10.1016/j.enbuild.2015.06.027.

Overeem, A. R., J. C. Robinson, H. Leijnse, G. J. P. Steeneveld, B. K. Horn, and R. Uijlenhoet. 2013. "Crowdsourcing Urban Air Temperatures from Smartphone Battery Temperatures." *Geophysical Research Letters* 40 (15): 4081–4085. doi:10.1002/grl.50786.

Pascal, M., K. Laaidi, M. Ledrans, E. Baffert, C. Caserio-Schönemann, A. Le Tertre, ... P. Empereur-Bissonnet. 2006. "France's Heat Health Watch Warning System." *International Journal of Biometeorology* 50 (3): 144–153. doi:10.1007/s00484-005-0003-x.

Patz, J. A., D. Campbell-Lendrum, T. Holloway, and J. A. Foley. 2005. "Impact of Regional Climate Change on Human Health." *Nature* 438 (7066): 310–317. doi:10.1038/nature04188.

Petitti, D. B., D. M. Hondula, S. Yang, S. L. Harlan, and G. Chowell. 2015. "Multiple Trigger Points for Quantifying Heat-Health Impacts: New Evidence from a Hot Climate." *Environmental Health Perspectives* 124. doi:10.1289/ehp.1409119.

Quade, E. 1975. *Policy Analysis for Public Decisions.* New York: Elsevier.

Robinson, S. E., W. S. Eller, M. Gall, and B. J. Gerber. 2013. "The Core and Periphery of Emergency Management Networks." *Public Management Review* 15 (3): 344–362. doi:10.1080/14719037.2013.769849.

Rosenthal, J. K., P. L. Kinney, and K. B. Metzger. 2014. "Intra-Urban Vulnerability to Heat-Related Mortality in New York City, 1997–2006." *Health & Place* 30: 45–60. doi:10.1016/j.healthplace.2014.07.014.

Ruddell, D. M., S. L. Harlan, S. Grossman-Clarke, and A. Buyantuyev. 2009. "Risk and Exposure to Extreme Heat in Microclimates of Phoenix, AZ." In *Geospatial Techniques in Urban Hazard and Disaster Analysis,* edited by P. S. Showalter and Y. Lu, 179–202. Netherlands: Springer.

Semenza, J. C., C. H. Rubin, K. H. Falter, J. D. Selanikio, W. D. Flanders, H. L. Howe, and J. L. Wilhelm. 1996. "Heat-Related Deaths during the July 1995 Heat Wave in Chicago." *New England Journal of Medicine* 335 (2): 84–90. doi:10.1056/NEJM199607113350203.

Solecki, W. D., C. Rosenzweig, L. Parshall, G. Pope, M. Clark, J. Cox, and M. Wiencke. 2005. "Mitigation of the Heat Island Effect in Urban New Jersey." *Global Environmental Change Part B: Environmental Hazards* 6 (1): 39–49.

Swan, M. 2009. "Emerging Patient-Driven Health Care Models: An Examination of Health Social Networks, Consumer Personalized Medicine and Quantified Self-Tracking." *International Journal of Environmental Research and Public Health* 6 (2): 492–525. doi:10.3390/ijerph6020492.

Toloo, G., G. FitzGerald, P. Aitken, K. Verrall, and S. Tong. 2013. "Evaluating the Effectiveness of Heat Warning Systems: Systematic Review of Epidemiological Evidence." *International Journal of Public Health* 58 (5): 667–681. doi:10.1007/s00038-013-0465-2.

Uejio, C. K., J. D. Tamerius, J. Vredenburg, G. Asaeda, D. A. Isaacs, J. Braun, A. Quinn, and J. P. Freese. 2016. "Summer Indoor Heat Exposure and Respiratory and Cardiovascular Distress Calls in New York City, NY, Us". *Indoor Air* 26: 594–604. doi: 10.1111/ina.12227.

Verma, I. M. 2014. "Editorial: Expression of Concern: Experimental Evidence of Massive Scale Emotional Contagion through Social Networks." *PNAS Early Edition.* http://www.pnas.org/content/111/29/10779.1.full

White House. 2014. *Big Data: Seizing Opportunities, Preserving Values.* Washington, DC: Executive Office of the President. https://www.whitehouse.gov/sites/default/files/docs/big_data_privacy_report_may_1_2014.pdf.

White-Newsome, J. L., S. McCormick, N. Sampson, M. A. Buxton, M. S. O'Neill, C. J. Gronlund, … E. A. Parker. 2014. "Strategies to Reduce the Harmful Effects of Extreme Heat Events: A Four-City Study." *International Journal of Environmental Research and Public Health* 11 (2): 1960–1988. doi:10.3390/ijerph110201960.

Winkler, M. S., M. Röösli, M. S. Ragettli, G. Cissé, P. Müller, J. Utzinger, and L. Perez. 2015. "Mitigating and Adapting to Climate Change: A Call to Public Health Professionals." *International Journal of Public Health* 60 (6): 1–2. doi:10.1007/s00038-015-0722-7

Zhao, Y., A. Ducharne, B. Sultan, P. Braconnot, and R. Vautard. 2015. "Estimating Heat Stress from Climate-Based Indicators: Present-Day Biases and Future Spreads in the CMIP5 Global Climate Model Ensemble." *Environmental Research Letters* 10 (8): 084013. doi:10.1088/1748-9326/10/8/084013.

Zimmer, M. 2008. "The Externalities of Search 2.0: The Emerging Privacy Threats when the Drive for the Perfect Search Engine Meets Web 2.0." *First Monday* 13 (3). doi:10.5210/fm.v13i3.2136

Preparing public managers for the digital era: incorporating information management, use, and technology into public affairs graduate curricula

Qian Hu

ABSTRACT

This study examines how current public affairs graduate programmes prepare students for governing in the digital age and offer suggestions for how to better incorporate information management, use, and technology into public affairs curricula in the United States. Through surveys of graduate programme directors and content analysis of course syllabi, this study shows that current curricula have failed to keep pace with rapid changes in the industry. Courses on information management, use, and technology need to balance their focus on technology with their focus on government. It remains a challenge to integrate information management, use, and technology topics into mainstream management and policy foci.

Introduction

The recent rapid growth of information technology (IT) has presented public managers with many new challenges in governance, giving rise to questions about how graduate programmes in public affairs,[1] policy, management, and administration are preparing future public managers for information management, use, and technology in a digital era. Over the past few decades, e-government research has been sharply criticized for having a lack of theory development and for being too focused on technology itself (Norris and Lloyd 2006; Yildiz 2007, 2012). Likewise, on the practical side, e-government projects face all kinds of challenges. The meltdown of HealthCare.gov is a recent example of an e-government failure. The multifaceted challenge facing HealthCare.gov demonstrates the existence of design–reality gaps in e-government practice, in which the federal government was critiqued for mismanaging contracts and failing to coordinate with the technical team to design and launch the massive service website. The website's failed launch sparked questions and doubts about the legitimacy of the Obama administration's signature policy initiative – the Patient Protection and Affordable Care Act. The unsuccessful implementation of IT impeded the accomplishment of such a major policy initiative. Another example is the lack of quality data that state governments encounter when embracing initiatives on big data (Barrett and Green 2015). Although the availability of big data brought enormous potential for understanding public service needs and improving public management, many state agencies do not have access to quality data to conduct analytics, and some agencies are reluctant to share data and collaborate with one another (Barrett and Green 2015). Other underlying causes of e-government failures may include a lack of technology capacity, untrained workers, and institutional barriers (Barrett and Green 2015; Coursey and Norris 2008).

Many e-government failures may be reconsidered through an educational perspective. The HealthCare.gov issue, the bad data problem, and many other e-government challenges may reflect a largely neglected issue in our graduate public affairs programmes – that is, a lack of robust and innovative curricula on information management, use, and technology for public managers. With a number of exceptions (i.e. Brown and Brudney 1998; Dawes 2004; Kim and Layne 2001), few studies have systematically reviewed the coverage of topics on information management, use, and technology in public affairs programmes. To fill in this gap in the research, this study examines the extent to which graduate public affairs programmes in the United States have prepared public managers for success in the digital era. In particular, this study addresses two questions: How do current curricula prepare public affairs students to governing in the digital age? And what needs to be done to better incorporate information management, use, and technology into public affairs graduate curricula?

In this study, I used mixed methods to collect both quantitative and qualitative data. I collected survey data from graduate programme directors at schools accredited by the Network of Schools of Public Policy, Affairs, and Administration (NASPAA). Furthermore, I conducted content analysis of syllabi collected from courses on information management, use, and technology. This study focuses on the intersection of management, policy, data, IT, and context. My findings suggest that more work needs to be done to better connect e-government with public affairs education and to incorporate topics on information management, use, and technology into mainstream management and policy courses. In closing, this study provides recommendations about creating new courses and updating existing curricula to cover the multidimensional governing issues that we face in the information era.

Literature review

To identify relevant literature, I used keywords – *e-government, e-governance, electronic government, digital government, open government, government 2.0, big data, informatics, information technology, and information management* – to search both general public administrations journals (e.g. *Public Administration Review, the Journal of Public Administration Research and Theory, Public Management Review*, and the *American Review of Public Administration*) and e-government journals such as *Government Information Quarterly*, and *Information Polity*. I also used keywords such as reviews, reflection, and summary to further identify reviews or reflection articles on e-government research and practice. Some classic textbooks, such as Garson's (2006) *Public Information Technology and E-governance: Managing the Virtual State*, were also used to identify e-government research dimensions and foci. Both the list of journals and the selection of keywords were not meant to be exhaustive. I conducted the literature search primarily to identify past and ongoing conversations on the topic of e-government.

E-government or digital government,[2] in a broad sense, refers to the application of IT to government operations, citizen engagement, public policy, and the provision of public services (National Science Foundation 1999). Although the use of IT is not a recent phenomenon, e-government research gained its momentum in the 1990s, along with the rapid advancement of IT. This section of the study begins with a discussion of the challenges facing e-government research and practice. It then reviews the major research themes or dimensions of e-government research, followed by a discussion of the coverage of information management, use, and technology in public affairs programs.

The challenges of e-government research and practice

Existing literature on e-government has focused on how IT can serve as platforms and infrastructure for improving public management, engaging citizens in governing processes, and transforming public services (Coursey and Norris 2008; Chen and Gant 2002; Garson 2006; Dawes 2008; Bretschneider and Mergel 2012; Yildiz 2007). Despite rapid development, e-government research and practice have received critiques from both researchers and practitioners for their overly technological focus, underspecification of concepts, lack of theory development, and disconnect from mainstream public administration research (Norris and Lloyd 2006; Yildiz 2007, 2012).

Researchers have noted that e-government research needs to be more focused on macro-level themes, such as the role of information and communication technology (ICT) in institutional change and reform in government, as well as cross-boundary interorganizational information sharing enabled by IT (Dawes, Cresswell, and Pardo 2009; Gil-Garcia, Chun, and Janssen 2009; Yildiz 2012). In recent years, there has been growing interest in the changes brought by emerging social media, informatics, and big data (Hu and Bryer 2014; Desouza and Jacob 2014; Johnston 2015). Researchers have called for more attention to the use of IT to facilitate interorganizational information and knowledge sharing (Dawes, Cresswell, and Pardo 2009; Gil-Garcia, Chun, and Janssen 2009; Guha and Chakrabarti 2014), to empower citizens, and to foster transparency, participation, and collaboration (Ganapati and Reddick 2012).

Although multiple groups of researchers have described a linear stagewise model of e-government evolution (e.g. Baum and Di Maio 2000; Layne and Lee 2001; Wescott 2001), actual e-government evolution has not been shown to follow a linearly progressive path. Coursey and Norris (2008), for example, found that e-government in local governments did not move progressively from information provision to online transactions, to service integration, and ultimately to transformation. They also discussed the fact that although most local governments were on the web by 2004, they have used their web presence primarily to provide information and nontransactional services (Coursey and Norris 2008). Their findings are echoed by Dawes's (2008) reflection on the challenges facing e-governance and Feeney and Welch's (2012) study of electronic participation technologies. Dawes argued that the greatest progress in e-governance lies in service and management improvement, whereas e-democracy and the exploration of ICTs for institutional reform have seen the least progress. A recent study by Ganapati and Reddick (2012) examined the adoption of open e-government initiatives by state governments. They found that in the three major areas of open e-government initiatives – transparency, participation, and collaboration – the chief information officers in state governments perceived greater strides had been made in transparency than in citizen participation and collaboration.

To assess how e-government has evolved, researchers have called attention to institutional arrangements that can influence e-government adoption and implementation. Fountain's (2001) technology-enactment framework, for instance, suggests that technology needs to be aligned with the needs and environment of an organization. A recent e-government review article also suggested that institutional and political barriers are the major contributing factors to low rates of e-government adoption (Savoldelli, Codagnone, and Misuraca 2014). Therefore, understanding e-government development requires a holistic approach that takes into consideration relevant technical, managerial, organizational, political, economic, social, and institutional factors.

Dimensions of e-government research

Researchers have studied e-government from different angles but have shared similar research approaches and foci. The following section highlights a few studies that discussed the foci of existing government research and discusses the commonalities and differences across these studies. Garson (2006) discussed the applications of IT to politics and policy separately from applications to public management. Under the politics and policy domain, he discussed e-democracy, the digital divide, information access, privacy, security, and regulation issues; within the management domain, he examined public information systems, IT procurement and contracting, and e-government models. Similarly, Reddick (2012) differentiated the external environment from the internal environment with respect to IT applications. He further categorized the application to the external environment into e-democracy, e-participation, and e-governance. Within the internal environment, he discussed e-government and organizational change and public management information systems.

Dawes (2008) suggested five interrelated objectives of e-governance: information-related policy frameworks, improved public services, effective government operations, enhanced citizen participation in democracy, and administrative and institutional reform (s87). Recent research by Moon, Lee, and Roh (2014) applied Rosenbloom's three competing approaches – managerial, political, and legal – to examine IT and e-government studies. The managerial approach focuses on the use of IT to provide and improve public services and to enhance governmental responsiveness; the political approach emphasizes the use of IT for enhancing government accountability and representation of public interests; and the legal approach considers IT as a tool for protecting privacy and providing access to information. Across these different approaches are the common foci on management issues and the political, and policy dimensions of e-government.

The conceptual framework in Figure 1 includes five key dimensions of e-government research and practice: management, policy, technology, data, and context (Andersen and Dawes 1991; Gil-Garcia 2012; Gil-Garcia and Pardo 2005). Different from the above-mentioned models, this framework highlights the data dimension, the technology dimension, and the context to which IT applies. Furthermore, this

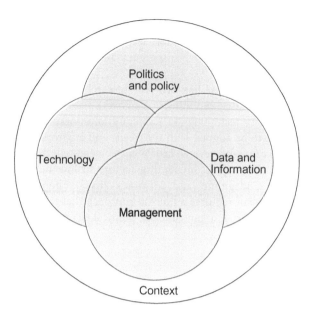

Figure 1. The key dimensions of e-government (adapted from Pardo, Gil-Garcia, and Dawes 2015).

framework demonstrates the overlapping and interdependent relationships among these dimensions.

The existing discussion (e.g. Dawes 2008; Garson 2006; Moon, Lee, and Roh 2014; Reddick 2012) presented frameworks for understanding the field of e-government research. Table 1 summarizes the key dimensions that are used for analysing IT courses in this study. I borrowed frameworks from Garson (2006) and from Pardo, Gil-Garcia, and Dawes (2015) and defined and redefined the five dimensions. I added the element of 'politics' to Pardo et al.'s framework to highlight the politics dimension that covers e-democracy and e-participation. I also added 'information' to the data dimension to differentiate data from information[3] and to highlight the importance of both data and information to organizations. The technology dimension in this study focuses on technology development, emerging technology, and the function and structure of IT. The data and information dimension highlights the large amount of data and information made available through IT. The context dimension is unique in noting the social, economic, demographic, and institutional contexts in which IT operates (Gil-Garcia and Pardo 2005). It also refers to the specific application domain. This framework is used to guide the content analysis of syllabi in this study.

Information management, use, and technology curricula in public affairs programmes

When examining barriers to e-government, Coursey and Norris (2008) highlighted that among the 'technical, political and organizational, legal, and financial' barriers (529), a lack of skilled IT staff stands out as a primary barrier identified by more than half of the local governments that they surveyed. This problem was raised in an earlier study: in their survey of public managers in Arizona state and local governments, Lan

Table 1. Five dimensions of e-government.

Dimensions of e-government	Primary focus	Examples of topics and subtopics
Management	Managing IT projects/resources, managing programme, services, and organizations through the use of IT to enhance management and improve services (Garson 2006)	IT and organizational effectiveness, information system management, planning, funding, and implementation of IT projects
Politics and policy	The use of IT for enhancing governmental accountability and representation of public interests (Moon, Lee, and Roh 2014) and for implementing public policy, and policy issues (Garson 2006)	E-democracy, e-participation, digital divide, information access, privacy, security, laws, regulation issues, information policy
Technology	IT development, emerging IT, function, structure, and systems of IT (Garson 2006)	Broadband technology, information management systems, geographic information systems, social media, database systems, Web-based situation awareness programmes, cloud-based solutions
Data and information	Information and data quality (Gil-Garcia and Pardo 2005), informatics, and data processing and analysis	Big data and analytics, open data, policy informatics, and information quality, intra-organizational information sharing, and interorganizational information sharing
Context	The social, economic, demographic, and institutional contexts, and the application domain (Gil-Garcia and Pardo 2005)	Implementation success factors, applications in emergency management, homeland security, cybersecurity, cyberterrorism, advocacy, public policy, government operations

and Cayer (1994) found that people with managerial backgrounds made up more than 50 per cent of public-sector chief information system manager positions. Both studies pointed to the need to better integrate IT education into graduate curricula in public affairs programmes.

Few studies, however, have systematically reviewed the current state of public affairs education to examine how public managers are prepared to utilize ICT in their daily management practice (cf. Brown and Brudney 1998; Dawes 2004; Kim and Layne 2001; Mergel 2012). Brown and Brudney (1998) surveyed NASPAA-accredited schools and departments of public administration and examined how graduate programmes provide instruction on managing and using information resources in government and how they cover IT concepts recommended by the Clinger-Cohen Act of 1996.[4]

Kim and Layne's (2001) study examined the connection between e-government and public administration education. They proposed emerging e-government topics to be incorporated into existing public administration curricula. Furthermore, they asserted that graduate programmes need to focus on special leadership competencies to lead e-government to service integration. Dawes (2004) reflected on public administration education and proposed key competencies on information strategies and systems that need to be covered in core public administration courses and in special topics. She noted that courses should cover the competencies of 'strategic thinking and evaluation' (aligning IT with organizational mission and goals, making informed IT investments, and evaluating the performance of IT projects), 'analytical skills' (conducting stake-holder analysis, needs analysis, process analysis, information policy analysis, and modelling), 'information stewardship' (data quality and data and information manage-ment), 'technical concepts' (fundamentals of information system design, security, databases, networking, and application development), and 'complex project manage-ment' (communication, coordination, negotiation, and risk management) (5).

Table 2 summarizes the key recommendations of previous studies on IT education in public affairs programmes. The common recommendation across these studies was to introduce IT topics to public affairs curricula through the core courses or indivi-dual IT courses. Better connections still need to be made to link IT development and public affairs education.

Table 2. Summary of studies on information technology education in public affairs programmes.

Author (year)	Key focus	Findings and recommendation
Brown and Brudney (1998)	Programmes' coverage of the IT concepts set forth by the Clinger-Cohen Act of 1996, focus in managing information resources in government: • 'Planning and coordinating information systems concepts • Information system life-cycles concepts • Evaluating information system outcomes • Developing information system policies • Integrating information sys-tems across organizational boundaries • Legal implications of informa-tion system technologies' (432).	• Less than one-third of the programmes covered the topics recommended by the CCA Act. • Recommended incorporating the NASPAA guidelines and developing three courses: • Strategic Information Resource Management • Information Resource Management Planning Methodologies • Information Policy (438)
Kim and Layne (2001)	• How to connect e-government and public administration education. • New topics of e-government in public administration curriculum. • New changes needed in exist-ing curriculum.	• Add e-government topics to public administration curricu-lum to adapt to the digital era • Develop a new leadership cur-riculum focused on competen-cies for integrating services vertically and horizontally using ICT (229)
Dawes (2004)	• Competencies that public managers need to 'build suc-cessful information strategies and systems in the public sec-tor' (5). These competencies include 'strategic thinking and evaluation,' 'analytical skills,' 'information stewardship,' 'technical concepts,' and 'com-plex project management' (5).	• Introduce information resource management in core courses • Foundation courses on infor-mation strategy and management • Special courses on policy, management, and applications (15)

Data collection and analysis methods

In this study, I used mixed methods to collect both qualitative and quantitative data. I sent a survey to graduate directors of NASPAA-accredited schools and conducted a content analysis of syllabi for IT-related courses. I conducted an Internet search to compile the contact information for all the graduate directors of programmes that are listed in the NASPAA 2014–2015 roster of accredited programmes. If the department or school did not have a designated graduate director, I collected the contact information of the director of the school or department itself. In total, 180 graduate directors were invited to participate in a self-administered online survey using Qualtrics. These graduate directors were asked to provide information about their course offerings on information management, use, and technology in their pro-grammes. They were asked whether they have individual courses covering these topics and whether their core administration, management, and policy courses incorporate these topics. They were also asked to identify the major dimensions of e-government covered in their courses and to evaluate the status of IT education in public affairs programmes on a Likert scale. Finally, survey participants were also asked to address an open-ended question about changes that need to be made to better prepare public managers for the digital era. The original survey questions are provided in Appendix A.

After the invitation to the survey was sent in July 2015, three rounds of e-mail reminders followed, and a total of fifty-two responses (28.9 per cent of those invited) were received. Despite the relatively low response rate, the programmes whose direc-tors responded to the survey are diverse. A list of the schools and departments that participated in the survey is provided in Appendix B. I used SPSS software (IBM SPSS Statistics 24 Software) to run descriptive statistical analysis on the quantitative data; for the qualitative data collected from the open-ended question, I used NVivo 10 (QSR International) and conducted open coding (Strauss and Corbin 2007) to identify common and unique recommendations for better integrating information manage-ment, use, and technology into public affairs curricula.

In addition, I wrote to the directors of the top thirty graduate public affairs programmes in the United States (per the U.S. News and World Report's 2012 rankings) to collect updated course syllabi on information management, use, and technology in public affairs (Public Affairs Ranked). Of those thirty programmes, seventeen offer courses on information management, use, and technology. When requesting syllabi, I provided a list of courses as examples (e.g. Digital Governance, E-Government, Information Management Systems, Public Information Management Geographic Information Systems, Social Media, Government 2.0, Big Data, and Informatics). After the initial e-mail request, two rounds of follow-up e-mail remin-ders, and one round of phone calls, I received twenty-five syllabi from twelve programmes out of the seventeen programmes I contacted.

I analysed the twenty-five syllabi to examine what topics had been covered in these IT-related courses and conducted a content analysis to examine how current public affairs programmes have incorporated information management, use, and technology into their curricula and how relevant courses have addressed the data, management, politics and policy, technology, and context dimensions of e-government. Using NVivo software, I conducted open coding to identify the common topics and themes covered in existing IT courses and to identify the gaps in IT education that need to be addressed. More specifically, the course title, course description, topics, and course schedule were coded to identify the main foci and course topics. Then, the course foci and topics were further categorized into the five research themes: management, politics and policy, technology, data and information, and context. To visualize the wide array of topics covered under the five dimensions and the intricate relationships among various topics, I developed a two-mode network using UCINET's NetDraw function.

Findings

In this section, I report my findings from the survey of graduate programme directors and the content analysis of course syllabi on topics related to information management, use, and technology. First, I discuss the individual courses offered by public affairs programmes and the coverage of IT topics in core management and policy courses. Then, I present a grouping of courses into the five interrelated e-government themes and display the main course topics on a network map. Last, I cover perceptions of IT education and recommendations for better integrating information management, use, and technology into graduate public affairs education.

Information technology courses and topics

As Figure 2 shows, of the fifty-two graduate directors who responded to the survey, twenty-nine (55.8 per cent) reported that their programmes offer individual courses covering topics on information management, use, and technology, and thirty programmes (57.7 per cent) cover these topics in their core courses. Geographic information systems, public (management) information systems, and information management are the most frequently reported individual courses among the twenty-nine graduate programmes. Graduate directors also noted that information management, use, and technology are covered in a wide range of core courses, such as introduction to public policy/management/administration, public organization

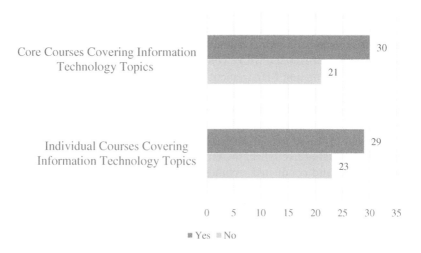

Figure 2. Information technology course offerings in public affairs graduate programmes.

management, public budgeting and financial management, human resource management, analytical techniques, and database management.

It has been more than a decade since the NASPAA technology committee recommended that public administration programmes add IT topics to their core courses (Dawes 2004). IT[5] topics are now covered in public management/policy/administration core courses in more than half of the programmes that responded to the survey. Yet it is surprising that fourteen (26.9 per cent) of these graduate programmes neither offer individual courses on IT nor do their core courses cover these topics. In the core management and policy courses, the majority of programmes cover applications and management of IT and policies related to IT; topics on the organizational and social impact of IT, however, receive relatively little attention (as shown in Figure 3).

In addition to the survey data, I also collected course syllabi from the top thirty graduate public affairs programmes in the United States, according to the U.S. News and World Report's 2012 rankings. Of these thirty programmes, seventeen (56.7 per cent) offer individual courses on IT (see Table 3), corroborating the percentage reflected in the survey results of NASPAA-accredited programmes. Although researchers have highlighted the importance of having one foundation course to introduce students to IT use, management, and policy issues (Dawes 2004; Kim and Layne 2001), more than 40 per cent of the top thirty programmes still do not have courses on IT.

Twenty-five course syllabi were analysed using NVivo to identify the coverage of topics in the courses. The course title, course description, topics, and course schedule were coded to identify course foci and the major e-government dimension covered. As Table 3 shows, the twenty-five IT courses cover a wide range of topics, with the majority (e.g. Digital Government, Managing Information and Technology, and Technology and Public Administration) covering the management, politics and policy, and technology dimensions of e-government. Relatively few courses discuss issues related to the data and information dimension and the context dimension. This finding is consistent with previous research suggesting that the managerial approach predominates in existing e-government research and that there has been increasing

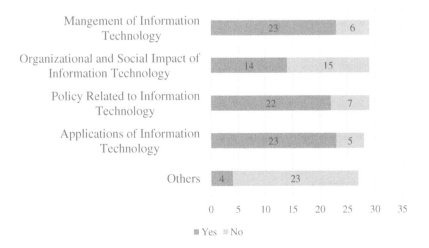

Figure 3. Topics covered in core management and policy courses.

Table 3. Individual courses on information management, use, and technology.

School and department names	Individual information technology-related courses	Management	Politics and policy	Technology	Data and information	Context
Syracuse University	• Digital Government	✓	✓	–	–	–
	• Technology & Information Management*	–	–	✓	–	✓
	• Social Media in the Public Sector	✓		✓	✓	
	• Geographic Information Systems			✓		
Harvard University	• Survey of Telecommunications and Information Policy		✓			
	• Media, Politics, and Power in the Digital Age		✓			
	• From MoveOn.org to Obama 2012: Digital Strategy in Political Campaigns*	–	–	–	–	–
	• The Internet: Governance and Power*	–	–		–	
	• New Media, Surveillance, Access, Propaganda, and Democracy		✓			
	• 2025 Vision and Information Policy Considering the Public Interest		✓			
	• Technology, Security, and Conflict in the Cyber Age		✓	✓		✓
	• Human Rights Advocacy Using Video, Social Media, and Participatory Media		✓	✓		✓
University of Kansas	• Managing Information and Technology	✓	✓			
The State University of New Jersey-Newark	• Technology and Public Administration	✓	✓	✓		✓
New York University	• Gov 3.0 Solving Public Problems with Technology	✓	✓	✓	✓	
University of Washington	• Digital Innovation Lab			✓	–	
	• Information Technology and the Policy-Making Process*	–	–	–	–	–
Ohio State University	• Social Media Strategies for Government and Nonprofits*	–	–	–	–	–
	• Government Information Systems	✓		✓	✓	
University at Albany	• Foundations of Government Information Strategy and Management	✓	✓	✓	✓	✓
	• Information Technology and Homeland Security	✓	✓	✓	✓	
	• Information Technology Innovation in the Public Sector*	–	–	–	–	–
	• Government Information Strategy and Management: A Selected Topics Seminar	✓			✓	
	• Simulating Dynamic Systems			✓		

Table 3. (Continued).

School and department names	Individual information technology-related courses	Management	Politics and policy	Technology	Data and information	Context
University of Texas – Austin	• Information Technology Policy for a Networked World*	–	–	–	–	–
	• Modern American Political Campaigns*	–	–	–	–	–
	• Policy Research Project – Social Media Use by Congressional Committees*	–	–	–	–	–
Arizona State University	• ePublic-Administration: The Use of Information for PA Professionals	√	√	–	√	√
Texas A & M University	• Information Technology In Emergency Management	√	√	√	√	–
University of Minnesota	• Public Information Systems Management	–	–	√	√	–
	• Strategic Social Media*	–	–	–	–	–
University of Nebraska – Omaha	• Emerging Technologies and Society*	√	–	–	–	–
	• Managing Information in the Public Sector	√	√	–	–	–
	• Telecommunications Management*	–	–	–	–	–
	• Information Security Policy and Ethics*	–	–	–	–	–
	• Information Technology Project Fundamentals*	–	–	–	–	–
University of North Carolina	• Strategic Information Technology Management*	–	–	–	–	–
Georgia State University	• GIS Applications for Planning	√	–	√	√	–
University of Delaware	• Information Technology Skills for Planning and Administration	√	√	√	√	–
	• E-Democracy in Theory and Practice*	–	–	–	–	–
University of Missouri	• Informatics and Governance*	–	–	–	–	–
	• Telecommunications Policy*	–	–	–	–	–

'√' means that the course covers the dimension. '*' means that the course syllabi could not be found for the courses on the websites or through contacting the department/schools. '–' means that these courses were not coded. These courses were included to present the types of courses offered by these schools, but the courses were not coded for the dimension due to lack of course syllabi.

interest in the political approach (Moon, Lee, and Roh 2014). It is not surprising that the technology dimension has always been one of the foci in e-government research and education (Yildiz 2012); in fact, e-government research has been critiqued for focusing too narrowly on technology itself (Lips and Schuppan 2009; Yildiz 2007). By contrast, courses on data and information, despite the growing need to use and manage big data (Desouza and Jacob 2014), are limited. A number of courses focus on the application of IT to specific contexts such as emergency management and urban planning, yet few courses focus on the internal and external contextual factors that influence the implementation of e-government projects.

Figure 4 presents a visual display of the course topics covered in the individual courses. These course topics were coded under the five interrelated e-government dimensions. The squares represent the different e-government dimensions, and the circles represent the course topics. The line connecting the square and the circle indicates that the topic (represented by the circle) is coded under the dimension (represented by the square). In total, sixty-five course topics were identified and coded under the five dimensions. The management dimension includes the most course topics (thirty-four), followed by the context dimension (twenty-three), the technology dimension (twenty-two), the data and information dimension (twenty), and the politics and policy dimension (nineteen). Some topics fall under more than one dimension; for instance, the topic of database design, structure, and management involves three dimensions – technology, management, and data and information.

Rapid development of information technology and its wide applications

Within the technology dimension, the topics not only include traditional IT such as broadband Internet, but also cover emerging technology such as cloud-based solutions, Web 2.0, social media, simulation and modelling, and web-based situation awareness programmes (as shown in Figure 4).

As the context dimension also suggests, IT is vital to a broad range of domains, such as organization management, policy implementation, and planning. Furthermore, individual courses include special topics to cover the application of IT in specific contexts such as cybersecurity, advocacy, energy, and emergency management. Despite the slow progress made in e-participation and e-democracy in practice, these topics have been covered in many IT courses, especially in general IT management or policy courses. This finding speaks to Moon, Lee, and Roh's (2014) conclusion that the political dimension of e-government has received increasing attention since the 1990s. The variety of topics covered under the technology and context dimensions reflects the rapid growth of IT over the past few decades, growth demanding that public affairs programmes prepare students with the knowledge and skill sets required to cope with the challenges and opportunities brought by emerging IT.

A wide range of topics has been included under the management dimension, from information system management to knowledge and information management, information strategy, needs assessment, planning, funding, and implementation of IT projects, as well as the impact of IT on organizational effectiveness, public services, government, and society. Under the politics and policy dimension, topics include e-participation, e-democracy, elections, the digital divide, security, privacy, information policy, and more. These topics address important management issues, politics, and policy aspects of e-government practice.

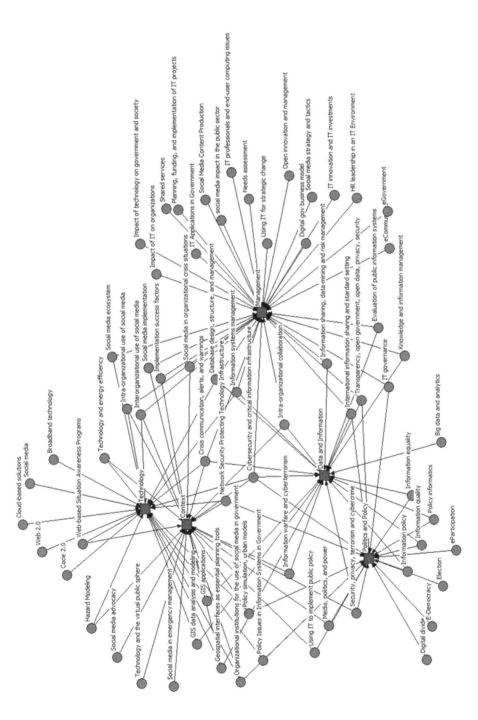

Figure 4. Course topics covered in information technology courses.

Table 4. Information technology education in public affairs programmes.

Items	Very behind	Behind	Barely keep up	Updated	Very updated	Total responses	Mean
Textbook content	4	17	16	10	0	47	2.68
	(8.5%)	(36.2)	(34)	(21.3)	(0)		
Faculty' knowledge base specific to	3	20	8	15	2	48	2.85
information technology	(6.3)	(41.7)	(16.7)	(31.3)	(4.2)		
Research on information technology	3	9	19	16	1	48	3.06
	(6.3)	(18.8)	(39.6)	(33.3)	(2.1)		
Overall quality of IT education in	2	19	18	8	1	48	2.73
public affairs programmes	(4.2)	(39.6)	(37.5)	(16.7)	(2.1)		

Numbers in the parenthesis indicate percentages.

Perception of information technology education in public affairs programmes

About half of the survey respondents noted that the overall quality of IT education in public affairs graduate programmes is behind the development of IT, as shown in Table 4. On a scale from 1 to 5 (1 = very behind, 5 = very updated), textbook content received the lowest score, an average of 2.68. At the time the survey was administered, only 20 per cent of respondents thought that IT education was up to date with the growth of IT overall.

Multidisciplinary and comparative approaches

The nature of the IT topics discussed here suggests a multidisciplinary approach (Yildiz 2012). Instructors teaching IT courses came from diverse educational backgrounds, including public administration, political science, law, business economics, business administration, philosophy, information science, system dynamics, geography, and regional planning. Most of the instructors were full-time faculty members within the department or school. Few practitioner-specialists and few faculty members from other disciplines engaged in teaching IT courses. In the open-ended question section, graduate directors noted that programmes could increase their use of practitioners to teach IT courses and partner with other departments – such as business management, information science, and computer science – to provide IT courses.

Faculty not only adopted IT books written by public administration scholars, such as *Public Information Technology and E-Governance: Managing the Virtual State* (Garson 2006), *Governance and Information Technology: From Electronic Government to Information Government* (Mayer-Schönberger and Lazer 2007), and *Managing Information in the Public Sector* (White 2007), but also used books from other disciplines. A few faculty members did not require traditional textbooks; instead, they used articles and updated online materials. One graduate director suggested that IT courses could move away from traditional textbooks and use open-access content.

Although a comparative approach may benefit e-government research and education (Yildiz 2012; Zhao 2013), few IT courses, if any, took a comparative approach. E-government projects often go beyond local and state government practice, requiring international cooperation. Understanding the impact of national culture on e-government development, therefore, has become increasingly important for e-government scholars and practitioners (Zhao 2013), yet only one of the courses considered in this study covered internationally focused topics such as information sharing and standard setting.

The role of NASPAA in information technology education

When asked how to integrate IT into public affairs curricula, graduate directors highlighted the important role that NASPAA can play. It was noted that NASPAA can 'insert more IT standards language into the expectations' and 'make [IT] [a] mandatory component of programs and add it as a competency.' One director noted that NASPAA can promote the importance of IT education at professional meetings and provide a venue to share successful practice:

> [NASPAA can] increase emphasis on IT and the graduate curriculum at the annual meetings. [NASPAA] can provide more specific examples of programs that have strengthened their IT offerings and applications.

NASPAA first developed its accreditation guidelines and standards for incorporating IT education in 1986, updating them in 2004. In 2009, NASPAA replaced those standards with five core competency domains, which do not explicitly discuss the requirement of IT education. NASPAA, as the membership organization and accreditation institution of programmes in public policy, public affairs, public administration, and public management, may play a leading role in establishing standards for assessing competency and proficiency in IT management, and may set expectations for IT education. Furthermore, NASPAA can also serve as an organizer for initiating research on this issue and share best practices at its annual meeting.

Discussion

Survey findings suggest that current IT education fails to keep pace with rapid changes in IT overall. Approximately 27 per cent of the fifty-two graduate programmes surveyed neither offer individual courses on IT nor do their core courses cover IT topics. Furthermore, course content analysis shows that a wide range of topics has been included in existing IT courses under the management dimension, the politics and policy dimension, and the technology dimension.

Yet the challenge of how to integrate information management, use, and technology with mainstream public management and policy foci remains (Meijer 2007; Lips and Schuppan 2009). IT courses need to balance their focus on technology with their focus on government. There also remains a lack of courses on managing big data and using IT for interorganizational information sharing and collaboration, and the coverage of e-government implementation and performance evaluation has been uneven in existing curricula.

One of the ongoing challenges that e-government research faces is the question of how e-government research can be 'better connected and grounded with mainstream public administration' (Yildiz 2012, 348). E-government research and teaching need to seek a balance between the 'e' focus and the 'government' focus (Lips and Schuppan 2009). Consistent with e-government research foci (Yildiz 2012), IT courses include many micro-level themes, such as e-government development and applications; however, more macro-level questions, such as the role of IT in government reform and institutional change in government (Dawes 2004; Yildiz 2012), deserve attention in IT courses. Although e-government development may require new leadership competencies to lead e-government transformation (Kim and Layne 2001), there is limited coverage of leadership issues in existing IT courses.

Furthermore, the emerging trend of cross-sector collaboration and multiorganizational structure demands that organizations share information and coordinate efforts. It has become important to teach students how to use IT to facilitate interorganizational information sharing and joint actions, a topic that is still missing from the majority of courses on information management, use, and technology.

Another issue is a lack of content coverage on e-government performance evaluation and on the social, economic, demographic, and institutional contexts in which e-government projects are implemented. Few courses cover the measures and frameworks required to systematically evaluate the impact of IT on government and society, and researchers have challenged the linear stagewise model of e-government evolution (Coursey and Norris 2008; Dawes 2008). The frequently cited four-stage e-government maturity model does not fully capture the complexity of e-government development (Coursey and Norris 2008). Much more progress has been made in the areas of management and service improvement than in the areas of citizen participation, service integration, democracy, and institutional reform (Coursey and Norris 2008; Dawes 2008; Baldwin, Gauld, and Goldfinch 2012). While a few courses cover implementation success factors, more attention needs to be paid to the complex contextual factors that influence the adoption and implementation of e-government projects. For instance, institutional capacity (Tolbert, Mossberger, and McNeal 2008), political support, organizational leadership, legal requirements, and financial sustainability (Coursey and Norris 2008) can have impact on e-government implementation.

Although there are relatively few courses on data and information, a few public affairs programmes cover data management, information use, security, privacy, and information quality and equality. The topic of big data and informatics and interorganizational information use, in particular, were found in two courses. With the advance of IT, a large volume of data has become available for storage, mining, and analysis to inform decision-making. Big data holds such great potential for improving public management and public services that big data initiatives have been made across federal, state, and local governments. Big data, notable for its 'volume, velocity, variety, and complexity' (Desouza and Jacob 2014), presents great challenges and opportunities to public managers for leveraging technologies, using information, and integrating resources. Yet coverage of how to manage information and data challenges remains limited in existing curricula.

Topics on information management, use, and technology need to be incorporated into public management and policy core courses. A policy course could discuss the privacy, access, and security issues related to IT management and use, for instance. Or an organization management course could cover how IT may influence organizational structure and decision-making processes. Students could benefit more from having individual courses on IT, and public affairs programmes could invite practitioners to teach IT courses and collaborate with other disciplines such as information science to offer courses on IT. At the end, this study also highlighted the role that NASPAA can play in establishing standards for IT education and providing venues for sharing best practices.

This study has some limitations. The findings of this study need to be generalized with caution as the response rate from the survey was relatively low. Despite the fact that a diverse group of schools and department responded to the survey request (Appendix B), future studies may invent more creative ways to increase the survey response rate. It might be helpful to have a support letter from institutions such as NASPAA or present this survey request to school or department directors at an annual conference. In addition, a bibliometric analysis of existing e-government literature may help expand the discussion on the key research dimensions of existing research, although it is beyond the scope of this study for now.

Conclusion

The rapid development of IT presents unprecedented challenges and opportunities for public managers and policymakers to govern in the digital era. The dynamic interactions among IT, management, politics, policy, data and information, and context will continue to be an important field for learning and action. It is often not the technology itself, but the lack of understanding of IT management, its use, and policy implications that leads to e-government failures (Dawes 2004). Many recent e-government failures can be re-evaluated and reflected on through an educational lens. It is worthwhile to assess how graduate public affairs programmes in the United States prepare current and future public managers to manage and use IT. To ensure successful implementation of e-government projects, we need well-trained public administrators who can work with computer engineers and other technology teams to translate public service requests into well-designed e-government projects.

This study is one of few research attempts to evaluate IT education in public affairs graduate programmes. This study contributes to the existing literature in multiple respects, and it extends previous research on IT education (e.g. Dawes 2004; Layne and Lee 2001) by applying mixed methods to collect both quantitative and qualitative data. This study not only captures perceptual data, but also collects course syllabi for in-depth analysis. The rich data collected enabled me to address the question of IT education from multiple perspectives. Furthermore, the systematic content analysis of course syllabi identifies the course foci, main topics, and gaps in in existing IT courses. On the basis of its findings, this study goes beyond simply describing the current curricula on information management, use, and technology in public affairs programmes: it further provides recommendations about updating existing curricula to cover the complex governing issues in the information era.

Notes

1. In this study, for the sake of simplicity, I use 'public affairs' as an encompassing term to include public management, public administration, and public policy.
2. In this study, 'e-government' is used in a broad sense. It is not differentiated from digital government or e-governance, though some researchers note clear differences among e-government, digital government, and e-governance (Dawes 2009; Garson 2006). For instance, some research argues that the term 'e-government' has a narrow definition, referring to the provision of public services via IT, usually through the Internet (Garson 2006). The term 'digital government,' coined by the National Science Foundation, refers to the use of IT to improve government operations, provide public services, engage citizens, and inform and support public policies (Dawes 2009; Garson 2006). The term 'e-governance' not only includes the use of IT for service provision and management improvement but highlights the use of technology for the 'democratic processes and the relationships among citizens, civil society, the private sector, and the state' (Dawes 2009, s87). 'E-government' has been used more frequently in existing literature, and it is used in this study interchangeably with digital government.
3. Although 'data' and 'information' are often used interchangeably, there are differences between these two terms. Data refer to the raw facts – or, 'representation of facts about the world' (Bardach and Patashnik 2015, 13). Information consists of data that have been processed to

have 'meaning' and to 'help you sort the world into different logical or empirical categories' Bardach and Patashnik (2015, 13). Differentiating information from data allows the researcher to pay attention not only to the necessity of data collection, but also to the importance of informatics – that is, processing data into information.

4. The Clinger-Cohen Act of 1996 (formerly the Information Technology Management Reform Act of 1996) requires federal agencies to improve the acquisition, management, and use of information resources by appointing an agency Chief Information Officer (CIO), redesigning their work processes, and linking information resource planning and investment to the budget process (McClure 1997).

5. The term 'information technology' in this study goes beyond technology itself, covering information management, use, and technology. In the original survey questionnaire, the term and its broad connotations were illustrated by examples. To be consistent with the question-naire and for the sake of simplicity, I use IT here, in Figures 2 and 3, and in Table 4 to refer broadly to information management, use, and technology.

Disclosure statement

No potential conflict of interest was reported by the author.

References

Andersen, D. F., and S. Dawes. 1991. *Government Information Management. A Primer and Casebook.* Englewood Cliffs, NJ: Prentice Hall.

Baldwin, J. N., R. Gauld, and S. Goldfinch. 2012. "What Public Servants Really Think of E-Government?" *Public Management Review* 14 (1): 105–127. doi:10.1080/14719037.2011.589616.

Bardach, E., and E. M. Patashnik. 2015. *Practical Guide for Policy Analysis: The Eightfold Path to More Effective Problem Solving.* 5th ed. Thousand Oaks, CA: CQ Press.

Barrett, K., and R. Green. 2015. "Bad Data: A Special Report (The Causes, Costs and Consequences of Bad Government Data)." *Governing* (July Issue) 24–31. http://www.governing.com/topics/mgmt/gov-bad-data.html

Baum, C. H., and A. Di Maio. 2000."Gartner's Four Phases of E-government Model." Accessed March 25 2015. http://www.gartner.com

Bretschneider, S. I., and I. Mergel. 2012. "Technology and Public Management Information Systems: Where We Have Been and Where We are Going." In *The State of Public Administration: Issues, Challenges, and Opportunities,* edited by D. C. Menzel and H. L. White, 187–203. Armonk, NY: M. E. Sharpe.

Brown, M. M., and J. L. Brudney. 1998. "Public Sector Information Technology Initiatives: Implications for Programs of Public Administration." *Administration & Society* 30 (4): 421–442. doi:10.1177/0095399798304005.

Chen, Y.-C., and J. Gant. 2002. "Transforming Local E-Government Services: The Use of Application Service Providers." *Government Information Quarterly* 18 (4): 343–355. doi:10.1016/S0740-624X(01)00090-9.

Coursey, D., and D. F. Norris. 2008. "Models of E-Government: Are They Correct? an Empirical Assessment." *Public Administration Review* 68 (3): 523–536. doi:10.1111/j.1540-6210.2008.00888.x.

Dawes, S. S. 2004. "Training the IT-Savvy Public Manager: Priorities and Strategies for Public Management Education." *Journal of Public Affairs Education* 10 (1): 5–17.

Dawes, S. S. 2008. "The Evolution and Continuing Challenges of E-Governance." *Public Administration Review* 68 (special issue): S86–S102. doi:10.1111/j.1540-6210.2008.00981.x.

Dawes, S. S. 2009. "Governance In a Digital Age: A Research And Action Framework For An Uncertain Future." *Government Information Quarterly* 26 (2): 257–264.

Dawes, S. S., A. M. Cresswell, and T. A. Pardo. 2009. "From "Need to Know" to "Need to Share": Tangled Problems, Information Boundaries, and the Building of Public Sector Knowledge Networks." *Public Administration Review* 69 (3): 392–402. doi:10.1111/j.1540-6210.2009.01987_2.x.

Desouza, K. C., and B. Jacob 2014. "Big Data in the Public Sector: Lessons for Practitioners and Scholars." *Administration & Society*. Advance online publication. doi:10.1177/0095399714555751.

Feeney, M. K., and E. W. Welch. 2012. "Electronic Participation Technologies and Perceived Outcomes for Local Government Managers." *Public Management Review* 14 (6): 815–833. doi:10.1080/14719037.2011.642628.

Fountain, J. 2001. *Building The Virtual State: Information Technology And Institutional Change.* Washington, DC: Brookings Institution Press.

Ganapati, S., and C. G. Reddick. 2012. "Open E-Government in U.S. State Governments: Survey Evidence from Chief Information Officers." *Government Information Quarterly* 29 (2): 115–122. doi:10.1016/j.giq.2011.09.006.

Garson, G. D. 2006. *Public Information Technology and E-Governance: Managing the Virtual State.* Sudbury, MA: Jones and Bartlett Publishers.

Gil-Garcia, J. R. 2012. *Enacting Electronic Government Success: An Integrative Study of Government-Wide Websites, Organizational Capabilities, and Institutions.* New York, NY: Springer.

Gil-Garcia, J. R., S. A. Chun, and M. Janssen. 2009. "Government Information Sharing and Integration: Combining the Social and the Technical." *Information Polity* 14 (1 and 2): 1–10.

Gil-Garcia, J. R., and T. A. Pardo. 2005. "E-Government Success Factors: Mapping Practical Tools to Theoretical Foundations." *Government Information Quarterly* 22 (2): 187–216. doi:10.1016/j.giq.2005.02.001.

Guha, J., and B. Chakrabarti. 2014. "Making E-Government Work: Adopting the Network Approach." *Government Information Quarterly* 31 (2): 327–336. doi:10.1016/j.giq.2013.11.008.

Hu, Q., and T. A. Bryer. 2014. "Exploring the Potential of Social Networking Sites for Public Service Professionals." *International Journal of Organizational Theory and Behavior* 17 (4): 401–427.

Johnston, E. 2015. *Governance in the Information Era: Theory and Practice of Policy Informatics.* New York, NY: Routledge Taylor & Francis Group.

Kim, S., and K. Layne. 2001. "Making the Connection: E-Government and Public Administration Education." *Journal of Public Affairs Education* 7 (4): 229–240.

Lan, Z., and J. Cayer. 1994. "The Challenges of Teaching Information Technology Use and Management in a Time of Information Revolution." *The American Review of Public Administration* 24 (2): 207–222. doi:10.1177/027507409402400206.

Layne, K., and J. Lee. 2001. "Developing Fully Functional E-Government: A Four Stage Model." *Government Information Quarterly* 18 (2): 122–136. doi:10.1016/S0740-624X(01)00066-1.

Lips, M. B., and T. Schuppan. 2009. "Transforming E-Government Knowledge through Public Management Research." *Public Management Review* 11 (6): 739–749. doi:10.1080/14719030903318921.

Mayer-Schönberger, V., and D. Lazer, ed. 2007. *Governance and Information Technology: From Electronic Government to Information Government.* Cambridge, MA: MIT press.

McClure, D. L. 1997. "Improving Federal Performance in the Information Era: The Information Technology Management Reform Act of 1996." *Government Information Quarterly* 14 (3): 255–269. doi:10.1016/S0740-624X(97)90004-6.

Meijer, A. 2007. "Editorial: Why Don't They Listen to Us? Reasserting the Role of ICT in Public Administration." *Information Polity* 12 (4): 233–242.

Mergel, I. 2012. "The Public Manager 2.0: Preparing the Social Media Generation for a Networked Workplace." *Journal of Public Affairs Education* 18 (3): 467–492.

Moon, M. J., J. Lee, and C.-Y. Roh. 2014. "The Evolution of Internal IT Applications and E-Government Studies in Public Administration: Research Themes and Methods." *Administration & Society* 46 (1): 3–36. doi:10.1177/0095399712459723.

National Science Foundation. 1999. "Digital Government Program Announcement NSF 99-103." Accessed March 15 2015. http://www.nsf.gov/pubs/1999/nsf99103/nsf99103.txt

Norris, D. F., and B. A. Lloyd. 2006. "The Scholarly Literature on E-Government: Characterizing a Nascent Field." *International Journal of Electronic Government Research* 2 (4): 40–96. doi:10.4018/jegr.2006100103.

Pardo, T. A., J. R. Gil-Garcia, and S. S. Dawes. 2015. "Call for Papers: Special Issue Topic: Digital Government and Public Management." Accessed March 15 2015. https://dgsociety.org/call-papers-special-issue-public-management-review

Public Affairs Ranked. Accessed May 25 2015. http://grad-schools.usnews.rankingsandreviews.com/best-graduate-schools/top-public-affairs-schools/public-affairs-rankings

Reddick, C. G. 2012. *Public Administration And Information Technology*. Burlington, MA: Jones & Bartlett Learning.

Savoldelli, A., C. Codagnone, and G. Misuraca. 2014. "Understanding the E-Government Paradox: Learning from Literature and Practice on Barriers to Adoption." *Government Information Quarterly* 31 (Supplement 1): s63–s71. doi:10.1016/j.giq.2014.01.008.

Strauss, A., and J. M. Corbin. 2007. *Basics of Quantitative Research: Techniques and Procedures for Developing Grounded Theory*. Thousand Oaks, CA: Sage.

Tolbert, C. J., K. Mossberger, and R. McNeal. 2008. "Institutions, Policy Innovation and E-Government in the American States." *Public Administration Review* 68 (3): 549–563. doi:10.1111/j.1540-6210.2008.00890.x.

Wescott, C. 2001. "E-Government in the Asia-Pacific Region." *Asian Journal of Political Science* 9 (2): 1–24. doi:10.1080/02185370108434189.

White, J. D. 2007. *Managing Information in the Public Sector*. Armonk, NY: M.E. Sharpe.

Yildiz, M. 2007. "E-Government Research: Reviewing the Literature, Limitations, and Ways Forward." *Government Information Quarterly* 24 (3): 646–665. doi:10.1016/j.giq.2007.01.002.

Yildiz, M. 2012. "Big Questions of E-Government Research." *Information Polity* 17 (3–4): 343–355.

Zhao, F. 2013. "An Empirical Study of Cultural Dimensions and E-Government Development: Implications of the Findings and Strategies." *Behavior & Information Technology* 32 (3): 294–306. doi:10.1080/0144929X.2011.644580.

Appendices

Appendix A

Survey questions

(1) Does your school/department offer individual courses covering information technology-related topics, such as Digital Governance, E-government, Information Management Systems, Geographic Information Systems (GIS), Social Media, Government 2.0, Big Data, and Informatics?
☐ Yes, please provide the title(s) of the course(s).
☐ No.

(2) Do the core management/administration/policy courses (such as Public Management, Public Administration, Public Policy, Human Resource Management, and Organizational Theory) cover information technology-related topics?
☐ Yes, please provide the title(s) of the course(s).
☐ No.

(3) Please check the information technology-related topics covered in the core courses offered at your school/department. Please check all that may apply.
☐ Management of information technology such as information resource management
☐ Organizational and social impact of information technology
☐ Policy related to information technology such as information policy, and privacy policy
☐ Applications of information technology such as social media, data management systems, geographic information systems
☐ Others, please specify.

(4) How will you evaluate the status of Information Technology Education in Public Administration/Affairs/Management/Policy/Service Graduate Programmes in the United States?

	Very behind the development of information technology	Behind the development of information technology	Barely keep up with the development of information technology	Updated with the development of information technology	Very updated with the development of information technology
Textbook content	☐	☐	☐	☐	☐
Faculty' knowledge base specific to information technology	☐	☐	☐	☐	☐
Research on information technology	☐	☐	☐	☐	☐
Overall quality of IT education in public affairs programmes	☐	☐	☐	☐	☐

(5) What needs to be done to better incorporate information technology into graduate curriculum? (Please type your comments in the box below.

Appendix B. A list of public affairs programmes that responded to the survey

Albany State University
American University
Binghamton University
California State Polytechnic University-Pomona
California State University – San Bernardino
Central Michigan University
Clark Atlanta University
Cleveland State University
Eastern Kentucky University
Florida Gulf Coast University
Georgia College & State University
Georgia Regents University
Harvard University
Indiana University South Bend
Kansas State University
Kean University
Long Island University – Brooklyn
Mississippi State University
Missouri State University
New Mexico State University
Ohio State University
Old Dominion University
Pennsylvania State University – Harrisburg
Rutgers University – Camden
Rutgers University – New Jersey
San Diego State University

San Francisco State University
San Jose State University
Syracuse University
Texas State University
Texas Tech University
Troy University
University of Tennessee – Chattanooga
University of Central Florida
University of Colorado – Denver
University of Connecticut
University of Delaware
University of Georgia
University of Missouri
University of Nebraska – Omaha
University of North Carolina – Charlotte
University of North Carolina – Greensboro
University of North Texas
University of South Carolina
University of South Dakota
University of South Florida
University of Utah
University of Vermont
University of Washington
Valdosta State University
Virginia Commonwealth University
Wichita State University

The programmes are listed alphabetically.

Index

Note: Figures are indicated by *italics*. Tables are indicated by **bold**. Endnotes are indicated by the page number followed by 'n' and the endnote number e.g., 20n1 refers to endnote 1 on page 20.

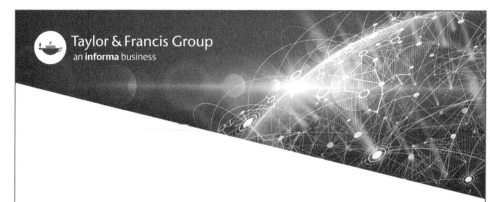